THIRD-SECTOR DEVELOPMENT

CHRISTOPHER GUNN

THIRD-SECTOR

DEVELOPMENT

Making Up for the Market

ILR Press an imprint of
CORNELL UNIVERSITY PRESS
ITHACA AND LONDON

First published 2004 by Cornell University Press
First printing, Cornell Paperbacks, 2004

Printed in the United States of America

Library of Congress Cataloging-in-Publication Data
Gunn, Christopher Eaton.
Third-sector development : making up for the market /
Christopher Gunn.— 1st ed.
p. cm.
Includes bibliographical references and index.
ISBN 0-8014-3991-4 (alk. paper) — ISBN 0-8014-8881-8
(pbk. : alk. paper)
1. Nonprofit organizations—United States.   2. Non-governmental organizations—United States.   3. Cooperation—United States.   4. Human
services—United States.   5. United States—Economic policy.
6. United States—Social policy.   7. United States—Cultural policy.
I. Title.
HD2769.2.U6 G86 2004
338.7′4—dc22
2003019948

Cornell University Press strives to use environmentally responsible
suppliers and materials to the fullest extent possible in the publishing
of its books. Such materials include vegetable-based, low-VOC inks
and acid-free papers that are recycled, totally chlorine-free, or partly
composed of nonwood fibers. For further information, visit our website
at www.cornellpress.cornell.edu.

Cloth printing   10   9   8   7   6   5   4   3   2   1
Paperback printing 10   9   8   7   6   5   4   3   2   1

Contents

Preface

Economic development is a pressing issue for poor communities in this wealthy nation. This book is about a different path to achieve that development. Investments from the private, for-profit sector have already bypassed poor communities, and any government assistance those areas have received has not been enough to ignite development. Another set of options is available, and it involves communities building the nonprofit and cooperative portions of their economies. Through organizations of what can be called "the third sector" jobs can be created, goods and services can be produced and delivered, and surplus from which to build can be retained and reinvested in the communities.

The terrain of this book is the United States. I use the term *third sector* as a label for organizations in the economy that are neither traditional for-profit businesses nor government agencies. They have similarities to what in international development work are called "nongovernmental organizations" (NGOs), but they are more than aid agencies. U.S. domestic third-sector organizations are well known in their familiar forms of hospitals, universities, social service agencies, and charities, and each of these organizations can contribute to development. Less familiar is a new generation of entrepreneurial nonprofits, cooperatives, and credit unions that have as one of their objectives building stronger local economies. While the book begins with an overview of the entire nonprofit world, its subject is these development-oriented organizations.

Chapters 1 through 3 provide a survey of the third sector and tackle the question of why development is a problem in a country with the resources and wealth of the United States. The focus is economic, but for some readers it may be considered political as well, since it has to do with class and inequality, among other issues. This is, then, a study in one aspect of local political economy. Before turning to profiles of organizations doing the work described here, basic criteria for assessing development are discussed in chapter 3.

Chapters 4 through 10 provide profiles of over twenty-five organizations that are contributing to development across the United States. They include nonprofits that have approval from the federal government to receive donations that are tax-deductible for the donors and other nonprofits without that privilege. They also include a mix of different kinds of cooperatives. I argue in the opening chapters that these organizations have important elements in common. Most importantly for place-based development, they tend to be grounded in local economies. These organizations can be launched with energy from social entrepreneurship and capital raised from a variety of sources.

No claim for a new holy grail will be made. There are shortcomings to use of these institutions, which are only as trustworthy as the people responsible for them. They require financial resources in a capitalist economy that starves them of capital for structural as much as (or more than) ideological reasons. Compared with the bigger players in the game, capitalist firms and governments, the third sector is small. Chapters 11 and 12 deal with public policy issues concerning this sector and how they might play a role in reshaping the direction of national social, political, and economic development.

One reason to pay greater attention to the third sector is that it is the fastest-growing part of the U.S. economy. At the national level it now makes up approximately 10 percent of economic activity—somewhat more if counting employment, somewhat less if counting the value of economic transactions. In some regions, cities, and communities the third sector is a far greater economic factor. For instance, a study published as this book was being completed shows that in the New York City economy the third sector (defined more narrowly than in this book) accounted for 11.5 percent of economic activity in the city and 14 percent of its employment (Seley and Wolpert 2002, 29–31). The study shows that during the 1990s in New York City nonprofit organizations were the fastest growing source of jobs. Their share of employment now outranks the city's signature financial, insurance, and real estate (FIRE) sector (32).

Why is this phenomenon so little known? First, it must be said that there is much literature on nonprofit organizations, numerous accomplished researchers are studying the field, and the Association for Research on Nonprofit Organizations and Voluntary Action (ARNOVA), which is made up of professional and academic researchers, is dedicated to it. Although it draws on this literature, this book begins with the question of development, especially where it is lagging in both rural and urban settings, and looks to see what new approaches using these organizations might have accomplished. Some of my prior writing has dealt with the world of cooperatives. The portion dealing with development has focused on what Hazel Dayton Gunn and I have called "alternative institutions of accumulation," alternatives to first-sector businesses. For healthy parts of the economy the process of capital accumulation goes on routinely. In poorer areas something else has to jump-start the process and keep the surplus, the newly generated capital, in the communities and available for reinvestment. This is the role that some dynamic third-sector organizations can play, along with their other generally good work. The organizations and the process are what this book is about.

Acknowledgments

Because this book reflects, and reflects on, the work of many people in third-sector organizations, it is to them that I owe my first thanks. Their commitments and inventiveness are described here, and I thank them for the time spent with me explaining their successes, failures, and aspirations. The two years of empirical work that went into the book were a pleasure because of conversations along the way with these remarkable agents of change.

Teaching at a liberal arts college (plural in the case of Hobart and William Smith) means that one's research and teaching often overlap. Before this book began to take shape I was able to initiate a course called Third Sector Economics. Thanks to the students who ventured into this new offering, to Hobart and William Smith for the environment and support to develop new courses of this kind, and for summer research funding to carry out some of the fieldwork for the book.

I frequently get to share ideas on local economic development issues with a remarkable group of faculty and students in the Department of City and Regional Planning at Cornell University. I began talking about the role of nonprofits, cooperatives, and credit unions in development with them several years ago, and those conversations helped stimulate what follows. My thanks to many occupants of West Sibley Hall for their ongoing engagement with these issues.

My greatest debt in this project is to Hazel Dayton Gunn. In addition to her own work she has been actively engaged as this book unfolded, responding with a fine critical eye and ear to the ideas, accompanying me on many site visits, and vetting draft material. To Hazel I am deeply indebted in so many ways.

Last, when I pitched the idea of this book to Cornell University Press, I received a very enthusiastic response from Frances Benson. She encouraged the project from the beginning and supplied an important part of the title. Many thanks, Fran. Thanks as well to Pat Coate and Ange Romeo-Hall for helping to polish the manuscript into the form that follows. Any remaining mistakes are of course my responsibility.

THIRD-SECTOR DEVELOPMENT

1

The Third Sector

The capitalist economy succeeds and fails, often at the same moment. Where it performs well it tends to be embraced as the only viable way to organize material affairs. Economic growth is capitalism's strength; problems such as income inequality and environmental degradation are troublesome but are often seen as manageable with growth or technological innovation. Where capitalism has yet to work its growth magic people in relatively poor communities and regions have two options: wait in the hope of being seen as attractive to capital or do something different. This book is about pursuing the second option.

Neither capitalist nor public, the *third sector* is the third element in the mixed economy of the United States. It consists largely of private organizations that act in the economic arena but that exist to provide specific goods and services to their members or constituents. These organizations act neither to enrich "owners" nor to provide high income to top executives. Some are used to protect entrenched interests, and others are used to do social good.

Nonprofit organizations fall into two broad categories: some serve only their members, and others perform a broad array of public services. The first group includes social clubs, political parties, labor unions, business associations, and cooperatives. In the United States they are typically incorporated under Internal Revenue Service 501 status and are exempt from federal and some local taxation. Nonprofits that meet public service criteria include religious organizations, social service providers, art and cultural organizations, foundations, and educational institutions. The fact that they serve public needs beyond their membership or create public goods can enable them to apply for U.S. IRS 501(c)(3) status. Contributions to 501(c)(3) nonprofit organizations are tax-deductible to donors, providing incentive for monetary donations to those institutions.

Table 1.1 contrasts the third sector with the first and second sectors, the two larger players in the economy: the private, for-profit sector; and the public sector. The *first sector* is the heart of the U.S. economy. Its most numerous organizations are small businesses, but its most important organizations by almost all other measures are large corporations. For-profit corporations exist to enrich those who provide them with equity capital, and in return those organizations provide people with goods, services, and jobs. The *second sector* consists of government organizations at the state, local, and federal levels. Government is (ideally) under democratic control and exists to do the business of its citizens. In general terms the relative proportions of economic activity by each sector in the United States are as follows: first, 65 percent; second, 25 percent; and third, 10 percent.

The term *third sector* is used broadly here to denote a mix of nonprofit and cooperative economic organizations and their activities.[1] For reasons to be discussed below, this is the fastest growing of the three major sectors in the U.S. economy. Cooperatives have been part of the economic and social history of the United States for over a century. They are best known in their consumer cooperative form but are still often unrecognized as representing a unique kind of business. For example, shoppers at Recreational Equipment Incorporated (REI) may not think about what sets this supplier of outdoor equipment and clothing apart from others, and the nation's more than seventy million credit union members may rarely recognize that they are being served by their own financial cooperatives. Workers' cooperatives have a long history in this country as well, especially in the plywood industry, but this form of co-op is even more obscure than the others.

Nonprofit organizations, while more familiar to many people than cooperatives, have received little attention in the economics and business literature, and they have only become a field for academic attention in recent decades. Mention nonprofits to most people and they think of their religious institutions, clubs, or the United Way. Many are surprised to hear of the more entrepreneurial side of this sector—for instance that the Green Bay Packers of the National Football League is a nonprofit organization. Irony abounds in the fact that the New York Stock Exchange—bastion of

Table 1.1 Sector Characteristics

Characteristics	Third Sector (Nonprofits and Co-ops)	Second Sector (Government)	First Sector (For-profit Corporations and Small Businesses)
Ownership	Private organizations and their members	Public	Private individuals and first- and third-sector organizations
Funding	Donations, grants, revenues, and loans	Taxes, revenues, and loans	Equity from investors; loans; retained earnings
Motivations	Serve general public or members	Provide public goods and services	Profit (return on investment)
Dispersion of net income	Retained for operations or asset development	To public coffers	Dividends to stockholders or retained earnings for growth
Dispersion of net assets if dissolved	Generally to other nonprofits; some conversion to private and for-profits (e.g., hospitals)	To other public agencies; to public coffers after privatization	Sale within private sector
Earnings taxed?	Generally not; yes in the case of for-profit subsidiaries and cooperatives	No	Yes
Property taxed?	Generally not; yes for for-profit subsidiaries and cooperatives	No	Yes, except when abatements are provided
Create jobs?	Yes	Yes	Yes
Range of compensation	Low to high	Moderate	Low to very high
Attract volunteer unpaid labor?	Yes	Limited	No

capitalism—is a nonprofit association. How it fits into the nonprofit world will be made clear in chapter 2. Internationally efforts to foster development and deliver humanitarian aid through the use of nongovernmental organizations (NGOs)—nonprofits—are better known.

The United States has a larger third sector than most other nations, for complex reasons that will be discussed throughout this book. Traditionally this has been the "caring" or "voluntary" sector responsible for social conditioning through religious, educational, and civic organizations and through philanthropies. But from this tradition a new breed of nonprofit and noncapitalist organizations has emerged that can serve communities facing needs created by capital's failure, neglect, or flight. The innovative use of these noncapitalist (and nongovernmental) organizations to stimulate development concerns more than just economic development, as it also intersects with current needs to revitalize communities and enhance civil society. Third-sector organizations are providing these needs in numerous fields of activity in all parts of the country. Diverse examples include arts organizations that help revitalize depressed downtown or industrial areas; credit unions that bring financial services to people whose only other local options are the pawnshop and loan shark; and child-care providers who organize their own company as a cooperative in order to provide both better care and better jobs.

Hybrids and Migration

The three sector designations used in this book provide a picture of the U.S. mixed economy, but that picture is unrealistically static and strictly delineated. Movement of resources takes place between these sectors, and organizations migrate between them. In addition important hybrid organizations incorporate features of two and even all three sectors.

Some of this overlap and ambiguity are captured in Figure 1.1, in which the three sectors appear as overlapping circles. The overlapping of third-sector and for-profit worlds, area "a" in the diagram, is exemplified by the for-profit subsidiaries of nonprofits, such as a real estate development project, and by the charitable foundation of a for-profit corporation. Area "b" is the hybrid world of third- and second-sector (governmental) operations, illustrated by the example of local development organizations that operate under the auspices of, and for, county or city development projects. Public, private-sector partnerships illustrate area "c" hybrids, which commonly

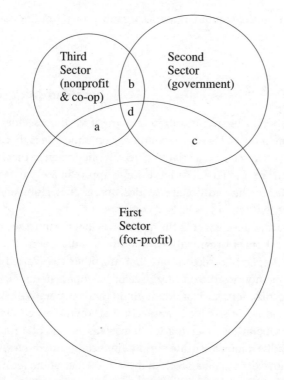

Figure 1.1. The three sectors and hybrid segments of the economy.

carry out local development and sometimes operate the new assets resulting from that development. The diagram has been constructed with an additional point of overlap, area "d," among all three sectors. While it is not common to find an organization that fits this space on the diagram, joint ventures between organizations in all three sectors make it relevant. In addition some of the more dynamic third-sector cases (to be encountered later in the book) demonstrate overlap and cooperation between the third and both other sectors.

Organizational migration between sectors occurs when a nonprofit organization converts to for-profit operation or when a cooperative is sold to private investors. Public-to-private migration occurs through the sale of public assets in the practice known as privatization. Migration between the second and third sectors takes place when public hospitals are converted to nonprofit operation. Funds and personnel also migrate among the three sectors. The point is that the economy is dynamic and fluid not just in its ability to grow but also in the combinations of organizations, funding, and tools it uses to get results.

Unheralded Initiatives

Why have people heard little about growth of the third sector and development initiated by it? There are several reasons, and one is that a more entrepreneurial third sector is a relatively recent phenomenon that has gained momentum in the past few decades. Prior to approximately 1975 this sector was dominated by the traditional charities, universities, clubs, and religious organizations that remain its largest components.

Another part of the answer to the question is that the third sector is a pastiche—a collection of organizations that are usually defined by their *not* being of the larger two sectors but that are otherwise varied in nature. Historically the nonprofit, voluntary sector has not generally been associated with organizations such as credit unions and cooperatives, which have been accounted for in small categories of their own. This continues today with some cooperatives referring to themselves as part of a fourth sector. However, credit unions are quite simply financial cooperatives, and cooperatives do not exist to make profit in the usual sense of the term. If a co-op makes a surplus (sometimes called profit) in any given year, it is either used for new investment in that co-op or returned to its members. No outside stockholders await their dividends or capital gains from owning shares of cooperatives. Lenders to them get interest but no managerial control. By adding these private, nonprofit organizations to an already eclectic group based on a neither-nor definition, a sector comes into view in a way that highlights new strategies for locally based development. Communities and individuals have recently recognized and acted on these options, and the results of their entrepreneurship deserve wider recognition.

Another obvious reason for the obscurity of this sector is that people live in a society (the United States especially) that has spent the past two decades emphasizing the primacy of the private for-profit sector and its use for development. The mantra of markets and privatization has been reinforced by the collapse of state-based socialism internationally and by powerful ideological campaigns at home. (These campaigns were of course often assisted by think tanks of the political right—nonprofits all.) Entrepreneurship has been celebrated in small businesses, dot.coms, e-businesses, and other forms, but rarely has the celebration taken account of new third-sector, and more social, forms of entrepreneurship. Since the accepted rationale for entrepreneurship is that it can make you rich, why pay attention to a form that won't?

One other reason for the obscurity of initiatives in the third sector deserves mention. Most of the cases presented in subsequent chapters highlight organizations and initiatives that are small (by Fortune 500 company standards) and local. Even if they have received national attention—and some have—it has generally been fleeting. They may matter enormously in their communities or even regions, but they do not have the national or global impact of, for instance, a new Microsoft. Why then discuss them as tools for development? The answer is simple: they create jobs, build linkages that encourage other start-ups, provide goods and services, and improve peoples' lives. This is development. And unlike organizations of transnational capital, these initiatives tend to be grounded in place. As communities seek stability in a world of change created by ever more mobile capital, this is a valuable contribution to development that can last.

Problems in the Third Sector

While this book applauds third-sector development, it does not idealize it. Associating terms such as *caring organizations, charities, trust-based organizations,* and others with nonprofit organizations can be misleading. People who manage nonprofits or serve on their boards know all too well the struggle these organizations face to meet their obligations to their communities and their staffs. They may not be the best employers in town, despite their mission statements, and they can go astray ethically or in choice of ventures. They are generally dependent on donations, and hence they may be subject to the whims of major donors. They can be hierarchical or dominated by one key individual. On balance they show some of the same positive and negative attributes of the organizations making up the two more dominant sectors. That does not preclude their being useful and sometimes downright inspiring.

This book is being written at a time when the news is full of scandals in the first sector. Corporate America is reeling from evidence of corporate wrongdoing, accounting malfeasance, and damaged reputations. The third sector has had its share of the same kinds of problems, but its smaller scale has meant that it did not gain as much attention in the news. Still, large problems have been visible. For instance, the disasters of September 11, 2001, were followed by a meltdown in the reputation of a nonprofit on which the nation depended to recover: the American Red Cross. Its decision to set aside some of the funds donated for victims of the September 11 attacks angered the public and led to the resignation of Dr. Bernadine Healy, its CEO. Subsequently the organization has come under heavy public and official pressure to be more open about its operations and finances (Strom 2002). In New York in early 2002 the vice president of the Local Initiatives Support Organization, a large and respected community development organization, was indicted for embezzling $1.8 million from one of the organization's subsidiaries (Pristin 2002). In Virginia, Jerry Falwell has attempted to use his nonprofit ministry to develop and build a large retirement community, Liberty Village, which would exclude gays and lesbians. Foundations provide shelters for private wealth because they supposedly operate for the public good, but their history suggests that some simply function as mouthpieces for their founders' views of the world (Dowie 2001).

Third-sector organizations are of this world, not of some idealized realm. They can be used for good and bad, and they require careful guidance. Since most of them operate with donated funds, they sometimes face censure from the public at large in the form of dwindling financial support. They also require some regulatory oversight, a topic discussed in chapter 11.

Local Initiatives in Global Context

People in this country have *almost* reached the point where writing about local economic initiatives is not dismissed as "useless because we live in a global world." We do live in such a world, but many a community is not being served well by the global economy. Rather than waiting for capital's sun to shine on them or trying to outbid their neighboring communities to entice capital to favor them with new investment, people who live in poorer communities—those missing the blessings of the global economy—may decide to take action for themselves. Because few individuals in these communities have the resources to step forward and take on the traditional role of private entrepreneur, collective action may be the answer. It can take public-sector form, and historically it has, even in the United States.[2] However, trends of recent decades (privatization, tax revolts, and strained local public budgets) have made this strategy more difficult. Public initiatives that can aid development, such as provision of adequate and high-quality public goods (e.g., education and transportation), should be part of any local development strategy. But another option exists, and it is often complementary to first- and second-sector initiatives. Nonprofit corporations and cooperatives have proven to be organizational forms within which collective entrepreneurship can take place and new capital can be formed. Initiatives of this kind cannot ignore forces that make our world more globally integrated, but they can work within that world to local advantage.

The multiple meanings of the term *globalization* can make it a muddle, with negative results. One appropriate meaning is that decisions that affect our lives can be made far away from us geographically and far from our control. Being reminded of this tends to be enervating, contributing as it does to feelings of inevitability and helplessness. But confronting this aspect of globalization is also instructive since it can help people understand more clearly what is given up when power is ceded to distant, nondemocratic institutions of capital accumulation. Globalization reflects capitalism's and modernity's shrinking of time and space. The pace of this several-centuries-old system has been hastened by modern communication media (themselves largely born of it) and by the ability to move capital electronically. Capitalism's history has been one of expansion—a relentless search for new sources of raw materials, labor power, and new markets for products. Beginning around 1990 with the collapse of the socialist system, the whole world became available for capital's efforts.

Markets create change, and throughout much of their history they have been applauded for doing so. True conservatives (rather than classical liberals, often mislabeled conservatives in the United States) have chafed at this aspect of capitalism and sought restoration of a more stable order. Since turning the clock back to early agrarian capitalism or feudalism is impossible, conservative agendas have emphasized the cultural front (e.g., family values, fundamentalist religion). Modern liberal critics of market-driven change see it producing winners and losers, and they seek to soften the blow to those displaced by the change. To many this is both a legitimate and an essential role for the community and the state in a modern, affluent society.

Communities as well as individuals win and lose in the great flux of markets, and it does them little good simply to attribute the cause to globalization. The prescription that generally follows from this diagnosis is that a community should find ways to attract its share of globally mobile capital, but doing so may involve compromises the community is unwilling to accept. Options often include relaxing environmental standards for producers, curbing union activity, spending public funds to build dedicated infrastructure for specific firms, or forgoing tax revenue from new investment for extended periods of time. Unless the community has unusual assets—for example, a highly trained workforce, abundant natural resources that are easy to use, proximity to cheap transportation, cultural amenities, an excellent climate—it will have little bargaining leverage. People need jobs, communities need tax revenues to finance essentials such as schools, and the world expects economic growth. For most local areas capital is in the driver's seat.

Confronting these aspects of globalization is not easy, but recognizing them and investigating all possible options in the face of them are essential. No argument will be made that communities should consider isolating themselves in a nostalgic retreat to some vision of self-reliance. There is much to be gained by trade, as long as its full costs are met and its benefits distributed equitably. What communities must do in the face of globalization is assess their strengths and weaknesses and then articulate what they want. This, of course, involves forums and processes of public dialogue and participation, which constitute some of the most important tasks for community leaders (elected and informal). With goals clearly specified, communities can use multiple strategies to achieve them. Attracting private investment and public funds for development will most likely be on the agendas of all communities organized enough to take action. An additional path of action for development is to use the third sector and its institutions. Communities are doing so with positive results. In the process they are shifting some of the control over their destinies back to the local level and countering some of the negative forces of globalization.

Systemic Problems

Is it hypercritical to point out the problems caused by or needs unmet in the capitalist system of production and distribution? After all, capitalism has allowed much of the world to develop in ways generally considered good. Capitalism, and to a more limited extent twentieth-century "socialism," produced material abundance. Both were quintessentially modern in their driving forces, including their determination to win control over nature (this argument is developed in Berman 1988). Capitalism delivered the goods faster, and it could coexist with representative democracy better than could the state-based form of socialism that emerged as a model from the Soviet experience. Capitalism won, so end of story? While some serious thinkers and best-selling authors claim that history is over, many others of us prefer to think that people create history every day and that there is work to do. Capitalism has been with us a relatively short time in human history, and it has been reformed and can be some more. It is also replaceable. However, given past experiments in doing so, it will probably take a clear and persuasive alternative to spur many people to sign on again for such a major leap.

Some of capitalism's failings and limitations provide the rationale for attempting to devise alternative ways by which society can reproduce materially. One failing and two limitations are relevant to this discussion. The failing derives from the term *development*. This is a label for what is needed by communities where poverty exists, and what we call poverty exists because capitalist development is notoriously uneven. It works for some but not all, and this is a failing.

The first limitation to be confronted is the presumption that production and distribution must be done by hierarchical organizations controlled by individual owners, which is accompanied by a hostility to alternatives. (This limitation will be explored in chapter 2 in a discussion of cooperatives.) The second limitation is a presumption about human nature: that the only incentive motivating people is the possibility of making a great deal of money and, based on this presumption, the construction of organizations based largely on financial motivation. These limitations are generally ideological in character, and their imposition has served to aid capitalism's systemic reproduction and stability. Dynamic third-sector institutions often prove them wrong, or at least incomplete. In broader social terms, however, both these limitations have constrained the selection of tools available for addressing the development problem.

If the tendency of market capitalism to create change is broadly recognized, so too is its tendency to generate inequality in its material outcomes. Evidence provided in the 1980s and 1990s in the United States illustrates the shift in income and wealth to be expected when markets are given freer rein (see chapter 3). The outcome of this process is that large segments of the population seem to be left out of periods of rising prosperity, at least until labor markets tighten to the point that lower-wage workers gain some bargaining power. At that point either the market economy trips over some aspect of its own good fortune (e.g., it builds too much productive capacity) and begins the slide toward recession or the central bankers smell inflation and engineer the recession themselves. Either way people are thrown out of work, the safety net is insufficient to the task of seeing people through to better times, and many slide backward in economic condition. When the economy begins to grow again, they are likely to be the last to benefit. Since these people tend to live together in class- and race-segregated places, the problem appears as a need for community economic development.

Two standard counterarguments (almost clichés) carry some force here—just enough to make them useful in maintaining class privilege. One is the familiar maxim "a rising tide lifts all boats." The truth in this saying is that general economic growth can eventually make all participants in the economy better off. True, seventy years ago few rural poor people had indoor plumbing or telephones and today most can afford them, but this truth calls for a more careful definition of poverty, one that recognizes its historical and relative dimensions. No contemporary society would tolerate a system that made a large portion of its citizens worse off in absolute terms, but people seem to be accepting one that does so in relative terms. Poverty is experienced by people in their relation to others, and the fact that life is slowly getting better for the poorest in society does not repair the damage of relative depravation.

The other popular argument against worrying about inequality applies the trickle-down theory. The argument is that as some people become wealthy they will create more demand for the skills of the poor, such as cutting the lawns and cleaning the homes of the wealthy, which serve as means by which the poor can improve their or their children's lives. The reality behind this metaphor lies in the low wages paid for this work and the poor community resources available to people who live in low-income areas. Without resources such as good schools these communities become incubators for new generations of yard workers and maids. The gap grows, and all that trickles down is reproduction of class-stratified society. The poor have little to offer in the new global economy except their need-based willingness to work for low wages, and they may well lose opportunities for that work to people in other regions of the world who are conditioned by their life histories to expect far less materially. For those with few skills, restrictions on semiskilled and unskilled immigrants may provide some protection. Yet even if a job is grounded locally by supplying services rather than the more mobile production of goods, employers (households or firms) will use all possible strategies in their quest for low-wage workers.

Does capitalism have to produce this outcome? Yes and no. Yes, it is a system whose lifeblood is profit, and profit comes from reaping more in value from people's work than the value the employer has to pay to them.[3] No, in the sense that society can set limits on the disparity in rewards to work or mandate a higher base limit of acceptable pay. The means for achieving these ends are well known and practiced throughout the world. The United States, always cautious to minimize "distortions" of market outcomes with regulation, uses those remedies sparingly and some of them not at all. Other capitalist societies use them to temper extremes in market outcomes (Goodin et al. 1999) and to assure that poverty is a temporary experience, should markets deal a person a bad hand, and not a lifetime or intergenerational experience.

Market capitalism is a human construct rather than the natural order. It serves those who own capital, and its more laissez-faire forms serve them more overtly. Reforms to the system that make it less harsh are society's choice as well, and they may or may not carry acceptable prices in loss of efficiency or slower growth. The global economy discussed above is competitive, and when a powerful nation in this global system sets lowest-common-denominator standards in how its version of capitalism functions, it pressures other nations to dumb down to those same standards in order to compete.

New Roles (and Old) for the Third Sector

Among the new and more entrepreneurial nonprofits that have emerged in the past few decades are many that have wrestled with the development dilemma and performed key roles to ameliorate it. The organizations have taken multiple forms, and chapters 4 through 10 of the book highlight their organizational variety and elaborate on the examples summarized here.

One of the roles of the new breed of nonprofits has been *to focus community energy, skills, and resources on development challenges.* This has often started with dialogues about what should be done to improve a community. While this conversation should take place in the public arena, that is not always the case. Even when it does, the limitations on public-sector activity can limit the conversation. Organizations such as community development corporations (CDCs) reopen it, often in more focused forms. (See chapters 2 and 9.) CDCs were created in the late 1960s by units of the U.S. Department of Labor and Office of Economic Opportunity. The first was Hough Area Development Corporation in Cleveland, Ohio, begun in 1968; within three years there were over thirty CDCs attempting to foster development in rural and urban areas. In their early form their mandates were broadly developmental, targeting numerous aspects of poverty eradication and infrastructure revitalization. As CDCs matured, many became more focused on specific goals, such as improving the housing stock or saving an urban commercial area. Large foundations signed on as major funders for this work.

While the conversations CDCs use to rally resources may be less inclusive than a public conversation at its best, they can make up for this shortcoming by greater focus on the specific problems and goals they target. Their results have been mixed. They provide, however, an example of an organization that can target community resources for problem solving and attract more financial resources in the attempt to solve them than the private or public sectors were providing.

Much more project-oriented third-sector initiatives abound, and their goal is usually *providing specific goods or services.* An example is the use of cooperatives to provide child care. (See chapter 9.) Cooperative child care exists in many communities in the United States. Communities seeking to establish them are assisted by organizations such as Parent Cooperative Preschool International (www.preschool.coop) and cooperative extension branches of land-grant universities. Child care provides a classic case of a service for which market failure exists.[4] The private sector is involved in providing child care, but it struggles to find a way to do so and make money. Primary and secondary education are provided by the public sector because of their positive externalities, and broad public benefit is strong enough that numerous wealthy countries make funding of child care a public responsibility as well. In the United States, however, much of it has been left to individual funding and provision.

There are private-sector responses to this problem, used primarily in cases when for-profit employers or nonprofits seek to provide benefits to employees that will enhance the hiring leverage of the firms. Local public-sector initiatives and public-private partnerships to address the need have also been implemented. The third-sector response has been for those facing the need to self-organize, incorporate as a cooperative or nonprofit association, locate physical space, hire staff, buy insurance, and manage their own child-care service. If society accepted responsibility for the care and education of preschool children, much of this initiative would be unnecessary, but until that day cooperative child-care arrangements can do the job. Even with public provision, this service might still work best under the local control of parents and direct providers, as it does with the cooperative structure, but with better tax relief to help defray the cost of this expensive service.

Another area in which new third-sector initiatives have been prominent is *transferring and enhancing specific skills*. While the skills have typically been aimed at expanding participants' ability to succeed in the job market, others, such as parenting skills and household money-management skills provided by credit unions and religious organizations, can be included as well. The latter are extensions of the kinds of skills that the Girl/Boy Scouts and YWCA/YMCA have provided in the past, but the new job skills aspect has often taken the form of on-the-job training organized by nonprofits carrying on activities such as renovating housing. Others, such as the Bidwell Training Center in Pittsburgh (see chapter 9), are provided by organizations created for this purpose.

Perhaps the most unusual role for entrepreneurial third-sector organizations is their use to *build productive assets that stay in the community*. This role has traditionally been served by the first sector, but as private investment has proven unpredictably fleet-of-foot, communities have welcomed organizations that can build assets that are more grounded in the community. Nothing is permanent, but a community-based organization that creates a pool of savings for use by area businesses and households, such as a credit union, or creates a new museum or science center for use by local residents and visitors contributes to development. Jobs and other benefits result: the credit union provides access to banking services that might otherwise be unavailable or more expensive, its physical space can provide a meeting place in which to launch other forms of collective entrepreneurship, and its financial assets can help fund the activity; the museum or science center may attract visitors who spend money (e.g., for meals, housing) that can enhance business development. In these scenarios the first priority for use of accumulated capital can be for worthy, financially sound projects in the community rather than for the best possible return in international financial markets.

Nonprofit organizations are not generally seen as accumulators of capital unless they are foundations, and then their purpose is presumably to give the assets away. The idea of asset accumulation by nonprofits and cooperatives takes a page from the book of private, for-profit organizations. The twist, of course, is that the assets may be held collectively, and those who provide them (and society in general) expect some resulting collective good rather than simply private monetary gain.

In the capitalist system entrepreneurship is usually assigned to private, for-profit players for a number of reasons. But this is also a function that is undertaken by both other sectors. The public sector is entrepreneurial in creating public goods, from the classic case of the lighthouse to the interstate highway system and airports. During periods of U.S. history when the federal government was more involved in fostering development, citizens gained not only massive assets such as the Northwestern hydroelectric projects but also public hospitals and universities. Third-sector activity is familiar in the form of churches, synagogues, and mosques; YWCA/YMCAs; private schools and universities; and more. What is new in the asset building of nonprofits today is that some of their assets are intended to produce revenue, from which the organizations can grow more assets that will be used to expand their work. The for-profit stock corporation has been the bedrock institution of accumulation under capitalism. By aiming to stimulate community development by similar means, nonprofits are clearly encroaching on the terrain of private capital. Their purpose, however, is different. By taking on development projects where private capital has failed to deliver, nonprofit organizations also continue their historic mission of doing public good.

2

Third-Sector Scope, Scale, and Purpose

Recent third-sector growth is intertwined with changes in the sector's historical role in the United States and changes in both the public and for-profit sectors during the last quarter of the twentieth century. Other elements of the story are the increasing demographic diversity within the nation and changing work responsibilities that have buffeted traditional patterns of voluntary activity. This chapter addresses both the shape of the sector and indicators of its growth and change.

Dimensions of the Sector

Counting the third sector—whether by the number of organizations in it, those who work in it, or the volume of its economic activity—does not yield certain numbers. The diversity of the sector and the independence of its organizations make it quicksilver for the statistician, and those who have spent careers documenting and studying the sector routinely wrestle with its dimensions. This chapter draws on the best of their work, augmenting and updating it when necessary.

Tables 2.1–2.4 provide a four-part sector overview that serves as a visual reference and summary. Across the tops of the tables are the basic categories of organizations found in the third sector, which are grouped as public benefit (2.1), funding intermediary (2.2), member benefit (2.3), and mutual benefit and cooperative (2.4) clusters. Features that help distinguish the organizations are arrayed vertically on the left sides of the four tables. The spaces of this simple matrix provide room for only a word or two to summarize what are sometimes close similarities or subtle differences among organizations.

By one count the number of nonprofit organizations jumped from 309,000 in 1967 to nearly a million thirty years later (Herman 1995, 1997). Paid employment in nonprofits grew 41 percent between 1980 and 1990, a pace more than double the growth of national employment in the same period (Salamon et al. 1996, cited in Weisbrod 1998, 2). Using the revenues of nonprofits as an indicator, their significance in the national economy jumped from less than 6 percent of gross national product (GNP, the most used measure of economic activity at that time) in 1975 to over 10 percent of GNP in 1990 (Herman 1995). The numbers clearly indicate growth in the nonprofit area of the third sector. The significance of these broad measures of growth will be explored after a survey of the sector in which evidence on growth will be considered for each group of nonprofits, credit unions, and cooperatives.

Public Benefit and Service Providers

Public benefit and service organizations make up table 2.1. The clusters in which they are grouped are commonly recognized as primary areas of activity for the sector. Organizations in these clusters often coexist and compete with the institutions of either the public or for-profit sector. For instance, nonprofit hospitals compete with for-profit and public hospitals for patients, and private universities coexist and compete with public universities for students and research grants. When the U.S. economy is described as "mixed," the reference often points to the interplay of the private, for-profit domain with the public, when in fact the third sector is very much a part of the mix.

Health Care

Health care organizations include hospitals, nursing homes, home health care providers, and specialized outpatient facilities, among others. In 1987, 85 percent of general medical and surgical hospitals were nonprofits that accounted for 91 percent of revenue in their group. Sixty-four percent of home health care services in 1987 were provided by nonprofits (Rose-Ackerman 1996, 709, tbl. 3), and almost half of HMO enrollments were in nonprofits (710, tbl. 4). Measurement of nonprofit nursing care facilities indicates that from a quar-

Table 2.1 Institutions of the Third Sector: Public Benefit and Service Providers

Distinguishing Features	Health	Education	Social and Legal	Civic	Arts and Cultural	Religious	Research
Purpose	Health care	Education services	Charitable services	Advocacy	Cultural enrichment	Spiritual enrichment	Increased knowledge
IRS Code	501(c)(3)	501(c)(3)	501(c)(3) and (c)(20)	501(c)(3)	501(c)(3)	501(c)(3) and 501(d)	501(c)(3)
Scope of service	Payers and public	Payers and public	Public	Public	Public	Members and public	Public
Governance	Board and officers	Board and officers	Board and officers	Board and officers	Board and officers	Board and officers	Board and officers
Open membership?	n/a	n/a	n/a	generally	generally	generally	generally
Donors receive tax deduction?	yes	yes	yes	yes	yes	yes	yes
Earnings taxed?	no	no	no	no	no	no	no
Examples	Hospitals; nursing homes	Private schools and universities	Alcoholics Anonymous; Red Cross	NAACP; ACLU	Arts councils; zoos	Any religious organization	UL Inc.; medical research
Volunteer labor used?	yes	no	yes	yes	yes	yes	no

ter to a third of the service was provided by nonprofits, depending on whether establishments, beds, or revenues are being measured (711, tbl. 5).

Counting growth based on change in revenue relative to change in gross domestic product (GDP) for the United States, the period 1977–96 was one of expansion for nonprofits in health care, along with the rapid expansion in expenditure on health care generally in the country. The major acceleration in the presence of the third sector in this period came about because such a large portion of the nonprofit sector provides health services (Salamon 1999, 68–69). Changes in the mid-1990s slowed growth in overall expenditures on health care as a percentage of GDP and have also influenced the role of nonprofits in the sector. Cost containment through controls on Medicare spending, managed care as practiced by many providers of funding for health care services, conversions of nonprofit to for-profit hospitals, and growth in specialized hospitals as compared to general hospitals—the old nonprofit mainstay—have all contributed to this trend. Still, general hospitals are the institutional heart of the system, and nonprofits make up 55 percent of those institutions, provide 64 percent of hospital beds, and receive 72 percent of the revenue for general hospital care (81).

The role of third-sector institutions in health care is changing. The industry is being reshaped to allow the profit motive supposedly to stimulate changes in efficiency, and the public sector's role has shifted from provision of services in the older public institutions to government funding of much of the country's health care, especially for the fast-growing older segment of the population. When large expenditures for facilities and technology are necessary and profit is made possible, nonprofits tend to be squeezed to the sidelines. Should conditions for profit become questionable, as they did for for-profit nursing homes that were overbuilt in some parts of the country in the 1980s, the presence of the nonprofits—with commitments beyond the bottom line—can strengthen.

Home health care was one of the fastest growing components of health care in the period 1975–96 (85). Whether measured by the number of firms, their employees, or their revenues, nonprofits have played a minority role in this field relative to for-profit institutions. (An example of a cooperative urban home health care provider will be discussed in chapter 7.)

Education

Education looms large in the traditional third sector, especially because of the role of nonprofits in higher education. Counting by institutions, nonprofits account for 69 percent of four-year colleges; the public sector accounts for 28 percent, and for-profits a scant 3 percent. A different picture emerges in looking at two-year institutions since nonprofits are only 12 percent of the total, the public sector accounts for 69 percent, and for-profit institutions claim 19 percent (Rose-Ackerman 1996, 710, tbl. 4). If students rather than institutions are counted, the public sector's larger role in higher education becomes more apparent.

The U.S. tradition of public education is strongest, of course, at the primary and secondary levels. Here nonprofits make up 23 percent of institutions but serve only 10 percent of enrollments, while public schools serve 89 percent (Rose-Ackerman 1996, 710, tbl. 4). The first sector has a small presence in this area because profits are hard to come by in such labor-intensive activity, especially when public provision is the rule. The point of public provision of primary and secondary education is, of course, that there is a good public outcome: the society benefits from having well-educated citizens.

The debate over whether public funds should be used for "choice" through a "voucher" system points to a potential growth area for nonprofit, private schools. Private school options are often encouraged on the basis that competition will be good for the overly complacent public schools. However, these options raise the specter of segmentation that attracts the students who, for a complex mix of reasons, can gain the most from private education and leaves the public schools struggling with the students who are potentially most difficult to educate. Public schools would then face increasing taxpayer resistance to funding them. For those who fear the worst from this change, the history of what has happened to public hospitals and access to health care looms as a chilling lesson for "choice" in education. (Use of vouchers in education is discussed in chapter 11.)

Education has not been an area of growth for nonprofits largely because the trend for this sector has been the reverse of the situation for health care. Government spending on education as a percentage of U.S. GDP has decreased in the past three decades (Salamon 1999, 96). The negative impact on nonprofits would have been stronger if U.S. spending on education were not so heavily weighted to higher education, the area of greatest strength for the nonprofits. High fee income to nonprofit providers, largely in the form of rising tuition charges, has kept them strong. For the wealthiest of these institutions growth in endowment income and surges in donations received in the 1990s have contributed to their strength.

Social Service Providers

Social service providers are in many respects the backbone of the nonprofit sector, and related *legal services* are a smaller part of this cluster. Social service providers are numerous, they are diverse, they often reflect the third-sector practices of voluntary giving of time and money, and they have traditionally filled much of the void created by government and market failure in provision of social services. By some estimates nonprofits account for 90 percent of employment in the sector (Salamon 1999, 23). In part this is because their work is fundamentally labor-intensive. Some derive much of their operating income by performing services under contract for federal, state, and local governments, and many are also beneficiaries of a regular flow of resources from federated funders such as the United Way. These organizations do much of U.S. society's caring work, for example providing shelter for the homeless, child care, teen recreation programs, and disaster relief. As important as the services of these agencies seem, they actually receive a small portion of total spending in the economy. In the mid-1990s total spending on social services was $74 billion, approximately 1 percent of the U.S. GDP (110).

Growth in the social services area of nonprofit activity has taken place in spite of declining governmental funding. The federal government's real-dollar spending on social services declined by 15 percent between 1977 and 1994 (Salamon 1999, 116). However, the number of social services agencies outside of government grew by 130 percent between 1977 and 1992; employment by these agencies grew by 140 percent, and their inflation-corrected revenues increased by 240 percent between 1977 and 1996. Fee-based work attracted for-profit firms, whose growth was faster than that of nonprofits in general through the period. Still, by the mid-1990s nonprofits made up a majority of establishments, received a majority of the revenue, and employed a majority of the people employed in this field (112).

Legal services in the United States are provided primarily by for-profit firms, but the development of legal support agencies for the poor in the 1960s marked the early expansion of legal service nonprofits. Growth in legal services has occurred primarily in the area of public-interest legal organizations working in consumer rights, the environment, and civil rights (Salamon 1999, 141–42). They are often linked by their work, and sometimes organizationally, to civic organizations.

Civic Organizations

Civic organizations allow for collective expression of citizens' voices. They are advocacy groups as traditional as the Daughters of the American Revolution and as contemporary as animal rights organizations. Groups seeking to strengthen their participation in society, such as civil rights organizations, fit into this category. Alexis de Tocqueville's 1835 observations about American "associations" are strongly reflected by organizations in this group, which is the focus of current advocacy for strengthening "civil society" and "social capital" (discussed in chapter 12).[1] Fundamental to the vitality of these ever-evolving organizations is that they remain relatively easy and inexpensive to form, which accounts for some of the informality that characterizes the third sector. They have been essential to the development of social movements across the political spectrum. Public-interest advocacy organizations serve a myriad of causes, from neighborhood development to pro- and antigun campaigns. When they aggregate people of common interests, they may simply provide member services, and then they overlap with member-service organizations. If they serve their members by extensive political action, they overlap with another cluster of nonprofits, political action organizations.

Civic organizations have grown significantly in recent decades. From 1977 to the mid-1990s the number of organizations grew 68 percent, employment in civic nonprofits grew 48 percent, and their revenue increased 216 percent (Salamon 1999, 140–41). The growth of the Worldwide Web has accelerated the pace at which like-minded people can find each other, agree to join in common causes, and form nonprofit organizations to serve those causes.

Art and Cultural Organizations

Art and cultural organizations are mainstays of the nonprofit sector, even though their numbers in the United States constitute only 8 percent of nonprofit organizations and 2 percent of nonprofit employment (Salamon 1999, 123). Data for art and cultural organizations are mixed with sports and recreation data. Much of sports and recreation are provided by for-profit private-sector organizations, but volunteer work for soccer, hockey, little league, and other sports is typically organized by nonprofits.

The art and cultural side of this arena of activity is the territory of live theater (with 62 percent of employment by nonprofits), orchestras and operas

(99 percent employment by nonprofits), and museums, art galleries, and zoological gardens (95 percent employment in the private sector by nonprofits) (Salamon 1999, 125). Artistic and cultural enrichment finds little provision from the for-profit side of the private sector because it often does not provide sufficient profit. Put another way, it requires subsidy, and private giving accounts for 41 percent of the operating income of arts and entertainment nonprofits (126).

Government provides only 14 percent of the operating income of nonprofits in the arts (Salamon 1999, 126), and much of that funding comes from state and local sources. In fact, where public funding exists it has in recent years led to some of the notorious squabbles between second- and third-sector institutions. Former New York mayor Rudolph Giuliani's contretemps over exhibits at the Brooklyn Museum of Art and earlier attempts by members of Congress to censor photographs exhibited using National Endowment for the Arts (NEA) funding reflect problems that emerge when public officials feel compelled to impose (their) standards as limits on what is considered "acceptable" artistic expression. Still, grants from public funds at all levels of government help sustain the arts.

Growth in establishments, revenues, and employment in arts and recreation have been substantial over the past several decades, and nonprofits shared in this trend. For the arts it was fueled by Ford Foundation efforts and NEA seed money in the 1960s and 1970s, private charitable support in the 1980s, and in the 1990s growth in entry fees, other charges, and revenue from commercial activities (Salamon 1999, 128–31).

Religious Organizations

Religious organizations are generally included in the group of public benefit and service organizations, although they can also be included in the category labeled "member-serving" organizations. Part of the reason for their inclusion here is that they do public good, such as providing means for transmitting a variety of religious teaching and morality throughout society and delivering social services, cultural services, and international aid. Many religious organizations deliver social services beyond their membership—sometimes in the hope of attracting new members as they do. This, of course, is one of the flash points associated with proposals to make religious organizations eligible for federal funding for their social work or to enable their social service units to bid for federal service delivery contracts. Historically, religious organizations achieve automatic 501(c)(3) status because of the legal implications of the First Amendment with respect to religious practice that bar the government from limiting religious freedom. The desire to protect this aspect of the "separation of church and state" gives many in the religious community pause about their organizations becoming federal contractors subject to legal restrictions usually imposed in those contracts. Arguments against allowing religious organizations to receive public money cut the other way, reflecting concern that religious organizations would find it difficult to refrain from proselytizing while doing social work. (These issues are discussed in chapter 11.)

There are approximately two hundred religious denominations in the United States. Their financial support comes primarily from private giving (86 percent), with the remainder from endowment income and dues (Salamon 1999, 152). The number of religious organizations in the United States may be seriously understated as a result of the fact that because of their distance from the state there is no one institution with which they must register or to which they must report.

By measures of revenues and employment religious organizations in the United States have not constituted an area of growth for the third sector (Salamon 1999, 154). Still, religious organizations make up approximately a quarter of the public-serving nonprofits, and they account for approximately 10 percent of nonprofit employment (23). Religious organizations dominate among U.S. nonprofits in the percentage of charitable donations they receive. While the magnitude is difficult to determine precisely, religious congregations are estimated to receive from 48 to 62 percent of the value of charitable giving done in this country (the low figure is from Salamon 1999, 25, tbl. 3.2; the high figure is from Hodgkinson and Weitzman 1994, cited in Rose-Ackerman 1996, 703.) The motivation for this giving is nobody's business but the donors', which adds to the ambiguity in whether religious organizations are primarily member-serving or social service organizations. Whether members give to save their souls or to do some good beyond themselves, religious organizations are solidly U.S. citizens' favorite recipients of monetary donations.

Research and Testing Organizations

Research and testing organizations make up the last group in this cluster. While small in number, basic research institutes such as those seeking cures for diseases provide a quintessential public good—the creation of new knowledge that can be disseminated to form the basis of new health care treatments or new products. Public-sector grants for some of the research done by universities are based on the same rationale—that their research will help society. This is work that is disconnected enough from marketable products that it does not attract for-profit investment in research and development (R&D).

Other organizations in this group provide consumer information through product testing. Examples include the Consumers Union and the Underwriters Laboratories, Inc. Consumers looking for impartial information before purchasing a product can use the information provided by the Consumers Union through its website or in its monthly magazine *Consumer Reports.* The magazine does not generate revenue from advertising, a source of funds that could undermine the organization's commitment to impartiality. Instead appreciative donors give money to the organization, supplementing revenues from its sale of information.

Donations

Taken as a cluster, the organizations arrayed across the top of table 2.1 represent the heart of the traditional nonprofit sector. Donations of time and money are one of its hallmarks. Ninety percent of the voluntary labor in the United States goes to nonprofits, and most of that goes to service-providing organizations. Most of the remaining 10 percent goes to schools in the public sector (Weisbrod 1998, 13). In addition, some economists count the gap between the incomes of people who work in nonprofits and potentially higher paying for-profit equivalents as donations of labor. Donations of money come primarily from individuals and go primarily to religious organizations. For 501(c)(3) organizations the donations that have tax-reducing benefits for the donors provide an indirect means of financing the private supply of goods and services that are valuable to society, not profitable enough to attract for-profit provision at desired levels, and not provided by the government.

Funding Intermediaries

Funding for the work of service-providing organizations can come from individual donors, institutional donors, and the government. Institutional donors make up the segment of the third sector portrayed in table 2.2.

The category of funding intermediaries contains institutions that are central to the workings of many other nonprofits because they exist largely to direct resources to them. *Federated funders* are active in most communities

Table 2.2 Institutions of the Third Sector: Funding Intermediaries

Distinguishing Features	Federated Funders	Foundations	Financial Intermediaries
Purpose	Fund nonprofits	Fund nonprofits	Provide assets for financial nonprofits
IRS Code	501(c)(3)	501(c)(3)	Various
Scope of service	Social service nonprofits	Nonprofits	Nonprofits
Governance	Public board	Private board	Private board
Open membership?	n/a	no	no
Donors receive tax deduction?	yes	yes	no
Earnings taxed?	no	yes	no
Examples	United Way	Gates; Ford Foundations	Boston Community Captial

and are best known in the form of the United Way, the American Heart Association, and similar collectors and distributors of funds. Federated funders help make the voluntary giving process more efficient, in part because they work with employers in major institutions to raise funds at the places of employment, often with payroll deduction plans. Their contributions can make up a substantial portion of the operating budgets of local service agencies, and they can therefore hold significant power over those agencies.

United Way, the best-known of the federated funders, struggled through the 1990s. Its number of donors dropped 20 percent in the years following 1992 publicity surrounding its national president's use of charity money for his own benefit. This scandal would have harmed any nonprofit, but fundamental changes were also buffeting United Way. Corporate downsizing cut into work-based donations, and the national trend in giving shifted to favor hospitals and educational and religious institutions. These shifts cut into funds available for charitable work in poorer communities at the same time that another round of federal cutbacks in social services were affecting the same communities (Johnston 1997).

Foundations

Foundations are private entities given special nonprofit status for their charitable distribution of money. They distribute income from their investment portfolios that were created from money put in trust for public bene-fit. The sources of their funding are wealthy individuals such as Bill Gates and the Rockefeller brothers, corporations, and—in the case of community foundations—often a broader public. The number of foundations grew dra-matically through the 1990s, yet many are comparatively small. Highly pub-licized new foundations launched by dot.com millionaires have had their portfolios constrained by the turbulent conditions within the sector. Larger foundations such as Ford, Kellogg, D. & L. Packard, and B. & M. Gates have seen their fortunes rise and fall with the stock market as well. The assets of the Packard Foundation declined by 25 percent from 1999 to 2000; the Lilly Endowment grew by 36 percent over the same period (Lewin 2001b).

Much like the wealth distribution within U.S. society, the wealth of foun-dations is concentrated: in 1998 the top 1 percent of foundations controlled over 60 percent of all foundation assets (United States Census Bureau 2000, tbl. 841). Independent foundation assets totaled $327 billion in 1998 (Foun-dation Center 2000). The majority of foundation grants (in number and dol-lar amount) go to educational institutions and human service agencies. Tax law requires foundations to give and spend at a level of 5 percent of their assets annually, including their operating expenses. This spending rate can be achieved as an average for a three-year period, providing them some ability to tailor giving to the ups and downs of investment portfolios or re-cipients' needs. Each foundation pays a federal tax of 1 percent of its annual investment income if it is maintaining or increasing its level of giving, and a foundation pays 2 percent of investment income if giving declines. In some years foundations have chosen to pay millions of dollars at the higher tax rate rather than give more to charities and other nonprofits (Abelson 2000). The taxes paid, of course, also benefit society.

While foundations gain considerable recognition for their philanthropy, the magnitude of their funding relative to total philanthropic giving in the United States is in the range of 10 to 15 percent. As summarized by the American Association of Fundraising Council Trust for Philanthropy in its Giving 2002 report, foundations accounted for $26 billion, or slightly over 12 percent of philanthropy in 2001. In the same year individuals gave $161 billion (76 percent), corporations gave $9 billion (4.3 percent), and bequests made up the remaining 8 percent (American Association of Fundraising Counsel 2002).

Other foundations in this category of nonprofits include corporate foun-dations, estimated to number 2,022 in 1998, and community foundations, estimated to number 437 in the same year (Foundation Center 1999, 6). Corporations use foundations to smooth the flow and tax benefits of their charitable giving over years of high and low income. Corporations get the same tax relief as individuals for their gifts to foundations, and like private (family) foundations they determine to which nonprofits their funds go and in what magnitude. Corporate giving is generally managed as part of the corporation's shaping of its public image.

The new major player among public charities in the United States is the Fidelity Charitable Gift Fund, begun in 1992. It extends Fidelity's money management for its clients to their charitable giving. Individuals place at least ten thousand dollars each with the fund, receive tax deductions in the year they do so, and direct the fund to make contributions in their names to their chosen recipients. If its rate of growth continues, the Fidelity Fund (which now has competitors) will soon be the largest charity in the United States (Lewin 2001a).

Community foundations are growing in number and assets. They are established to aggregate contributions for use in support of nonprofits in the community or in some cases in areas as large as a state. In 1998 community foundations made up approximately 1 percent of foundations, held approximately 6 percent of foundation assets in the country, and accounted for 7 percent of foundation giving (Foundation Center 1999, 6). The wealthiest among community foundations, the New York Community Trust, typically counts among the largest ten U.S. foundations.

The nonprofit organizations in table 2.2 are deemed public service providers and accorded 501(c)(3) status, which makes donations to them tax-deductible for donors. Of course, this incentive stimulates giving at the expense of the public coffers. The rationale for this privileged tax treatment is that the public good done by the organizations is at least a match for what government could do with the revenue and that society's pluralistic needs are better met by this system of funding.

Member-Serving Nonprofits

Nonprofits whose primary purpose is to serve members appear in table 2.3. As is the case for third-sector institutions shown in tables 2.1 and 2.2, the variety in this category is large. The organizations that represent the capital-labor divide at work and in society—labor unions and business organizations such as chambers of commerce—are included here. Country clubs, bowling leagues, and fraternal organizations are social in nature

Table 2.3 Institutions of the Third Sector: Member-Serving Organizations

Distinguishing Features	Fraternal, Social, and Recreational	Labor Unions	Business and Professional	Political	Political Action
Purpose	Social	Collective action	Collective action	Advocate and elect	Shape policy
IRS Code	501(c)(7) and (8)	501(c)(5)	501(c)(6)	527	501(c)(4)
Scope of service	Members	Members	Members	Members	Members
Governance	Board and officers	Board and officers	Board and officers	Board and officers	Board and officers
Open membership?	Limited	Limited	Limited	yes	yes/no
Donors receive tax deduction?	no	no	no	yes— limited	yes— limited
Earnings taxed?	no	no	no	no	no
Examples	Clubs	UAW; SEIU	ABA; AMA	Parties and associations	PACs

and are organized as 501(c)(7) and (8) nonprofits. The American Association of Advertising Agencies and the National Rifle Association belong in this cluster. Political parties (527 nonprofits) and political action organizations (PACs) intended to influence public policy exist to serve the interests of their members.

Unlike the social service group, member-serving organizations generally do not have the ability to provide their donors with the advantage of deducting contributions from their incomes in order to reduce their personal taxes. (PACs, discussed below, are an exception.) What remains without the donor tax deduction advantage for these organizations are the other benefits of being nonprofit organizations: they do not pay taxes on their income, they generally pay no taxes on property they own or sales tax on purchases they make, and they can generally take advantage of subsidies such as reduced postage rates. They face the usual restrictions on nonprofits as well: none of their assets can be transferred to the advantage of private individuals, and commercial activities they may engage in for fund-raising can generate income that is deemed taxable.

The nonprofit status of the New York Stock Exchange (NYSE)—the apparent anomaly noted in chapter 1—can be clarified in this discussion of member-serving nonprofit organizations. In existence since 1792, the NYSE received the current form of its nonprofit status in 1971. It is organized to serve the interests of its members, to provide an efficient marketplace, and to "serve as a forum for discussion of the relevant national and international policy issues" (New York Stock Exchange 2003).[2] Stock and bond dealers (brokerage firms) are this nonprofit's members, and the benefits they gain lie in their ability to do business in the exchange. Membership is limited and has value to firms that could make money through serving customers who want to buy and sell securities. There is a market for membership, and firms pay for the entry tickets ("seats") for doing business in this exchange. Regulation of the industry, a hot topic in the wake of the financial scandals of 2001–2, is the responsibility of the federal Securities and Exchange Commission (SEC).

Labor Unions

Labor unions serve their members as nonprofit 501(c)(5) organizations. Their principal revenue flow is members' dues, which support an institutional means by which workers can elect to have collective voice in their dealings with employers. Unions, and labor-management relations in general, are regulated by the National Labor Relations Board (NLRB). Unions may maintain pension funds for their members, but if they do they are organized as separate entities and regulated under the 1974 federal Employment Retirement Income Security Act (ERISA).

Union decline in recent decades has had several causes. A changing set of jobs and work relations has evolved with the shift from a manufacturing to a service-driven economy. Employer opposition and an NLRB dominated by Republican appointees have made it more difficult for employees to unionize. Unions were slow to adapt to change and slow to strengthen organizing efforts among women, minorities, and service-sector workers. New efforts in these areas have slowed the decline in union representation in the workforce from what it might have been, but the existing more than two hundred unions in the United States represent only 13.5 percent of the labor force, down from 20.1 percent in 1983. The figure is 9 percent for the private sector. The public sector's 37.4 percent union membership is concentrated in state and local government (United States Census Bureau 2001d).

Unions can serve employees of nonprofit organizations, but in that work they often face burdens not encountered in their work in the for-profit sector. The burdens include a history of "sacrifice" and the ability of management in the nonprofits to draw employees into the ranks of its "donors" by paying submarket wages. The May 2000 strike by employees of the Museum of Modern Art in New York pitted lower-paid staff members against senior staff and wealthy trustees of, and donors to, the organization. Wealthy patrons of the arts do not spring to mind as supporters of labor's cause, and this confrontation exposed some of the difficulties of organizing employees of nonprofits. In higher education unionization efforts at Harvard and Yale have pointed up similar problems.

Business and Professional Organizations

Business and professional organizations with 501(c)(6) status might be thought of as unions for the middle class. Engineers of different specialties (e.g., the Society of Automotive Engineers), attorneys (the American Bar Association), and physicians (the American Medical Association), among others, use them to promote their interests. Local chambers of commerce exist to serve their business communities and the interests of those communities. More broadly the National Association of Manufacturers, the U.S. Chamber of Commerce, and the American Federation of Labor–Congress of Industrial Organizations (AFL-CIO) exist to serve their members.

Political Organizations

Political organizations were among those groups highlighted by de Tocqueville in 1835. By recent count over six thousand of them exist (Salamon 1999, 22, fig. 3.1). They range far beyond the dominant two parties in the U.S. electoral system, providing voice for those who feel that their interests are not well represented by mainstream politics. Some are formed as incipient parties hoping to make it to the main stage. Others exist to rally support for ideas or goals rather than to engage in electoral politics.

Political Action Committees

Political action organizations are the notorious PACs, whose 501(c)(4) status is officially labeled "social welfare organizations." Law limits the amount of direct political action that charitable nonprofit organizations can engage in, so they may develop parallel 504(c)(4) organizations for this purpose. For-profit corporations are free to lobby, but the funding for their lobbying is often done through nonprofit agents as well. Political action

Table 2.4 Institutions of the Third Sector: Mutual Benefit and Cooperative Organizations

Distinguishing Features	Credit Unions	Mutual Insurance	Consumers' Co-ops	Workers' Co-ops	Agricultural and Other Co-ops
Purpose	Financial services	Insurance	Goods and services	Jobs and income	Inputs, processing, marketing
IRS Code	501(c)(1) and 501(c)(14)	501(c)(15)			521
Scope of service	Members	Members	Members	Members	Members
Governance	Member board	Member board	Member board	Member board	Member board
Open membership?	yes	yes	yes	no	no
Donors receive tax deduction?	no	no	no	no	no
Earnings taxed?	no	no	no	yes	no
Examples	Navy Federal; Alternatives	State Farm	REI, food co-ops	Plywood mfg.s	Sunkist Growers; Ocean Spray

nonprofits are created to fund attempts to shape legislation and influence the votes of elected officials. The means by which money is given to them, who (individuals, corporations) gets what tax relief from giving to them, and how they are to be regulated are central issues in the political process. Court testing of recent campaign finance reform is taking place as this is being written, and it will affect the shape and behavior of these organizations. By Lester Salamon's count of organizations registered under IRS 501(c)(4) status, 140,000 of them existed in the mid-1990s (Salamon 1999, 139).

Mutual Benefit and Cooperative Organizations

The fourth major grouping of third-sector organizations is less well known than and often not considered related to the nonprofits described above (see table 2.4). For both reasons and since this book counts them as an important part of the third sector, they are described in greater detail than were the more familiar organizations already presented.

Mutual benefit and cooperative organizations belong in the third sector because they do not fit well within the first (for-profit) and second (public) sectors and because they have characteristics that link them to nonprofit third-sector organizations. They are most clearly not public institutions funded by taxes and governmental in nature. They differ from for-profit corporations in that they do not exist to enrich equity holders who have no direct activity with them other than supplying capital. While in the case of workers' cooperatives they operate to generate income for their members, the members are "patrons" who produce within the organization.

Credit Unions

Credit unions are the most familiar of these organizations because seventy-nine million Americans (approximately 30 percent) are credit union members (National Credit Union Administration 2002). Credit unions are organized by member-owners to provide themselves with financial services, and they are chartered under either state or federal law. North American examples date from the early twentieth century, and in the United States their current legal standing dates from the Federal Credit Union Act of 1934. Historically they are related to nineteenth-century English cooperative principles and nineteenth-century German credit cooperatives (Isbister 1994, chap. 2). They have typically been organized to serve members who are employees of organizations such as Kaiser Permanente (a nonprofit), the I.B.M. Corporation, or branches of government (e.g., the U.S. Navy), and they also serve members of professional organizations such as the Airline Pilots Association.

Originally credit unions provided their members with safe places for savings and low-cost loans, but as the world of consumer finance expanded, their services developed to include a broader mix of consumer lending, mortgages, credit cards, and more. When a credit union's revenues from providing services exceed the costs they incur in any given period, that credit union makes a surplus—often called a "profit." This "profit" differs from that of a conventional bank in that the credit union's surplus cannot be distributed directly to the organization's owner-members. The surplus can be used to enhance the financial stability of the organization, to build other assets such as a physical facility from which to operate, to expand services to members, or for some other use determined by the membership and its elected board of directors. Another difference between a credit union and a typical bank is that credit union members vote for their board of directors on the basis of one vote per member, whereas votes for a bank board are allocated based on shares of ownership. Unlike banks, credit unions depend on volunteers among their members to set policy and safeguard the organization while members of the board oversee that policy.

The number of credit unions in the United States used to be far higher than it is today, as many were closer to savings clubs in character. While their numbers have declined from nearly twenty-five thousand in the late 1960s to nearly ten thousand today, the number of members they serve increased from twenty million to over seventy-five million in the same period (Mishkin and Eakins 2000, 510–13). The total assets of credit unions are in the neighborhood of $400 billion, less than the assets of any one large international "mega-bank" such as Citigroup. Credit unions account for approximately 10 percent of consumer deposits and 15 percent of consumer loans (509). Their scale highlights the different outcomes for organizations designed to serve their members as compared to those intended to accumulate assets for their owners.

Some credit unions have been designed specifically to foster economic development in poor communities. Begun in the 1960s, these development-based credit unions won expanded federal deposit insurance for small credit unions with few financial assets in 1970 and created the advocacy organization called the National Federation of Community Development Credit Unions (NFCDCU) in 1974 (see chapter 10). This category of credit union can open membership to the unemployed and marginally employed who live in poor communities. The communities are typically those that banks have decided against serving with retail outlets and where that void has been filled by pawnshops, loan sharks, and check-cashing services. As alternatives to those businesses, community development credit unions offer better services at lower cost to residents. They also provide banking services that can make it more feasible for small businesses to regain footholds in these communities. At the broader institutional level they provide an excellent example of an alternative institution of accumulation (a topic addressed in chapter 3; a portrait of a community development credit union is provided in chapter 6).

Mutual Insurance Companies

Mutual insurance companies have a long history in the United States. Organized as 501(c)(15) nonprofits, they have generally accounted for a small percentage of the insurance industry compared to the percentage represented by for-profit insurance companies (Mishkin and Eakins 2000, 550–51). They are similar to reciprocal insurance companies that maintain subscriber savings accounts as a source of capitalization, but they are quite different from those organized as "stock" or for-profit companies. Mutual insurance companies share several characteristics with credit unions and cooperatives. They exist to provide for their members' protection and benefit—true to the idea of insurance as risk sharing. Recent years have seen rapid change in this portion of the insurance industry, as major mutual insurance companies have engaged in "demutualization" to become stock companies. MetLife and John Hancock Financial Services are two industry giants that have gone this route. Prudential Insurance, tainted by mismanagement and scandal through much of the 1990s, completed the process in 2002. The largest of the mutual insurance companies, State Farm Mutual, has yet to do so, although as a possible step in this direction it launched the for-profit State Farm Bank after passage of the 1999 Financial Services Modernization Act (the Gramm-Leach-Bliley Act).

In the typical demutualization process member-owners of the mutual insurance company receive stock for their position as company members—generally based on the size and longevity of their policies. The rush to demutualize has been a part of the privatization trend of the past two decades, and its rationale is that large companies need access to equity markets for capitalization and expansion. Expansion is driven in part by the reshaping of the entire financial sector of the economy by mergers, acquisitions, and the elimination of separate spheres of commercial and investment banking activity that had been mandated by the Banking Act of 1933 (the Glass-Steagall Act). In the case of smaller mutual insurance companies, demutualization has sometimes been accompanied by little compensation for policyholders (owners) and big payoffs for top management who gained stock options previously unavailable in this form of organization (Paltrow 1998). It is early to assess fully the impact of these changes, but they have eliminated a part of the third sector and incorporated it into the profit-seeking world of big capital.

The last columns of table 2.4 distinguish three categories of cooperatives: consumers', workers' (producers'), and agricultural and other co-ops. Cooperatives do not have as large a presence in the United States as they do in some other nations.[3] Co-ops are represented internationally by an advocacy organization called the International Cooperative Alliance (ICA), begun in 1931 and based in Switzerland. Co-ops trace their history and operating principles[4] to the Rochdale consumer cooperative, founded in Rochdale, England, in 1844. Three operating ideas form the heart of most cooperative activity: members who use a cooperative own it; democratic control is assured on the basis of one vote per individual member; and services are provided at cost to members (Isbister 1994, 26–27). Workers' cooperatives are different enough that they do not reflect the third of these principles, as will be made clear below.

Consumers' Cooperatives

Consumers' cooperatives are the most common form of this kind of business and the form that attracts the largest membership. They are open to all, easy to join, and usually require a nominal membership fee. They actively seek the involvement of their members in governance matters and are expected to report their financial conditions and performance to their members on a regular basis. Those who manage co-ops work for their member-owner-customers. U.S. advocacy, education, technical assistance, and financing for cooperatives are available from a number of sources operating at the state, regional, and national levels. Consumers' cooperatives provide housing, child care, home energy, food, burial services, clothing and sporting equipment, health care, and a host of other goods and services to millions of members in the United States. They have been successful and—just like traditional businesses—they have failed.

Older Americans know cooperatives through either food-buying co-ops formed during the 1930s or the rural electrification co-ops started in the same era. A later generation encountered them as sources of "natural" foods during the 1960s and 1970s at the beginning of popular concern about excessive food processing and additives. Some of the informal storefront co-ops or bulk-buying food clubs of the 1960s have been transformed into large and successful retail co-ops, and rural electric co-ops still maintain a large percentage of U.S. electric transmission capacity (see chapter 9). The retail world of food co-ops has provided the basis for cooperative distributor-wholesalers to meet their needs.

Consumers' cooperatives, particularly the food co-ops among them, share key attributes with third-sector nonprofit organizations, including the use of voluntary labor. Members volunteer in an effort to keep costs and prices low, and volunteer work has strengthened the role of co-ops in building community. When volunteer work has run into conflict with members' time constraints, two types of membership have evolved. Those who choose to contribute the required number of voluntary hours of work receive a discount on store prices, and those who do not work in the co-op pay "regular" prices—the same that nonmembers pay if they shop in the store.

Nonmembers are usually allowed to use a co-op as if it were just another grocery store, but they do not share in the end-of-year distribution of surplus that goes to members.

Workers' Cooperatives

Workers' cooperatives are sometimes known as producers' cooperatives because their members produce in them. Unfortunately agricultural cooperatives are often called "production co-ops" or "producers' co-ops" as well. For clarity in this book cooperatives will be called "workers' co-ops" when their owner-members work in them and "agricultural cooperatives" when they exist to process and market the products of their member producers or provide inputs for them.

An aspect of the porous border of the third sector deserves mention here. It requires a distinction between workers' cooperatives and worker-owned firms that places the co-ops in the third sector and counts the worker-owned firms as part of the for-profit sector. The distinction is that workers' co-ops adhere to principles of cooperation, including (equal) voice provided to worker-members by their participation in the work of their firms. Worker-owned businesses base voice (votes) on relative capital ownership—the number of stock shares held. This distinction puts worker-owned firms in an unusual (and interesting) corner of the traditional capitalist world of commerce,[5] whereas workers' co-ops more closely reflect the principles of democracy and equality associated with the third sector.

Workers' cooperatives are the least common and the least well known type of co-op in the United States, although they have existed here since the first was founded by carpenters in Philadelphia in 1791 (Gunn 1984, 30). Their largest presence in an industry has been in plywood manufacturing in the Northwest, where they have been active since 1921 and have accounted for over 20 percent of softwood plywood production at some points in the industry's history (Gunn 1984, chap. 4; 1992; Pencavel 2001). These firms are owned, managed, and staffed by their members. It has been common in their history that the core, and generally a majority, of their workforce consisted of owner-members of the firms and that supplemental workers have been hired as needed. Where used, hired employees create a two-tiered work world, with only owner-members sharing democratic control and any surplus generated by the co-op.[6]

While consumers' cooperatives seek to deliver desired goods or services to members at good prices, workers' cooperatives exist to sell their goods or services in the market in order to provide income and job security to their members. Workers own the firms; make their policy decisions on a one-person, one-vote basis; and appoint or hire managers. Capitalization for these firms is usually provided by members as they join the organizations or paid over time from members' earnings. A workers' co-op typically distributes regular paychecks to members and sets aside a part of its earnings for expenses, taxes,[7] new capitalization, and reserves. At the end of an accounting period earnings not needed for other purposes are paid to owner-members. Reflecting the co-op heritage, this distribution is generally based on patronage—the hours worked by individual owner-members or their pay for the accounting period.

Workers' co-ops have a mixed record of success, as do all small businesses. Historically they have been bedeviled by underinvestment and a lack of finance capital. Workers typically do not have large amounts of savings with which to capitalize a firm. Workers' co-ops seem like strange creatures to banks. Their internal "owners" are numerous and equal, and managers may have less authority than banks are used to seeing. These problems provided part of the rationale for the founding of the National Cooperative Bank (described in chapter 6). While most of its activities have been directed to other forms of cooperatives, it also provides a broad range of financial services to workers' co-ops.

Throughout most of the history of workers' co-ops the financial structures they have adopted have contributed to their problems. If capital paid in by members was held collectively and no financial return other than improvements in productivity or value-added resulted from it, owner-members were likely to resist further investment (Gunn 1984, app. 2). Advances in theoretical understanding and practice made by and for workers' co-ops in the 1970s have helped solve these problems. The conceptual advance came from economists' close study of the problem (Vanek 1977, chap. 9), and the actual advance in practice came from the remarkable success of the Mondragon group of industrial co-ops in Basque Spain. Both recognized that owner-members would have to retain a claim on at least some of the capital they paid into the co-op and that their invested money should be paid a limited return consistent with the Rochdale principles. Collectively held assets should be built from surplus. Most of the forces working against member investment could be resolved by including these features in the financial structure of the firms; co-ops could then capitalize at magnitudes that enabled them to compete in industries with advancing capital-labor ratios.

Challenges remain for this form of co-op. Perhaps the most difficult to surmount is that members of workers' co-ops often live with high amounts of financial risk. Like those of the small businessperson and the farmer, their jobs and much of their life savings may be tied to the same organization. One of the next breakthroughs in fostering development of workers' cooperatives will be to develop funding intermediaries that can hold equity positions in a portfolio of them yet not interfere with their internal management. The co-op principle of a fixed return on invested funds would apply here, but that is an unusual stipulation when the financial entity would be an equity holder in organizations that face considerable market uncertainty and risk. It is difficult to resolve the contradiction between needing a venture capital fund for workers' co-ops and requiring the fund to play a low-key role in management and accept a fixed return on its capital with no possibility of large payoff (the carrot for the typical for-profit venture capitalist). Through the work of the Cooperative Development Institute (www.cooplife.com) in Greenfield, Massachusetts, and other organizations, attempts are being made to conceptualize and launch such a fund.

Agricultural Cooperatives

Agricultural cooperatives provide insight into another gray area of the third sector. Ambiguity arises because even though these are cooperatives, in their actual operation most of them behave like traditional for-profit corporations. These firms exist to provide inputs to or process and market the produce of their members, who are agricultural growers (farmers and large corporations). They grew out of traditional advantages of cooperation among farmers, providing joint ownership and operation of processing equipment and factories that individual farmers would be unlikely to be able to build for themselves. They also provided many a farm producer with freedom from the market power that privately owned processors had over them at harvest time and provided income from capturing the value-added in processing.

Today the big-business character of agricultural co-ops comes in part from the scale of facilities needed for some processing operations, but more fundamentally it results from the need to market the resulting products. Approximately 30 percent of U.S. farm products are marketed through cooperatives (National Cooperative Business Association 2003). The names of cooperatives that are well known to the public are familiar because of the advertising they do and the outlets they have created for the products they make. Many valuable brand names belong to major co-op producers: Welch Foods is owned by the National Grape Cooperative Association; Birds Eye frozen food is a product of Pro-Fac Cooperative; the Blue Diamond name in almonds is Blue Diamond Growers Cooperative; Ocean Spray is the brand of Ocean Spray Cranberries Co-op. These co-ops compete in a world of giant transnational corporations such as PepsiCo (Tropicana brand) and Nestlé, and they tend to adopt their modes of behavior.

Another example of the buying and marketing side of this group of cooperatives is ACE Hardware, a supply co-op for independent hardware stores with over $2.9 billion in wholesale sales to member stores in 2001. It allows volume purchasing and national advertising that enables its independently owned member stores to compete with Lowe's and Home Depot.

Of the largest one hundred co-ops in the country forty are in agriculture. The largest, Farmland Industries, sold $9 billion in feed, seed, fertilizer, and other farm necessities in 2001. In May 2002 it filed a petition for voluntary reorganization under Chapter 11 of the U.S. Bankruptcy Code. Indications are that its expansion in the 1990s left the company with too much debt and that it now plans to pare down to concentrate more on the food aspects of its business (Palmer 2002).

Being a co-op in the world of big business has inherent disadvantages, especially when it comes to raising large amounts of equity capital. Co-ops cannot sell stock on equity markets, the typical path to new capitalization for business. Their need to distribute surplus to their members limits their ability to build a large amount of retained earnings. Without a large equity pool they find it difficult to borrow in large amounts. The National Cooperative Bank has provided them some relief by offering lower-cost loans than they would face with other lenders, but they are still doing battle in a world into which they fit awkwardly.

The boards of directors of agricultural cooperatives consist of farmers. Some are from traditional family farms and some run major agribusinesses themselves, and they have a strong track record of developing brands that consumers know and trust. Because of changes in consumer habits such as demand for single-serving juice containers—the changes themselves often encouraged by advertising—the co-ops have to respond quickly, join the advertising juggernaut with its high costs, and compete. This trend has hastened substitution of business principles for cooperative principles. The National Cooperative Business Association (formerly the Cooperative League of the United States) is the nonprofit association representing these large co-ops. It has joined with other, more grassroots organizations in an attempt to be part of a cooperative movement in this country while it advocates for and serves its member co-ops.

According to the National Cooperative Bank there are nearly 50,000 co-operatives in the United States, including housing co-ops, and they serve nearly 120 million members. The recession of 2001 certainly slowed co-op growth: among large cooperatives the revenue of the top 100 co-ops remained the same from 2000 to 2001 (National Cooperative Bank 2003).

Are agricultural co-ops a part of the third sector? On one hand the answer might be yes and they could be claimed as flagship institutions. They answer to their members and provide important services to them while providing scales of operation that keep their members capable of competing with major private-sector firms. On the other hand their size and business practices make them a tenuous fit with the Rochdale principles. Because of their history and their potential to serve more than just capital owners they are counted here as part of the third sector.

Why Third-Sector Growth?

Trends in the data cited in this chapter reflect growth in absolute terms and growth relative to both other sectors. Writers on the nonprofit components of the third sector have offered several explanations for the growth. The first is the diverse population of the United States. Heterogeneity has meant that one-size-fits-all government programs to address needs have been less viable here (Weisbrod 1988, 25–31). With new rounds of immigration enriching the nation in recent decades newly diverse needs have meant new cultural challenges, and new nonprofits have emerged to meet these needs. This explanation may be credible for the United States, but international comparisons are reminders that it is not the whole story. History and politics also matter.

The ideological tendency in the United States favoring restricted state activity has produced a comparatively impoverished public sector, as John Kenneth Galbraith argued decades ago (1958, 198–99; 240). From this nation's English roots in law and custom its citizens have inherited both suspicion of the state and an inclination toward using associations to share interests and solve problems.[8]

Ambivalent feelings toward the federal government gained momentum in recent decades and fueled the related trends now known as privatization and devolution. Both have accompanied the attempt to diminish the size of the national government and its "intrusion" into the activities of the private sector. Privatization has led to the contracting-out of services that had been provided by government. *Devolution* is the label applied to attempts to move to the state and local level those activities that had been the responsibility of the federal government. Devolved responsibilities newly assigned to state and local governments may or may not have been funded by the national government. State and local governments were often engulfed in tax-reduction campaigns, and they were institutionally unprepared to provide the services required. Devolution and privatization have created new opportunities for private-sector—both for-profit and nonprofit—initiatives to win contracts to provide (mostly) services. Social services such as job training and drug treatment have been primary areas for growth of contract service delivery. Job training has been central because of the emphasis on eliminating "welfare" and expanding opportunities for paid work. Both the historical emphasis for nonprofit organizations to do "caring" work and the fact that they were already engaged in delivering social services made them natural candidates for these contracts. In this arena they could compete well with for-profit providers.

Both increased diversity of the population and the trend toward privatization have created a paradox. At the same time that social needs were perceived as growing, the government institutions that people had counted on to respond to the needs (at least since the 1930s) were constrained (Weisbrod 1998, 20). From this paradox an avenue of growth for nonprofits was created. Part of the paradox is the paucity of resources for the work at hand, and this plays to both a strength and a weakness of nonprofits. Nonprofits deliver at rock-bottom cost partly because of volunteer labor and partly because of moderate rates of pay for their staff members. Add the fact that they do not need to pay taxes or return profit to stockholders and this creates a growth situation for nonprofits based on these "competitive advantages."

Another reason for the growth of nonprofit activity stems from their efforts to raise revenues by providing goods and services that are unrelated or only marginally related to their missions. This is an area of activity in which the entrepreneurial side of nonprofits has been most clear, and it is related to their attempts to deal with the funding paradox described above. Costs of production have risen for nonprofits because much of what they do is labor-intensive. Technological advances that helped goods-producing industries make productivity gains that could help reduce costs of production are less readily applicable to services such as counseling, health care, and education. Facing rising production costs and attempting to keep the cost of their services in reach of their target recipients, nonprofit institutions have developed revenue-producing initiatives. A gift shop at a museum is one example; a more significant example in terms of revenue is the housing provided by universities to their students. This commercial activity is a thorn in the side of for-profit competitors who provide similar goods or services, and it has made nonprofits the target of campaigns to restrict their activities.

In summary, the third sector is a large, diverse, and in many respects dynamic part of the U.S. economy. The sector's historical mission has been to fill the cracks and repair the damage of a system that delivers success and failure. It has done this well, but it can do more. The next chapter explores the major failing of the U.S. economy—its uneven pattern of development—and what third-sector institutions have done and can do about that. It considers their potential to be catalysts of new activity in the mixed economy: badly needed new organs of development rather than Band-Aids.

3

Development and the Third Sector

Development—understood in the limited sense of increasing production of goods and services—comes about primarily through private, for-profit activity in a capitalist economy. The second sector complements this activity by providing essential physical, legal, and regulatory infrastructure. The presumed role of the third sector has been to clean up the mess that results from this arrangement. However, by the end of the twentieth century leading institutions of the third sector were taking on new roles in the quest for development. What brought the change about? This chapter explores the concept of development, why it is an issue in a wealthy country, and what new roles third-sector institutions might play in that development. The aim is to provide insight into the forces prompting new third-sector initiatives.

Development and Uneven Development

It is common to criticize economic measures of development, especially the single measure of growth of gross domestic product. Reducing the phenomenon of development to one indicator—growth in a nation's, state's, or county's production of final goods and services—sometimes simplifies too much to be useful. The figure leaves out accounting for what (not how much) is produced, omits "externalities" that should count against and sometimes for the sum used as indicator, and leaves out unpaid activities essential to life. Recent feminist analysis and development of "quality of life" indicators in this country and elsewhere have attempted to redress the shortcomings of measuring development by one indicator.[1] Other thoughtful people have long argued for less material approaches to the issue—those that would emphasize enhanced forms of community, ecology, or spirituality, among others.

Along with positive outcomes material development has a long history of creating negatives: pollution, congestion, conspicuous consumption, overwork, people left behind, loss of community—the list is long. Still, in the casual cost-benefit assessment of development as more goods and services, people tend to think the benefits outweigh the costs. At a minimum development is seen as providing new ways of using resources and new technologies that could ameliorate the negative outcomes of the process. With this optimism development as more goods and services (with some of the services providing damage repair) goes forward. If the repair cannot be provided within the first-sector quest for profit and if society cannot agree to provide it through collective government action, then repair falls to the third sector. This provides reason for the "subsidies" of donated funds and labor that characterize the sector.

There is a larger negative outcome to pursuing development in this way, which is that people and the places they inhabit are often left out of it. When the nation last lost faith in the ability of the mixed capitalist system to provide universal development, the sector that provided relief and rejuvenation was government. From the Great Depression through the 1960s the second sector played a key role in stimulating the delivery of goods and services. When the first sector could not deliver, government attempted to do so. The results were mixed, but gains were made and the system as a whole grew. When the performance of the system faltered in the 1970s, new answers were harder to find and government was gradually labeled the problem. Decades of ideological and practical maneuvering over reducing government's role in the economy ensued. Economic performance as measured by GDP lagged for some time, accelerated in the late 1990s to the extraordinary mid-century levels, and then faltered again. It is unclear what will follow the economic stumble of 2000–2002, but it is clear that when the next serious recession—a normal occurrence for the systems—is encountered, people will be ill-prepared. The second sector will have to gear up quickly, which will be difficult since relief programs were dismantled in the 1980s and 1990s and government resources are now in demand for "security." Come the next serious recession the third sector will be called on to perform Herculean efforts. With a broad and deeper mix of needs before this country it will be even more difficult to see the pockets of underdevelopment that continued through the growth period of 1995–2000. They are the system's dirty linen.

Why talk about development in a country as rich as the United States? By most generalized measures of economic performance and product the United States is exceptionally well off. The answer, of course, is that deep pockets of poverty—relative and absolute—persist in this wealthy country. The "rising tide lifts all boats" argument criticized in chapter 1 would hold true only if a society made certain that it did, which would take collective action, sharing of resources, and domestic forms of aid and "nonmarket" investment. Unwilling to do these things, citizens of the United States live with existing development problems.

Even in the best of times for growth-as-development in the United States, the post–World War II decades, urban and rural underdevelopment persisted. It should not be surprising that the same holds true today after a short period of strong growth in the latter half of the 1990s. What can be done about it? The answer from most official quarters is "Not much," especially if it involves public funds. Even if the funds were made available, there is little agreement about what could be done with them. This mix of willful and real ignorance has created a vacuum in which discussion of the problem does not take place at the national level. The common advice is to keep breathing until globalization brings a magic wand to each neighborhood, town, or region. Frustration with this nonapproach has shifted attention to local and regional efforts to solve problems that are impossible to ignore when observed at these levels.

The reasons for uneven development are difficult to explain, tied as they are to history of how the country developed, what groups had and have power, and how people and capital move about the economy. Two approaches help to illustrate it today. The first is to consider the implications of disparities in economic and quality-of-life indicators for subregional spatial areas. The second is to observe national disparities in income and wealth distribution. Both help sustain uneven development and, with that, the need for third-sector repairs.

Local disparity in the outcome of economic activity is readily apparent to any person who travels between communities. A commute between a wealthy suburb and the upscale office district of a city normally takes one through poor urban and suburban areas. If the commute is from the poor areas to work in the homes of the well-off, the disparity cannot be missed. Evidence in the form of data is readily available from county and state statistical sources, from the *Statistical Abstract of the United States* found in most public libraries, or from numerous state and federal websites. An easy example can be found within the state of Connecticut, the wealthiest in the United States through much of the 1990s as measured by per capita income. Within this wealthy state are urban areas of remarkable mixes of wealth and poverty (e.g., Hartford and New Haven) and mostly poverty (e.g., Bridgeport). Connecticut also has rural poverty, especially in its northeastern counties. Looking beyond income, indicators such as high school drop-out rates, rates of infant mortality, and crime rates show similar patterns that are repeated in every other state in the nation.

Among the many differences between well-off neighborhoods and poor communities are what can be called life opportunities. Conditions in the poorer communities lead to lagging intergenerational transfers of life's resources there relative to those in other communities. Disparities are apparent in nutrition, environmental hazards, education, health care, time and resources for parenting, and more. Setbacks delivered on children are difficult to correct later in their lives. The case for the problems can be argued in relative terms (Michael does not get as good an education in East Hartford as Johnny does in West Hartford) and in absolute terms (inadequate nutrition, pure and simple).[2]

Evidence on income distribution and its trends is readily available and often summarized in the press. Information on wealth distribution is less well reported and more controversial when it is. The usual portrayal on income involves the array of data into fifths (quintiles) of families and the percentage of aggregate national income each receives. The technique provides a picture of basic income distribution and, if used consistently over time, its trend. In table 3.1 the 2000 data are in the first column, followed to the right by data for 1990, 1980, and 1970. Included in the bottom row are data on the shares of income going to the 5 percent of families with the highest income. In the thirty years of this data the 20 percent of families with the highest income saw a 22 percent rise in its share of national income; the 20 percent of families with the lowest income experienced shrinkage of 33 percent in its share. The 60 percent of families with the lowest income, a solid majority, saw its income position worsen, while the income of the top 5 percent of families increased by 40 percent.

The trend is clear: income has become more unequally distributed in recent decades. More specific data indicate that deep divisions by race and

Table 3.1 U.S. Income Distribution: Percentage Shares of Aggregate Income Received by Each Fifth and Top 5 Percent of Families

	2000	1990	1980	1970
Lowest fifth	3.6	4.6	5.1	5.4
Second fifth	8.9	10.8	11.6	12.2
Third fifth	14.9	16.8	17.5	17.6
Fourth fifth	23.0	23.8	24.3	23.8
Fifth fifth	49.7	44.3	41.6	40.9
Top 5 percent	21.9	17.4	15.3	15.6

Sources: U.S. Bureau of the Census, *Statistical Abstract of the United States, 1996,* 467, tbl. 719. Statistics for the year 2000 are from http://www.census.gov/hhes/www/img/incpovoo/fig12.jpg [23 July 2002].

gender exist as well, but with some hopeful signs that these disparities are diminishing. The outcomes presented in table 3.1 are largely indisputable, although the reasons for them are debated at length. Connecting this picture of distribution with the areas of poverty (underdevelopment) addressed above, and understanding that the spatial living arrangements defining most communities are those of segregation by class and race, one powerful outcome of uneven development is seen. In a market system, consuming goods and services requires money. When those who have it tend to live in the same geographic areas, the delivery of goods and services is skewed to those areas.

Data on wealth distribution have gradually become more readily available and help explain facets of uneven development as both cause and effect. The most recent data at the time of this writing was from 1998.[3] Total wealth is distributed among the population as illustrated in table 3.2. The wealthiest 1 percent of households hold (own) 38 percent of the wealth in the nation (or the nation's wealth). The wealthiest 10 percent of households (the 1 percent just cited and the next 9 percent in wealth holding) hold 71 percent of the wealth, and the remaining 90 percent of households hold the remaining 29 percent. The bottom 40 percent of households own 0.2 percent—virtually none—of the wealth in the nation. What the lower 90 percent of wealth holders do "own" is approximately 70 percent of the liabilities measured in the society. The percentage of wealth held by the wealthiest 1 percent of households in the United States remained relatively steady from 1945 until the early 1970s and then began to climb. That percentage rose dramatically in the 1980s. Markets tend to reward those who can most readily take advantage of them to make (more) money. Progres-

Table 3.2 U.S. Wealth Distribution: Percentage of Household Wealth Holding by Asset Categories and Net Worth, 1998

	Top 10 Percent	Remaining 90 Percent
Stocks	82	18
Bonds	91	9
All assets	63	37
All liabilities	30	70
Net worth	69	31

Sources: Doug Henwood, "The Nation Indicators," *The Nation,* 9 April 2001, 8; "Measuring Privilege," *Left Business Observer* 78 (1997):3. Data for bonds are from 1995.

sive taxation can ease the ensuing growth in disparity if society can muster the will to make it work. When it cannot do so, trends emerge such as that experienced in the last two decades in the United States.

While communities are segregated by income and race, they are also segregated by wealth holding because wealth holding is fundamentally linked to class. Wealth is income-producing property. It provides income in addition to wages or salaries (except for those people who have so much wealth that they do not have to work), and it provides means by which to make down payments on homes (the most common vehicle for saving among the "middle class"), pay for children's university educations, or survive life's calamities. Individuals who do not have it and those who do are separated spatially, and those areas populated by people with little or no wealth are the underdeveloped areas in need of new economic activity. Without financial assets residents of underdeveloped areas are less or unlikely to be able to start businesses, assure quality educations for their children, have life insurance, or own homes. Poor communities lack assets. While much of the attention paid to them in recent years has emphasized "cultural" assets, often with racist and/or classist overtones, what is really missing in them and has been missing over the long haul is a modicum of wealth.

The problems of underdevelopment that provide incentive for much of the activity of third-sector institutions could largely be eliminated given more equitable distributions of income and wealth in the country.[4] But U.S. citizens are so conditioned by the rhetoric of growth at any cost and rising tides that they have been moving in the opposite direction. Large boats and yachts have been lifted for two decades. By the time a period of prosperity begins to lift rafts and rowboats the system is frequently subjected to a cooling-off period through tighter monetary policy. The development process in the United States often bypasses poorer communities, but the negative impacts of recessions do not.

Dynamic organizations of the third sector have taken up the challenge of development for poor communities. Recognizing how unlikely development is for many of these communities under current conditions, they attempt to jump-start the process by begging resources, combining them in innovative ways, devoting extensive time and energy to creating new initiatives, and performing sometimes daring entrepreneurial feats. Judged against the scale of better-off communities in periods of economic growth, their results could be called meager. But judged against the continued stagnation of poorer communities even in times of growth for the economy as a whole, their results are impressive. They create jobs, train people for jobs, provide health and child-care services, provide financial services, help communities get organized, attract resources that would otherwise bypass the communities, and more. They also help repair civil society, shape social capital, and reflect social entrepreneurship.

Before turning to criteria that can be used to address whether or not these organizations are successful, an irony should be highlighted. If third-sector (or third- and second-sector) strategies for development work, they make themselves unnecessary. Capital will be attracted to communities on the rise, and it will be profitable to offer services and recruit employees there.[5] So if they are successful, development strategies obviate themselves and the profit motive takes over. Capital avoids paying for its mess, except by taxes or donations. Society could choose to spread income and wealth more evenly by systematically eliminating the pockets of poverty that result from capital's neglect or abuse. Instead the United States, almost uniquely among wealthy nations, has chosen to condone the poverty quietly. The prices paid are shattered lives across generations and the costs of the struggles needed to revive the areas of neglect.

Good Development and the Third Sector

What needs to happen to make life better for people in poor or disadvantaged communities, and what can third-sector institutions contribute to making these things happen? In arguments made above, the criterion of economic growth was used to summarize the development process even while recognizing its limits. Here the argument turns more specific and concrete, seeking initiatives by third-sector institutions that can improve people's lives. The outcome should be more growth for the economy, especially if for-profit institutions join the process, but this growth will be the *result* of numerous starting points. In the best of cases it will result from assuring that fundamental needs are met for those who have not yet enjoyed their fulfillment. With development will come the realization that growth will have to be regulated and constrained, as it is in wealthier communities.

While a long list of good criteria for third-sector activity could be constructed, five that are both essential and achievable are highlighted: creating and retaining social surplus; providing jobs at a living wage; operating in environmentally sustainable ways; creating dynamic linkages, multipliers, and spin-offs; and meeting basic needs.

Social Surplus Creation and Retention

For development of any kind to take place social surplus creation and retention must occur. Social surplus is the financial wherewithal for future development that can be set aside from a period's productive activities and used to capitalize the next round of production. Using an agricultural analogy, it is seed grain for the next crop. In modern capitalist societies social surplus is most clearly recognized as income to property—the wealth addressed above. Poor communities lack it because they lack financial resources and the usual institutions for resource accumulation. In poor communities poor families have a difficult time saving, struggling local businesses cannot build capital, and much of the larger business community and its institutional infrastructure has abandoned the area; capital accumulation cannot take place. Needed are new institutions that can serve to aggregate capital or changes in existing institutions that will allow them to do so. The sources of the capital can be local small savers and business owners, traditional nonprofits such as local religious institutions, or outside sources that might provide capital for the new initiatives that can foster development.

Social surplus is often created in poor communities, but it does not stay there. Every time a meal is sold at a fast-food restaurant, something is bought at a convenience store, or laundry is done at a coin laundry social surplus may be created. But social surplus generally accrues to those who own stocks, bonds, and real estate. The figures cited above reflect the concentrated holding of wealth, and those who own wealth rarely live in poor communities. More typically they own the buildings (individually or institutionally) and collect the rent from those who live there. They own stock in the fast-food restaurant chain that serves the neighborhood and collect the dividends and stock appreciation that go with ownership.[6]

Nonprofits, credit unions, and cooperatives can perform the roles of capital accumulation and social surplus retention in poor communities. Nonprofits have typically done this by attracting philanthropic donations and using them to aid poorer communities. Useful as it was, the aid often took the form of short-term infusions that left little on which to build. More helpful forms of aid leave an asset in place that can generate new surplus—the source of the money for the original aid. Nonprofits can provide an asset such as new community infrastructure or help develop better job skills among residents. Community development corporations can develop housing, collect rent, and use the surplus from its operations to finance new development in the area.

Credit unions can provide for aggregation of savings that can be put back to use in the community in the form of loans. Community development credit unions (CDCUs) can attract funds from wealthier institutions for deposit and use within the CDCU's target area. Both kinds of credit unions provide financial services at nonpredatory rates, leaving the customers they serve with more disposable income than they would have had after paying the check casher or loan shark.

Cooperatives, when they can be successfully started and run in poor areas, provide new institutional means of accumulation along with the service of, for instance, a neighborhood grocery outlet. If they grow they generally use the accumulated funds locally to serve their members. Cooperatives and credit unions can also create jobs.

Providing Jobs at a Living Wage

Jobs, no matter what their character, are essential for development. Unemployment rates dropped dramatically in the 1990s but still remained high in many poorer communities, where not having a job is one of the surest ways to be poor. While the upstate New York county in which this book is being written had an unemployment rate of 3.2 percent in 1999, an adjoining, more rural county's rate was double that figure. Poor urban areas typically endure double and triple the rates of unemployment that the nation experiences, and for urban young adults in poor areas the multiple can be even higher. Given these conditions and the shrunken safety net for the jobless, any job creation has to be counted as good.

Better, however, would be jobs that offer employees paths or ladders for growth and that could be performed under healthy conditions and pay more than the downsized minimum wage. Assessed in constant 1997 dollars, the value of the minimum wage peaked in the late 1960s at nearly $7.00. By 1997 it was worth $5.15, and its purchasing power has shrunk since then (Mishel et al. 1999, 189–91). Until the late 1970s the minimum wage for full-time work paid an annual income close to and sometimes above the federal poverty rate for a single person. Because of its eroding value, since the early 1980s it has provided between 70 and 80 percent of that amount (Levin-Waldman 2001, 122–23, tbl. 4.2; 180, fig. 6.1).

Nonprofit and cooperative organizations often deliver jobs that are not hazardous and that offer potential for growth, but they have sometimes been laggards in providing good pay. For co-ops the squeeze is that members want low prices; for nonprofits it is that they operate under tight budgets, address community needs that they may overreach to meet, and operate on donated funds. Add to these influences their history of voluntary labor, much of it supplied by women, and service-sector work and there is a clear tradition of low pay in the sector (Preston in Odendahl and O'Neill 1994). Change has already occurred for many nonprofits because of diminished voluntary labor and the substitution of paid labor. Service-sector compensation varies enormously. The high end is populated by hospital surgeons, for instance; at the low end change is more difficult to realize but essential if nonprofits are to play effective roles in development.

A grassroots movement for what is generally termed a "living wage" has enlivened the debate over wages in many U.S. communities over the past decade (Pollin and Luce 2000; Pollin 2002). Alternatives Federal Credit Union in Ithaca, New York, demonstrated the ability of a third-sector institution to initiate and sustain a campaign for a living wage (coorganized with the local labor coalition). By surveying local bank wages and paying approximately 20 percent more, with better benefits, officials at this credit union thought that they offered "progressive" entry wages. While sponsoring a living wage campaign Alternatives Federal Credit Union learned that its "better" entry wage did not measure up to the "livable" standards determined by analysis of local living costs. With member, board, and senior staff approval the credit union raised its entry wage, which meant constraining the income of its top staff members. Better entry pay and staff solidarity won out, and the credit union's 2001 wage for member service representatives was $9.05 per hour, with substantial health benefits, for a 37.25-hour work week (Hochman 2001, 1–2). A major goal of the living wage campaign in the same city has been to coax two of its largest employers, a college and a wealthy university (both nonprofits), to pay living wages for their entry-level jobs. If they do so, their action will pressure other employers to pay better wages as well.[7]

Low wages entail subsidy by poorly paid staff to the goals of third-sector institutions, as explained in chapter 2. Wages that are below living costs in the general economy mean subsidies to employers in the other sectors as well. For-profit employers who often oppose increases in the minimum wage, and may also lobby against government "handouts" to the working poor, ignore the fact that the low wages they pay qualify the workers receiving them for government benefits that keep them alive and able to work. Programs such as food stamps are paid for by all taxpayers and serve as a social subsidy to any employer who pays a wage so low that it makes employees eligible for them. There is clear rationale for subsidies to many third-sector organizations: they provide some form of public good or service, and they do not exist to enrich owners. The rationale for public subsidies to private-sector for profit employers is more difficult to discern.

Operating in Environmentally Sustainable Ways

Environmental sustainability seems a heavy burden to place on the activities of third-sector institutions that are often struggling for resources. However, since they are locally based and their actions affect local residents this is a criterion that can pay big benefits at home.

The best-known summary statement of sustainability comes from the Brundtland Commission. Its explanation of sustainability as "development which meets the needs of the present without compromising the ability of future generations to meet their needs" has been a touchstone for rethinking production-at-any-cost forms of development. Because few third-sector organizations produce goods, they have an advantage in meeting this goal. For those producing agricultural products, rethinking soil-depleting and water-contaminating forms of production is taking place largely through the organic growers movement. However, decisions taken by organizations delivering services are not exempt from scrutiny with this goal in mind. Are work-area heating and cooling handled in ecologically sound ways? Are incentives offered to encourage employees or members to walk, bicycle, or use public transportation to get to work or to their credit unions? As William Shutkin has pointed out, one clear linkage between engaged members and staff in third-sector institutions and the ecology of their lives is the very processes by which they take responsibility for their environment (Shutkin 2000, chaps. 3, 8).

Creating Dynamic Linkages, Multipliers, and Spin-Offs

Linkages, multipliers, and spin-offs help build development from a dynamic third-sector institution to others that can foster new activity. Linkage refers to the ability of one organization to help another accomplish its mission. Examples include providing an organization physical space for a start-up period, a low-cost loan, staff training, or technical assistance. Linkages can foster expansion of both organizations by, for instance, cross-recruiting food co-op and credit union members and making the credit union's ATM machine available within the food co-op. Child-care providers can work closely to meet the needs of the staff members of other third-sector institutions, thereby solidifying their own user base.

Growth can be an encumbrance for third-sector institutions that exist to serve members or a particular constituency. As operations grow and diversify, logic may point to spinning off part of the operation to a new, independent third-sector provider. Alternatively, where commercial operations have been built to bring revenue to the third-sector organization, an arrangement that could make sense might spin off a for-profit firm with appropriate compensation to the nonprofit and a contractual obligation to share net revenue with the nonprofit for some period of time.

Multipliers are ratios used to measure how much change in income takes place in a particular economy because of a change in expenditure. With the multiplier more is better. When third-sector institutions bring new resources to a region or neighborhood and use them to pay staff or for some other resource for their activities and then the recipient of those expenditures spends them in the local economy, economic development accelerates. Third-sector institutions have no special advantage here, but the new activities they initiate serve to stimulate development in the same way that new activities do when initiated by either of the other sectors. What may set the third-sector organization apart from for-profit activity is that a surplus it is able to generate will likely be put back to work locally rather than paid to some distant corporate account and eventually corporate owners. Spending money in the community with other community-based organizations and businesses expands local multipliers. For poor communities local reinvestment is crucial for sustaining development momentum that can attract other new investment—from any source.

Meeting Basic Needs

The last of the criteria, meeting basic needs, is a part of what most non-profits and cooperatives do. The mission of many nonprofits is to repair the damage and fill in the gaps resulting from the economy's normal operation; for most cooperatives the reason for being is meeting members' needs.

The mixed capitalist economy is often described as one of choices for those who have resources. Basic needs can be met by a living wage, and above that level of income a person's most basic choice is the classic one between work and leisure. Opposing forces are at work here, with a massive attempt by marketers to blur the line between wants and needs, and burgeoning opposition from movements to simplify people's lives based on the growing sense that they are trading them away for work and unnecessarily high levels of material consumption (Schor 1991; Schor and Holt 2000, pt. 7). For people whose income does not provide for basic needs this debate has little meaning.

Basic needs could be met by personal choice in a world of living wages or sufficient savings, or by public provision of sufficient resources to allow such choice through, for instance, progressive taxation and transfers. Third-sector institutions provide many of the essentials of life and more in ways that can help people gain maximum satisfaction from their incomes. Participation requires income, and income comes about from development.

Basic Needs and Development

The term *basic needs* can be understood at the biological level of food, shelter, clothing, and not much more. It can also be understood in terms familiar from the twentieth century: sustaining people and providing the education and health care to make them productive members of society. The fact that the bar for this term can be raised is one sign of a society's progress in provisioning itself. The chapters that follow address the basics of food, housing, and health care, but they also address needs such as energy, financial services, the arts, and information. In this sense basic needs are defined in terms consistent with life in the early twenty-first century.

The wealthy can use third-sector institutions to serve a broad range of their interests, but the concern in this book is how these institutions can be used to ameliorate the most negative effects of uneven development. Along with a retransfer of wealth that has often been drained from them poor communities need the relaunching of a dynamic process that benefits their residents directly. If achieved, development takes place and community members gain greater mastery over their own destiny. This creates the conditions for other choices that matter in life.

The roles played by third-sector organizations in providing for basic needs serve to organize chapters 4 through 9 of this book. The criteria for good development outlined above will be used to evaluate the first organization profiled in each of these chapters.

4

Food

C
ompared to the other basic needs used to organize the case chapters of this book, food ranks with water (see chapter 9) as most essential to life. The structures and processes people use to produce and distribute food are staggeringly diverse, as are contentious issues in production, distribution, food ecology, and nutrition. Nonprofit organizations and cooperatives play numerous important roles in this sector.

The food industry is experiencing rapid change and has been doing so since the era of family farm production. Trends affecting the industry today are business concentration in larger food producers, wholesalers, and retailers; the rise of genetically modified food products; and the ongoing pressure on farmers either to join major integrated production and distribution chains or face being made redundant. These trends create new opportunities for third-sector organizations such as new generation cooperatives (NGCs). They also create a backlash: resistance in the form of initiatives for community-supported agriculture (providing consumers subscriptions to the output of farms) and local farmers' markets (often featuring specialty farm products).

Commuting to work through rural agricultural land and observing it for over two decades has provided this author with an education in some of the changes taking place in food production. In general over this time the farms have become fewer and larger. Often farmhouses were abandoned and replaced with mobile homes for employees; barns were torn down or left to fall down. Eventually the mobile homes proved mobile, and the property they rested on was converted to croplands. These croplands exist in large tracts, as hedgerows have been torn out to allow for longer-distance runs by larger tractors and harvesting equipment. Crops are uniformly planted, generally free of weeds and pest damage because of the use of herbicides and pesticides, and quickly harvested. Fewer people now live on this land. These changes have taken place for decades. They are described well in John Steinbeck's *The Grapes of Wrath* and in John Ford's film based on the book.[1]

Today less than 2 percent of this nation's workforce produces more food than its citizens need for domestic consumption[2] and tax dollars pay farmers not to produce. For farmers who have long fought to protect their independence it is surely a mixed blessing that today more than half of U.S. net farm income comes from government support (Harl 2001). Much of this public money goes to large corporate farms, but it is still a sign that people in the United States have neither figured out how to produce food well in a system driven by corporate profit nor developed sufficient alternatives to such a system. Citizens in general understand why family farms have to be protected from the boom and bust of markets, but they have difficulty with the rationale when those tax dollars go to a production system increasingly dominated by big corporations.

At the other end of the system from production are consumers, and creating change in consumers' food desires is an area of activity for numerous third-sector organizations. If the industry leaders' advertising were completely effective consumers would value speed and convenience above all. By doing most of the preparation the industry gets to add value, which if accompanied by increasing volume aided by advertising (if it works) allows it to make more money. The idea of cooking food "from scratch" recedes into history, nostalgia, or hobby. Countering this trend is consumers' desire for food that has natural flavor and nutritional value and that perhaps even connects them with its producers. Retail food cooperatives build on this counterforce, as do farmers' markets, community-supported agriculture, and the "slow food"[3] movement.

Farmers' markets are a counterforce to several of these trends and are typically operated as nonprofit corporations. They are associations of sellers, and in that characteristic they are similar to the New York Stock Exchange. Estimates place their number in the United States at twenty-eight hundred in 2000, a 63 percent increase from 1994 (Agricultural Marketing Service 2002). Today, however, small-scale venues for direct marketing of food face a fundamental challenge: a lack of farmers (Hu 2002). Suburbanization has driven them far from major metropolitan areas, and many farmers prefer growing to selling.

Farmers' markets allow producers (farmers) to eliminate the wholesalers and processors in the food marketing system, to deal directly with their customers, and to deliver food fresh from its production site. The costs to the farmer are primarily in the time that a person has to spend doing the selling at the market site. For consumers, farmers' markets generally mean improvement in the quality and freshness of the foods they buy there, community contact and interaction in the market setting, and perhaps lower food prices. The downside for the consumer is the time it takes to go to the farmers' market in addition to shopping for other kitchen needs.

Urban public markets generally emphasize food but often without restrictions used in some markets to make sure food is locally grown or that unprepared food makes up a majority of what is sold. While most farmers' markets operate a day or two a week in temporary spaces, another way of operating an urban market is reflected in the nonprofit Portland Public Market (PPM) in Maine's largest city. Its source range for products is the entire state of Maine, and it operates every day from an architecture-award-winning building that makes use of Maine wood and stone. Formed in 1996 and opened in 1998, the market has as its multiple missions to support Maine agriculture, help revitalize downtown Portland, support small businesses, and "celebrate our region's agricultural and food traditions" (Spitzer 2001b). Sales for the market shops, which occupy seventeen thousand square feet of space in the thirty-seven-thousand-square-foot building, were estimated to be $8 million for 2001. By negotiated agreement the market pays approximately $56,000 per year in property tax (Spitzer 2001a). It would take farmers' markets many years of self-taxing or rental income before they could build a $6 million facility, and this market clearly caters to a clientele with substantial disposable income. The bulk of PPM's cost was funded by a gift from Elizabeth B. Noyce through the Maine Community Foundation. The vision was hers with inspiration from several indoor markets, such as the Pike Place Market in Seattle. Noyce; her financial adviser Owen Wells; Ted Spitzer, a consultant on market operations throughout the United States and president of PPM's management company; and public officials of the city of Portland made the market a reality.

At the opposite end of the scale from the typical small producers of public and farmers' markets are agribusinesses that operate in the areas of food production and distribution. On the production side in the United States four firms accounted for 82 percent of beef packing and 75 percent of sheep and hog production in 2000 (Greider 2000b). Concentration in food retailing has accelerated, with the five leading retailers accounting for 19 percent of sales in the United States in 1992, 33 percent in 1998, and an estimated 42 percent in 2000 (Harl 2001). Concentration in retailing is strong in the United States by region, and it is growing globally (Greider 2000b, 11–18). In the face of these trends and successful ads telling busy consumers that they should save time by using "fast food" (Schlosser 2001) and "convenient" processed foods, convincing consumers to shop at farmers' markets and cook from scratch resembles swimming upstream.

Factors leading people back to less processed food are concern for the health effects of overprocessed food and the search for healthier diets. Nonprofit and governmental organizations regularly caution people to improve their health by choosing wholesome diets and exercise. Organic foods constitute a rapidly growing niche of the industry and one that has been served by cooperative markets and farmers' markets retailing directly. Today sophisticated chains are providing organic foods as a specialty line along with their regular corporate fare. Meanwhile cooperatives spend time and money reintroducing their members to food preparation with minimally processed ingredients and developing linkages with growers who want to produce less manipulated foods. Like so many consumer trends, this is often led by people with time, money, and basic education enough to take note of health gains that can be realized by a better diet.

The national problems of obesity and related conditions are brought on by the eating and exercise habits of a wide range of people. The poor are particularly at risk because economizing on food expenditures leads to consumption of refined carbohydrates that often use sugar and salt for flavoring. Fast-food outlets have downplayed fresh fruit and vegetables, although they are slowly changing to provide more healthy alternatives. In many poorer urban neighborhood markets, and ironically in many rural areas as well, good fresh produce is hard to find.

The organizational profiles that follow highlight food retailing through a successful cooperative and food as aid distributed through a food bank run by volunteers. But food has to be grown before it is distributed. A recent success among agricultural producers' cooperatives illustrates how providing enhanced value-added for growers improves their chances of surviving as independent producers.

Dakota Growers Pasta Company

It has been widely reported that farmers in the United States receive a dwindling portion of the value of the food consumed here. Whereas in 1980 the percentage of the value of food sold in the United States received by U.S. farmers was just over 30 percent, in 1998 it fell below 20 percent (United States Census Bureau 2001b). Making farming viable for independent producers requires reversing this squeeze. If corporations can enter the food processing and distribution business and reap good profits, why cannot farmers organize to do this for themselves? The answer is that it has been done, and the evidence lies in the large producers' cooperatives discussed in chapter 2. They are examples of vertical integration initiated from the bottom—by the producers. But can new co-ops be created today that serve the same purpose, even in the face of food market domination by transnational corporations? The new generation cooperatives indicate that they can. Dakota Growers Pasta Company (DGPC) provides striking evidence of the impact a third-sector producer can have on farm producers, affecting not only the viability of their rural living areas but also economic development where its processing and distribution facilities are located.

DGPC was formed in 1991, and its production began in 1994. Its members were farmers who grew number 1 hard amber durum wheat in the northern Midwest. In less than a decade it became the third largest maker of pasta products in the United States and the only pasta company in the world that produces its own wheat. In 2002 it converted to a conventional corporation, which will allow the public to own stock in the company. The sale of stock will enhance the equity side of the company's balance sheet and allow it to expand its operations further.

This organization of eleven hundred U.S. farmers opened membership to Canadian producers in 2001. It already sold its product there under the Unico label, and in the United States it provides store-brand pasta for major U.S. chains such as Kroger. In addition to its regular line of pasta and its own brand name, Dakota Growers has developed a line of organic pasta by helping its members become certified organic farmers (Dakota Growers Pasta Co. 2000).

DGPC's members are largely located in North Dakota and northern Minnesota, with a few in Montana. This region has been hard hit by diminishing rural population and job losses. When the co-op was started, its headquarters and processing facility were built in Carrington in the center of North Dakota and of a large durum wheat growing area. Carrington is in Foster County, which lost nearly 14 percent of its population between 1980 and 1990 (Zeuli et al. 1998). The population of the "city" of Carrington, whose population is over half the county's, had shrunk to 2,132 people in 1992, a 19 percent drop from 1980 (Zeuli et al. 1998, 8); by 2000 it was back up to 2,268 (North Dakota State Data Center 2003). The city is also home to Dakota Central Telecommunications Cooperative and Northern Plains Electric Cooperative.

While using cooperatives to deliver basic utilities is a familiar part of U.S. rural development, Dakota Growers was different. One of the most widely recognized new generation co-ops (NGCs), it served as a model for the creation of new producers' cooperatives in bison, beef, potatoes, dairy, and other farm goods. NGCs began in the Midwest with a co-op of sugar beet growers, American Crystal Sugar Co., which was purchased and reorganized as a co-op in 1974 (Centre for the Study of Co-operatives 2000), and Minnesota Corn Processors. Both were based on California developments in agricultural cooperatives (Patrie 1998).

The story of NGCs is based on the concept of vertical integration in agricultural production. Farmers who produce "commodity" outputs are at the mercy of mass markets, and their products are likely to end up in mass-produced and low-priced foods. In basic commodity markets prices fluctuate in ways that make planning and preparing for a new growing season's crops difficult, and for most of the products in mass markets the end result is eroding prices. The incredible efficiency of U.S. farming has benefits (low prices to the consumer) and costs (erratic business conditions and high capital needs for farmers, degradation of land and water). Vertical integration connects producers to the processing and marketing of their output—areas of important value-added for food products. It enables them to build brand names based on quality because they control production techniques in the field and factory. This is the history of branded products of co-ops such as Sunkist, Riceland, and Sun-Maid.

William Patrie was rural development director for the North Dakota Association of Rural Electric and Telephone Cooperatives. This large older-generation co-op association funded him to spur development throughout the state and provided the key link between two generations of co-ops. Support from rural electric and phone co-ops, the Bank of North Dakota (state-owned and founded in 1919; see www.banknd.com), and the St. Paul Bank for Cooperatives was vital. Their initiative helped the creation of sixty-seven new cooperatives between 1993 and 1998 that ranged in size from fifteen to two thousand members (Patrie 1998, 5).

What sets NGCs apart from earlier agricultural co-ops are their share structures and their planning rationale.[4] They generally begin with the idea of farmers capturing more value-added from their products and with an investigation of appropriate scale for a processing plant given available technologies and likely market potential. The co-op is then structured to attract enough growers to supply the plant. When that number of members is achieved, the co-op is closed to new members until and unless the processing facility is expanded.

The share structure for these co-ops generally consists of three types of shares. The first and most typical of the co-op tradition is the *membership share*, which gives the holder, who must be a producer of the agricultural product, the right to vote on a one-member, one-vote basis to control the co-op.

The second type is *equity share*, which is unique to this form of co-op and raises the start-up capital necessary for building or acquiring the processing plant and entering the business of processing and marketing. This share gives members "delivery rights," both the right and obligation to provide the co-op with a "unit" of the raw commodity (a bushel of durum; a bison) for processing. This is called a delivery contract in that the obligation runs two ways: for the co-op member to deliver, and for the co-op to accept delivery and pay for the unit delivered. A contract regulates time of delivery to make best use of production capacity and to assure quality. Members typically contract only a portion of their output to the co-op, enabling them to meet its high quality standards with their best products and to meet their quantity commitments. If a member cannot deliver what was contracted, the co-op has the right to acquire it from another producer and charge the cost to the equity account of the member that did not deliver (Patrie 1998, 3).

The third type is called the *preferred share*. It enables nonproducers to invest in the co-op with a financial instrument that resembles a cross between a bond and preferred stock. The investment gets fixed return and may have a limited life. Voting rights may attach to this share but only under limited conditions described in the organization's bylaws. This share is designed to enable outsider stakeholders, for instance members of the community who want to support the new enterprise, to invest in it.

Several key objectives are achieved by this pragmatic structure. One is that members provide most of the capitalization. In the case of the bison co-op reported by the Centre for Co-ops at the University of Saskatchewan, 180 founders paid $100 Canadian each for membership shares and then purchased a minimum of ten equity shares for $250 each, providing approximately half of the start-up costs. Equity shares are tradable,[5] and they can be passed on to the next generation of farmers in a family. Debt to finance the co-op fully can then be found through local lending institutions, specialized regional loan funds, the National Cooperative Bank, or local individuals and organizations that support likely development brought on by more prosperous farmers and the jobs of the new processing facility. Members who have substantial investment in their co-ops are likely to be attentive to the success of those co-ops.

The economic impact of Dakota Growers has been substantial. The plant began operations in January 1994 and by 1997 employed 274 full-time staff in Carrington, of whom 231 were hourly workers and 43 salaried (Zeuli et al. 1998, 11). The co-op purchased two pasta plants in Minnesota and built a distribution facility in Fargo. Production capacity expanded steadily through the late 1990s. By 2002 the co-op employed 435 people. It produces over sixty shapes of pasta made from its own (its farmers') semolina, and the mill's other products are durum flour and durum wheat midds, a by-product of the milling sold in pellet form for animal feed. In pasta production durum represents over half the cost of product sold, and this money goes directly to member growers. Even with intense price competition in the dry pasta market sales grew steadily through the 1990s, and by 1998 the co-op had paid out $2.7 million in patronage dividends (net revenues) to its member farmers (Zeuli et al. 1998, 11). Its stock shares, originally priced at $3.85 each—the price of durum at the time—split two-for-one and have sold for as much as $15.00 each (Patrie 1998, 4).

The reasons given for the conversion of Dakota Growers to allow conventional corporate stockholders are familiar in the history of cooperatives. Market forces make growth necessary to gain production and marketing efficiencies needed to be competitive. Co-op members may not be able to supply the capital needed for this growth, so the co-op must turn to the traditional route of building capital through the sale of equity shares to the public. In the statement announcing the member approval of the sale, the co-op cited dramatic changes in its market structure and the need "to make operational investments to remain competitive" (Charles Dalrymple quoted in Dakota Growers Pasta Co. 2002). An example of these changes was provided in the form of the departure of Borden Foods from the pasta market and with it the implication that Dakota Growers missed an opportunity to acquire some of its production capacity for lack of capital (Dakota Growers Pasta Co. 2002). The new company plans to continue use of what are termed Series D Delivery Preferred stock shares to assure its farmers (former members, now corporate stockholders) delivery rights for their wheat. Whether new stockholders who are not farmers will eventually gain enough strength in the company to diminish the protection farmers now have remains to be seen.

Dakota Growers and Good Development

How does Dakota Growers measure up against chapter 3's criteria for good development? Its years of operation as a co-op provide the basis for this assessment, with notes about possible implications of the co-op's conversion to a traditional corporation.

Social Surplus Creation and Retention

Social surplus creation and retention are enhanced in two ways by the presence of Dakota Growers as a co-op. Most obvious is the improved economic condition for member farmers in the sense that they gain a greater share of the value-added from producing wheat; this made their farms more profitable. In addition social surplus was created in the processing and distribution of a finished product. Part of that surplus was invested in new facilities and capacity, and a substantial portion of it was distributed to member farmers. If its new form is successful these farmers may have valuable stock shares to sell.

Particularly in the processing portion of this operation employees of the co-op create a major part of the surplus. In this case the co-op members who appropriate the surplus are analogous to the owners of a traditional corporation. With the conversion conventional stockholders and farmer stockholders will share this surplus.

As a regionally owned co-op Dakota Growers has the social surplus creation and retention properties that fit a classic sectoral and regional strategy for development. Surplus resulting from the co-op's success has been returned to producers in the rural area of its members' farms, and the portion created in processing and distribution has either been reinvested in the region or distributed to regional owner-members. This surplus is the wherewithal for future development in the region. With the conversion more surplus may or may not be created. Since ownership of the firm is likely to be more spread out geographically, the net distributional effect for the region is difficult to predict.

New Job Creation

New job creation was clear in the processing and distribution centers of the co-op and in its headquarters administration and marketing operations. For a co-op in existence less than a decade to produce hundreds of full-time jobs with benefits is impressive. The situation for jobs on members' farms is more ambiguous. New jobs may or may not result from the enhanced income to farmer-members. Each makes separate decisions about whether and how to reinvest those funds, and given the increasing capital intensity of farm production much is likely to be invested in labor-saving equipment.

Environmental Sustainability

Environmental sustainability is a criterion for which Dakota Growers, and most other forms of large-scale agricultural production, get mixed results. The product is renewable by definition, but problems arise from the way in which it is grown. In the northern Midwest wheat is close to a monoculture for much of the year. Controlling the quality of its production requires extensive use of herbicides and pesticides, some portions of which remain in the soil and find their way into groundwater, rivers, and lakes. Machine and chemical-intensive agriculture takes a toll on the earth.

Processing pasta is a relatively clean industrial operation, the by-products of the process can be used productively, and the final product is benign. Compared to many other foods pasta is easy to transport and store, and it has a long shelf life.

Growing demand for organic products and the entry of Dakota Growers into this market create the possibility for diminishing some of the negative impacts of wheat production. People wielding hoes are not going to return to these farms, but if the organic market grows, the use of some manufactured herbicides and pesticides in the region will diminish.

Linkages and Multiplier Enhancement

The success of Dakota Growers in the area of linkages and multiplier enhancement has important implications for the region. To the extent that owner-members' incomes are enhanced they have more money to spend. An improvement in multipliers has probably occurred because of the co-op, but this claim requires evidence that the improvement in farmers' income has been spent locally or regionally. Such an improvement can continue under the new corporate form as well. Positive economic linkages have been made by bringing more production into the region and thereby expanding need in the area for storage, marketing, and transportation activities.

Meeting Basic Needs

The last of the five criteria used to assess the contribution of an organization to development is the question of whether it supplies a basic need. In the case of Dakota Growers the answer is unambiguously positive. Pasta is considered a staple food, it is inexpensive, and it is a healthful food if consumed in moderation.

In sum, Dakota Growers must be judged to have had a positive impact on development in a region of the country suffering slow growth and depopulation. It and many of the other new-generation co-ops of the region are clear examples of what third-sector organizations can do to create jobs and enhance value for regions that are largely by-passed by the flow of for-profit corporate investment. The success of Dakota Growers provided the basis for its new for-profit form of operation, which should continue to enhance the regional economy.

Hanover Consumer Cooperative Society, Inc.

Retail food co-ops have come and gone over the past century, and some of the failures have occurred in what were considered flagship representatives of this form of retail business.[6] One that has survived and prospered is the Hanover Consumer Cooperative Society in Hanover and now in West Lebanon, New Hampshire. Founded in Hanover in 1936 as a food-buying club, the co-op now consists of two full-service retail stores, a food commissary to serve them, a gas station, and an auto service center. The gas station is also a convenience store. The term *convenience store* conjures images of junk food, but Hanover Consumer Co-op carries an abbreviated list of the same goods (most of it decidedly healthful) sold in its two grocery stores.

A walk through Hanover Co-op's West Lebanon store, opened in 1999, produces surprises for several reasons. First, the design is a mix of functional and architectural attractiveness as pleasing as anyone is likely to encounter in a large-box store. Spaces feel open rather than cramped, and aisles are wide. Second, people are not used to finding a co-op in a new small shopping mall, even if that mall is carefully sited in a wooded area. Third, the reflexive "political correctness" of products often associated with food co-ops seems muted here. White-bread hot cross buns reside with the artisanal whole-grain breads from local bakeries; jug wines are offered alongside decidedly upscale domestic and imported bottles. A full array of red meats is presented in cases near the free-range chicken and fresh seafood, and a deli and prepared-food area are well stocked and busy with customers. Yet this is not a co-op that hides its identity. Areas of consumer information for co-op membership and nutritional information are replete with literature and well staffed, and the co-op name and symbol are prominent on the doors of both facilities.

Hanover Co-op has over twenty thousand members. In 2000 it had net sales of over $42 million, a remarkable figure in its rural and small city area of the upper Connecticut River valley. Some of its members are staff of the Dartmouth-Hitchcock Medical Center near the West Lebanon store, and others are students and faculty at Dartmouth College in Hanover. Joining the co-op costs $50, but the membership fee can be paid from deductions from any patronage dividends that would be due the member, thus requiring no money up front to join.

High-profile food co-op failures are clearly on the mind of Terry Appleby, the general manager of Hanover Co-op. He began his report in the May/June *Co-op News* with two paragraphs on the probable cause of the demise of the Palo Alto Co-op in California, which was formed at about the same time as the Hanover Co-op. Appleby's article and one he cites in the *San Francisco Chronicle* attribute the failure of the Palo Alto Co-op (and the Berkeley Co-op before it) to two causes: diminished commitments of members who felt increasingly pressed for time; and "waning activism" (Appleby 2001, 2; Herel 2001). The term *waning activism* is vague. If it refers to less overt political engagement over the past two decades as compared to the late 1960s and early 1970s or the mid-1930s when many co-ops were formed, it may be an appropriate term, but other kinds of activism—about food and its sources, about new forms of community involvement—should have helped promote the trend for cooperative food stores.

Co-ops cannot create new energy for activism among their communities and members, although they may create organizational contexts within which it can flourish. As businesses they may respond in other ways. Meeting the needs of members who feel squeezed for time by increasing space and staff time devoted to developing appealing yet healthy prepared foods is one, and Hanover's expansion into these lines of food led it to create a new "commissary kitchen" in a location convenient to its stores but with less costly space than at the retail sites. At the end of 2000 the co-op kitchen operation employed twenty-two members of the entire organization's approximately three hundred full- and part-time employees. Is this strategy paying off? The commissary kitchen opened in mid-2000. While its impact on the co-op as a whole cannot be extracted from overall data, in 2000 the co-op experienced nearly 8 percent growth in food sales (the food industry average increase was in the 2–3 percent range) and 9 percent growth for all sales, including gasoline, the price of which became sharply higher during the year (Appleby 2000, 5). In 2000 the co-op had income of $114,860 and net income after state and federal income taxes of $77,213 (11).

Despite a successful year for sales growth and the West Lebanon store becoming profitable in March 2000, the year ended with a membership vote to accept the recommendation of management and the board of directors not to pay a patronage refund for the year. Earnings were used to pay down debt and add to retained earnings. According to Appleby, the other major "investment" made by the co-op was in its staff. He credits tight labor markets for encouraging upward wage adjustments (Appleby 2001). From his manager's viewpoint the rise in pay rates brought the benefits of reducing turnover and increasing productivity measured as labor costs as a percentage of sales. In addition pressure to respond was brought about by recognition that departmental managers' time was increasingly being used to hire and train new staff (Appleby 2000). Score one for the tight labor market of the time. Member activism on the issue of compensation, if present, may have taken the form of a living wage campaign. A co-op manager's life is never easy, as members typically want to feel that they are treating their employees well but also want reasonable prices. Price containment requires cost containment, and staff compensation is a large portion of the cost of the retail food business. For the Hanover Co-op in 2000 wages and benefits totaled 55 percent of total costs and expenses (Hanover Consumer Cooperative Society 2000, 11). The manager is squarely in the middle of this quandary.

Hanover's operations for 2001 produced another in a long string of surpluses and a patronage refund of over $200,000. Patronage refunds are paid from a co-op's surplus and therefore diminish the organization's tax bill. At the time of Hanover's annual meeting in the spring of 2002 members were asked to consider donating their patronage refunds to the community charity of the co-op, reaping a small tax benefit themselves and providing funds for regional nonprofits (Maker 2002). The co-op has reached a level of stability and success that enables it to develop this other vehicle for community development.

Kauai Food Bank, Inc.

The island of Kauai is near the western end of the inhabited islands of Hawaii. To many people Kauai suggests paradise, but several factors keep this from being true for residents there: one is that it has a large low-income population; the other is that Kauai imports 90 percent of its food. Agricultural production there has been largely sugar cane. Food is expensive if it is grown outside the Hawaiian Islands, with transportation and spoilage major factors affecting its price. Low-income residents and an expensive necessity add up to a need for help.

The Kauai Food Bank resembles many other food aid organizations in the United States. Founded in 1992 after Hurricane Iniki, it is a 501(c)(3) that collects food and monetary contributions and distributes food to needy residents, many of them children and the elderly, of Kauai and Niihau. It is part of the distribution chain of the Oahu-based Hawaii Food Bank, a certified affiliate of America's Second Harvest. What sets it apart from many food banks is that it has taken on the role of encouraging food production on Kauai, including teaching production skills and then buying its producers' products for resale to hotels, resorts, and other outlets.

Using Internal Revenue Service data from GuideStar (see chapter 10) to assess the scale of operations of the Kauai Food Bank in 2000, financial information indicates that the food bank took in $1.5 million in contributions in 2000 and expended $25,000 more (GuideStar 2002). Its liquid asset base and its inventory of food dropped substantially but remained over $100,000 each. Administrative services for the organization, such as payment to a CPA for financial record keeping and reporting, cost the organization the relatively small sum of approximately $26,000. Volunteer labor for operations as diverse as food transportation and fund-raising makes the food bank viable.

The executive director of Kauai is Judy Lenthall, 1999 winner of the Harry and Jeanette Weinberg Foundation's Aim for Excellence Award, given to honor directors of the best nonprofit organizations in the state. The monetary portion of the award was $25,000, and it was used to purchase a refrigerated truck for operations and disaster food relief.[7] The same year the organization also received a Harry Chapin Self-Reliance Award (World Hunger Year 1999), and it has continued to be recognized with other awards. Reflecting the open information flow of many nonprofit organizations, the minutes of the Kauai Food Bank's board of directors are posted on its website (www.kauaifoodbank.org).

This food bank engages in education for food production by operating its own farm, Hui Mea'ai, which comprises three acres on ancient Hawaiian homelands. Translated, the name of the farm means "the club of things to eat." The farm is envisioned as both a community development project and a source of food security for the island residents. In 1999, its second year of operation, Hui Mea'ai produced over thirty-two thousand pounds of food, and it was a financially self-sufficient and profit-making operation by 2001 (Center for Corporate Citizenship 2002, 1). The food bank buys grade A produce from graduates and growers of Hui Mea'ai and distributes its produce to over sixty commercial customers. Among them is the Kauai Marriott Resort and Beach Club, which buys approximately 25 percent of its produce from Hui Mea'ai at a cost of $800 to $1,500 per week (7).

Kauai has areas of fertile soil and abundant rainfall.[8] Among the issues confronted by organizers of Hui Mea'ai were the decline in food production skills on the island and the accompanying changes in the population's diet. Confronting these issues brought opportunities for cultural restoration and improved knowledge of diet. More practically, moving bulky and perishable food from growing areas in California, the likely source for much of the imported food, to an island one hundred miles northwest of Honolulu was loaded with logistical problems. Rejuvenating local food production provides jobs, lowers some food costs for consumers, leads to investigation of nearly lost cultural connections to different foods and their production, and provides some measure of security in the aftermath of damaging storms. By launching the farm Kauai Food Bank became more than a charitable distributor of food aid. While this is not exceptional for a third-sector organization, the emphasis on education for and development of food production skills provides the organization with an unusual role in development.

5

Housing

Housing needs are defined by climate-based requirements for physical shelter and by cultural and economic variables. Household composition, family size, income levels, and costs associated with urban, suburban, and rural settings all play roles in shaping basic housing options. How housing needs will be met derives from both culture and the structure of the economy. In the United States the basic sources are found in the market, with suppliers and consumers of housing interacting in transactions that have particular national character. A powerful part of the American dream includes home ownership, and for a clear majority of households this housing portion of the dream is met. Individual home ownership in the United States is the norm. After the percentage of households living in their own (or banks') homes slipped to 63–64 in the 1980s, the rate rebounded to 67–68 percent levels by 2000–2001 (United States Census Bureau 2001c).

Common in market-based systems of provision, this remarkable achievement is accompanied by abject failure. A hallmark of the failure is homelessness, accompanied by a history of poor quality housing in the form of urban tenements or rural shacks. Typical recommendations are that housing should use no more than one-third of a household's disposable income. For a household consisting of a person or people who have little or no income (people living on unemployment insurance, elements of public assistance, the minimum wage, or low-end social security payments) the market cannot provide housing unless more basic needs, such as food, are forgone by that household.

Typical as well for market systems of provision is that housing options for high-income individuals are plentiful. For middle-income members of society home ownership can be a struggle to achieve, but paying off a mortgage and owning a home can provide a long-term savings vehicle that may help fund life in retirement years. Whether it is actually a "good investment" depends on too many circumstances to allow a blanket conclusion.

Housing for people of low and moderate income is the challenge in the United States. The inability of low-income people to afford housing reflects market failure. Textbooks for courses on the principles of economics abound with cautionary tales of how interfering with the market through rent control programs, as many cities have done, can discourage developers from supplying rental housing, driving up its price. The same textbooks rarely mention alternative sources of supply, or the need for them, because normal market incentives are not sufficient to produce housing affordable for people living on low or moderate incomes. Public provision of low-income housing has been tried in various forms, and despite its shortcomings it has housed many people for many years. Housing for the elderly that is subsidized by governmental agencies is considered more acceptable, in part because most people know that social security does not provide enough for decent housing and other necessities of life and because many people have little in the way of income from pensions or from substantial savings for retirement years.

Housing created by third-sector organizations that addresses the needs of low- and moderate-income people is one focus of this chapter; another is innovative uses of nonprofits to encourage forms of housing that are alternatives to the typical "dream" suburban stand-alone home. While the stand-alone home provides housing for people with means, as a system of housing it contains pitfalls. One is the sprawl in land-use patterns now drawing national attention. Another is the related automobile-dependent way of life associated with the single-family, suburban home. For most in the United States homes and automobiles have been the ultimate consumer goods. Their consumption has been heavily subsidized by government with income tax deductions for mortgage interest and by public road building, to cite the most obvious examples. For a growing number of elderly people in this nation individual suburban homes and private transportation make little sense.

Manufactured-Housing Cooperatives

Having one foot in the door of home ownership can be a painful experience. For people who have chosen manufactured homes (often called mobile homes or trailers even when they are rarely moved) a compromise from the norm of full home ownership is created when the land on which their home is located is rented. This makes owners captive tenants vulnerable to eviction notices that may mean they either have to sell their homes or move them at great expense. For those living in the proverbial trailer park land-lords can sell the facility, cut back on maintenance, institute new fees for basic needs such as water supply or sewage service, or simply raise rents steeply each year. In many states until quite recently park landlords have had the right to enter tenants' homes at any time and without notice (Bradley 2000). So for many the first step toward home ownership, and one of the few low-income options other than renting, presented major prob-lems.[1]

Cooperative ownership and management of the land on which mobile homes are located solve some of these problems. This arrangement places owners in a position analogous to that of owners of a unit in a typical urban housing cooperative or a condominium. Under cooperative ownership of land both the quality of life in the physical surroundings of the home and its value are dependent on decisions made in common with other home-owners in the location. Unscrupulous landlords are banished from the equation.

Factory-manufactured housing has a checkered reputation, and in its early days it was generally inferior in quality to housing constructed on-site. Its problems included dangerous aluminum wiring, a high percentage of flammable building materials, poor insulation, and lack of sufficient means for tying the home to the ground at its site. This hardly seemed to be hous-ing that should be championed. But market pressure, self-regulation in the industry, and state and federal regulation have improved its quality. Mass consumption is essential to lowering the cost of a basic need such as hous-ing and mass production in a controlled factory environment is a time-tested method of achieving the Fordist outcome of lower prices. Building in a factory setting can produce higher quality products than those built in the field. Overcoming the worst uniformity of mass production through niche marketing and optional variations in manufactured housing helps to satisfy some of consumers' desires for more-tailored products. In 2001 man-ufactured and mobile homes numbered 8.8 million in the United States, or 7 percent of housing units (United States Census Bureau 2001a).

An example of a conversion to cooperative park ownership can be found, improbably perhaps, in the state of New Hampshire. This state's reputation derives from its independent-minded voters, their Republican leanings, and the state's famous license plate motto "Live free or die." Who knew that this slogan might refer to being free of landowners' power to control the use and value of what might be a person's largest financial asset: his or her home? States such as Florida and California have a longer history of co-op parks and more of them, but the New Hampshire example is instructive.

The first conversion in New Hampshire did not involve a villainous landlord; it did involve a nonprofit community loan fund handled by people with the foresight to see an innovative solution to a very real problem of low- and moderate-income housing. The New Hampshire Community Loan Fund was in its formative stage when the lending opportunity arose (Bradley 2000). It developed out of personal conversations between a resident of a small trailer park in Meredith, New Hampshire, and a founding board member of the loan fund. The problem originated in 1984 when an elderly couple who were owners of the small park needed to sell it in order to move the husband into a nursing home. The woman struggled with running the park yet did not want to give up her home on the same property. With land prices near New Hampshire's largest lake escalating rapidly, sale of the park seemed the best way out. For residents the likely outcome was sale of the land to a developer and the end of their leases. Several of them approached local banks to inquire about buying the property, but none had access to the credit needed to take on the financing. The key conversation to begin imagining the park as a resident-owned cooperative took place between one of the residents and Rebecca Storey, a student at the Community Economic Development Program at New Hampshire College.[2] Formation of a cooperative organization of tenants followed, and with legal assistance they began negotiating with town officials over much-needed septic system repairs and arranging with the owner terms of a buyout that would leave her where she wanted to be—in her home. The deal involved a below-market price for the property in exchange for a low-cost lifetime lease on the home.

Banks proved the stumbling block. Five area banks were approached, and each refused to lend for the deal. Factors cited for the refusals were the low income of residents, their lack of management experience, the need for repairs to the property, and the lack of a down payment. In addition the bankers were unfamiliar with how a cooperative works (Bradley 2000). Storey and others at the New Hampshire Community Loan Fund agreed to make this project their first loan, and the Meredith Community Cooperative became a reality in June 1984 (3). The successful transfer of ownership was quickly followed by removal of accumulated debris at the park, installation of a new water pump to regulate water pressure, and repair of the septic system. Residents began taking better care of and investing in what was theirs. A report on this cooperative park sixteen years after its creation describes it as debt free and charging the lowest monthly rent of any park in the state (Bradley 2000).

Changes in management of New Hampshire mobile home parks began before this successful innovation, and continued during its early years. The statewide Mobile Homeowners and Tenants' Association (MOTA) lobbied the state legislature to create a strong manufactured-housing park tenant-landlord law, passed in 1973. With advocacy by MOTA and the N.H. Community Loan Fund, a law passed in 1988 provided park residents the right of first refusal in cases of parks being sold. By 1994 MOTA managed to shift adjudication of violations of the state housing codes relevant to manufactured housing out of the state's district courts, where cases were costly for tenants to pursue, and into a newly created Manufactured Housing Board. The first two of these reforms and shifts in power combined with the powerful example of the Meredith Center Cooperative success led to formation of two more cooperative parks in 1986. Funding for them was made possible by the New Hampshire Housing Finance Authority.

By 2001 New Hampshire had forty-nine cooperative manufactured-housing parks containing almost twenty-three hundred units of housing (New Hampshire Community Loan Fund 2001). Banks were brought into the lending process for them by the role of the N.H. Community Loan Fund as provider of senior subordinate debt, which filled the gap between what banks would lend and the down payments that members of a new cooperative could afford. Early bank loans were made with interest rates varying annually, a difficult situation for co-op members who sought more predictable monthly payments. The Federal Home Loan Bank of Boston eventually instituted a fixed-rate community investment program for its member banks, and this money became available for cooperative parks. More recently Housing and Urban Development's (HUD) Community Development Block Grant program and U.S. Department of Agriculture's (USDA) rural development program have provided low-cost loans and grants for the environmental improvements that new cooperative owners made to their parks. This helped accomplish the initial cleanup of problems left by previous private owners who were milking their properties (New Hampshire Community Loan Fund 2001).

Banks came to see the real property improvements that resulted from cooperative ownership and perhaps to understand cooperative governance as similar to New England town democracy. In fact one large cooperative park,

Greenville Estates, makes up 20 percent of the population of the town of Greenville and has a larger population than some New Hampshire towns (Bradley 2000). More important to the banks, cooperative parks generate a steady stream of income from monthly membership (rent) payments, just as private parks or other rental properties do. The real education for banks has come from seeing that people of modest incomes can manage their own affairs. New Hampshire Community Loan Fund and New Hampshire Legal Assistance have played key roles in assuring that training for cooperative management has been available to people as they learned to become owners sharing responsibility for management of these parks.

Mobile home parks used to be small businesses, but they are being influenced by the same trend of consolidation affecting other industries. National chains such as Clayton Homes and Champion are emerging, and investors can often win control of a park by paying a high price for it and then raising rents. If the tenants cannot pay, the land may be sold to a developer for commercial or residential development. In many states tenants being displaced for other use of land have no protection other than an eighteen-month notice that they will have to move their homes. Nonprofit organizations and cooperatives are increasingly used to acquire parks as strategy to protect affordable housing. Manufactured homes can be a viable alternative to rental housing when their owners also own the land they are on and collectively control the land and community within which they are located. Cooperative land and infrastructure ownership provides means to this end. The movement to this form of home site cooperative became simpler for others to accomplish with the 2001 publication by Consumers Union of *An Introductory Guide to Manufactured Housing Park Cooperatives and the Services of the New Hampshire Community Loan Fund,* written by the staff of the New Hampshire Community Loan Fund (New Hampshire Community Loan Fund 2001). The nonprofit Consumers Union is publisher of *Consumer Reports.*

Cooperative Manufactured-Housing Parks and Good Development

Parks for manufactured homes have traditionally been private developments, with developers providing land and infrastructure for housing. Homeowners typically provided their own manufactured homes or bought homes already sited in the park. Once in the park they were captive rent-payers with less mobility than tenants of rental housing and thus potentially less able to avoid exploitation. Through rental payments developers accumulated social surplus. If unscrupulous they had the ability to capitalize on their advantageous position.

Social Surplus Creation and Retention

In the case of cooperative manufactured-housing parks social surplus creation and retention are shifted to residents. By gaining collective control of the land and infrastructure on which their homes are located, they stop paying rent and begin to invest in their own collectively held property. If they stay as resident members they enjoy greater ability to manage their affairs with other community members, improvements in the surroundings they might make, and higher disposable income from any reductions in housing costs they are able to realize. If they sell their homes in place the buyers become new members of the cooperative. Through the selling price a seller reaps the benefits of being able to offer the low membership fee (land rental rate) and the improved physical surroundings and infrastructure to a new member. The value of the home being sold is enhanced by any community improvements that are made.

Cooperative ownership provides collective control and democratic governance over social surplus that would have flowed to the private owner of the park. Comparing the normal economic situation of residents of park-situated manufactured homes with that of business owners of parks, the co-op strikes a small-scale blow for more egalitarian use of social surplus and against its concentration in a small number of hands as parks are consolidated. Of course most transitions of this kind require bank and/or loan fund financing, and interest is paid for use of that money. Interest payments typically cause surplus to flow from those with few resources to those with many, but this is a deal with an end to it whereas paying rent is not.

Job Creation

New job creation is not a likely outcome of cooperative manufactured-home parks. Many manage their affairs with elected and voluntary labor, which may be a good exercise in getting to know the neighbors and expanding skills useful in civic society but does not create good paid employment. Many established manufactured-home co-ops employ managers and staff but probably in no greater number than would a private owner.

Environmental Sustainability

One of the features of cooperative ownership of the parks that has most endeared them to state and local regulatory officials is owners' concern to solve environmental problems facing their communities. Families with a voice in managing these cooperatives live and have children growing up in them. Improving water quality, sewage and waste removal, and other environmental factors is both in their interest and within their control, and they can often find forms of public advice and assistance to get the jobs done. Improvements add to their cost for the property, but the incentives for residents are their own health and environmental enhancements. The private park owner faces increasing costs to undertake these improvements, and unless rents are raised the only incentive for doing so might be avoiding fines or other legal action.

Surprisingly, manufactured homes in a well-designed park may be more environmentally benign than a similarly designed conventional housing development. Homes located on concrete pillars, pads, or crawl space foundations produce less impact on the land than those built on fully excavated basements. While removal of housing units and infrastructure is unlikely in either case, removal of a manufactured mobile home could more quickly yield a return to natural conditions than removing or filling full-basement foundations. Given that removal of neither is likely while population is growing in a region, both forms of housing can be designed for minimal impact on land, drainage, water, and other environmental concerns.

Linkages and Multipliers

Conversion to cooperative parks can enhance linkages and multipliers. Linkages can be affected by the potential for low-income people to manage their lives and better afford their necessities. An improved mobile home park means higher tax revenue for local government and schools. Engaging people in running their own communities has encouraged their greater involvement in local public administration and strengthened their skills for citizenship participation (Bradley 2000, 5–8). Multipliers from spending are enhanced locally to the extent that savings on monthly membership costs, lower than previous rental costs, get spent in the community rather than flowing to absentee owners or a distant corporation.

Meeting Basic Needs

The last of the criteria to assess good development is meeting basic needs, and the improved ability of people to provide themselves and their families with decent housing through cooperative manufactured-home parks is obvious. Until society chooses either to make better housing options available to people with low and moderate incomes or to raise all incomes, this strategy can improve lives.

Kendal Communities

Housing needs change as people age. The successful, affluent lives of professional and middle-income households are reflected in the typical U.S. suburban home, which has grown in size even as households have become smaller.[3] Those who are entering the later years of their lives often find themselves with more space than they need and more maintenance responsibilities than they want. Some hang on, not wanting to leave neighbors, conveniences, or the memories of their lives in the home. A wrenching change may come when one is unable to function well without assistance and others, if present in the household, are incapable of providing it. The move to a nursing home is seldom welcomed, but it is reality for approximately 1.6 million people in the United States (United States Census Bureau 2000b, tbl. 208).

Nonprofit organizations have played a significant role in developing alternate solutions to the housing problems many people encounter in their late years. People who own their homes have assets, and those assets can be traded for better housing options if they exist. The Gray Panthers have promoted small-scale and community-based sharing of large homes among the elderly. The group homes they advocate enable owners to continue living in their homes because they are joined by others who can help share the cost of keeping it up, provide companionship, and potentially create the resources to provide for group acquisition of basic services.

For those who can afford them continuing-care retirement communities offer a larger-scale alternative to group homes. They combine housing, health insurance and health care funded by Medicare and resident group insurance, and many services that make life easier for the elderly. They provide housing in private units of compact scale supplemented by extensive common spaces. The architecture of these facilities is designed to minimize physical barriers to activity. The term *continuing care* means that they provide on-site health services and nursing facilities so that residents can stay in the communities even if they become incapacitated.

The Kendal Corporation, a nonprofit operator of continuing-care and residential retirement communities for the elderly, was founded in 1971. It is a Pennsylvania-based organization created and still largely run by members of the Religious Society of Friends (Quakers). Kendal has continuous-care facilities in Pennsylvania, New York, Ohio, Virginia, and New Hampshire. Most are in college or university towns. Kendal also operates two residential retirement communities in Pennsylvania. Two additional communities are in development: one in Sleepy Hollow, New York, and the other in Granville, Ohio. The parent corporation for all properties collects operating fees from each of its locations. For the fiscal year ending 31 March 2001 these operating fees provided the corporation with an annual income of $2.6 million (Kendal 2001, 26). Two of its affiliated communities showed small operating losses for that year.

Several controversial matters stand out when considering these communities. First, they discriminate on the basis of age, nationality, physical mobility at entry, and (implicitly at least) wealth and income. Age and nationality are controlled since residents of the continuing-care facilities must be eligible for Medicare. That means that they must be sixty-five years old, and Medicare is available only to people who are U.S. citizens by birth or naturalization. Joining a continuing-care community includes purchase and ongoing maintenance of housing space and shared common space for recreation and health care, various meal plans and cleaning services, health care supplements to Medicare payments (similar to supplemental health insurance for those who qualify for Medicare), and a promise of on-site continuous care (much like an in-house nursing home). For these reasons buying into one requires a major financial commitment—more than the majority of Americans can afford.

A startling feature of Kendal continuous-care facilities stems from how they are financed. Each new resident pays an "entry fee" to acquire the right to occupy an existing living unit varying in size from a studio to a two-and-a-half-bedroom apartment or attached "cottage." A resident does not "own" the unit in the traditional sense of real estate property rights; it is the property of the community. In 2003 units in Ithaca ranged in price from approximately $100,000 (studio, single occupancy) to $340,000 (two bedrooms and den, double occupancy), about the range for good quality residences at the time in the same area. This purchase price and a substantial monthly fee (from approximately $2,000 for the smallest single-person unit to $4,600 for the largest unit for two people in 2003) finance the community (Kendal 2003). The entry fee may be paid with the sale of a house, but monthly fees would require substantial income from a retirement plan or investments. Hence life at Kendal might be described as "socialism for the well-heeled." It is more precisely a community insurance arrangement for rest-of-lifetime acquisition of residential services, group health care, a meal a day, other services, and long-term care (if needed) rolled into one. The entrant has to be active and ambulatory and reasonably expected to continue that way for a year in order to join the community.

To make it possible for people of limited means to become community members Kendal communities operate a charitable fund to subsidize residents' fee costs. The mutual insurance aspect of the operation involves the commitment to provide long-term care for all, paid for by all, including those who do not need it.

Kendal's continuous-care arrangements have won national recognition for their quality and for their innovative techniques to eliminate physical restraints in treating patients who may be prone to wander or fall. A good staff is vital to make this kind of community work. Kendal employment practices are linked to Quaker principles of participation, dignity, and individual development. Cooperative work practices and careful economy are goals, even when the two might seem to be in conflict. For employees the community goals include "fair wages, good benefits, on-site child day care, sick leave, and a pension plan" (Kendal 2000, 16–17). Funding for employee work-related education and on-site training are available, and education through teamwork is considered a normal part of work. Staff pay in a typical Kendal community starts at seven dollars an hour with full benefits for the least skilled positions (Bibbie 2002).

Kendal's retirement communities are significant additions to the areas in which they are located. Their benefits for these areas are obvious: jobs in construction and staffing, adding or keeping relatively high-income consumers in the community, and offering local residents who can afford them the chance to move to such facilities without leaving their own communities. In an age of "prison Keynesianism," when communities compete to attract state and federal jails in the name of jobs and local development, serving the aging in this way is an attractive alternative.

A key issue for housing developments of this kind and the communities in which they locate is whether or not they pay taxes or reasonable alternative fees to support local public services and education. When some retirement communities bar young people from living in them in order to escape the need to pay for their schools, overt economic apartheid is the result. Nonprofit retirement facilities and nursing homes typically pay property taxes. Kendal's literature states that its policy is to "pay fair and reasonable real estate taxes without adding a significant burden to municipal services" (Kendal 2000, 19). In its Ithaca, New York, location the tax amount has been contentious. The community has contested its assessment by Tompkins County repeatedly. The most recent court suit by Kendal contested an assessment of $38.3 million, which would produce a combined local property tax bill of $1.2 million (Higgins 2001). That amount would constitute over 10 percent of the Ithaca unit's annual operating expenses (Kendal 2001, 27). On the one hand the publicity surrounding attempts by upper-middle-class people, many liberal university retirees, to get their taxes lowered has not been good press for the community. On the other hand, when through this news story it became public knowledge that a nearby successful shopping mall with national chain anchors and over sixty retail shops at the time was assessed at a value of $44.3 million and a large Ithaca nursing home was assessed for $7.8 million, it appeared that the Kendal community had a point. By late 2002 the dispute was unresolved.

Substantial financial challenges face those seeking to create this form of community. Land must be acquired and buildings made ready for occupancy before substantial revenue begins to flow. Since most residents count on selling their own homes to pay the initial entry fees, bridge financing is essential. Because the first entrants have to be healthy enough to have promise of independent living for at least a year, the costly continuous-care facilities can begin more slowly even if a few residents end up needing the care in less than a year. Careful actuarial and financial planning are needed to assure that continuing-care commitments can be met without raising the general costs beyond reach of sufficient numbers of present or future residents. Again, these are part intentional communities and part insurance plans. Kendal Ithaca's monthly fees have risen at a rate above the general inflation rate (Kendal 2002, 10–11), largely due to the high rate of inflation in health care and prescription drug costs.

Quaker roots and principles set the Kendal community apart from many retirement communities and residential developments for the elderly. Those principles emphasize independent living and resident participation in setting policy for the facilities, and they seek to expand older people's sense of good health, security, and the potential yet to be realized in their lives. In many respects Kendal communities embody another form of the American dream having to do with how life is lived. It could be argued that these should be national or global goals, but with Kendal at least they are being created for those who are willing and able to enjoy them in a community setting.

EcoVillage at Ithaca

Cohousing provides a different model for quality housing than the stand-alone suburban home. As a concept it had its start in Denmark in the late 1960s. Its aims are to overcome the sense of isolation that can accompany life in a suburban subdivision and increase residents' participation in designing and managing their communities. Individual living units provide space for cooking and entertaining, but there is also common space for community gatherings, meals together, child care, and other activities. Housing units are often clustered, leaving land for green space, gardens, or recreation. Most communities seek a mix of ages in their populations (Cohousing Network 2002).

As its name implies, EcoVillage attracts cohousing residents with a concern to protect the environment as best they can in the housing and community choices they make. This cooperative community began through a series of discussions in Ithaca, New York, in 1991.[4] A housing cooperative was formed in 1992, and residents moved into its first residential neighborhood in 1996 and 1997 (EcoVillage at Ithaca, n.d.). Each household owns shares in the cooperative, and a proprietary lease links the shares to a particular unit. The nonprofit that started EcoVillage bought 176 acres of open fields and woodlands, of which only 7 acres are now being put to use for the first and second clusters of housing.

Ithaca is a small city of thirty thousand in a largely rural setting in the Finger Lakes area of upstate New York. Home to two large nonprofit educational institutions, Cornell University and Ithaca College, it attracts residents who have thought about improving the way in which they live and demonstrating to the world that new ideas can be made practical. Not surprisingly, Ithaca has a history of cooperatives.[5]

EcoVillage is a blend of cohousing cooperative and intentional community. Its future residents were its developers. They acquired the land, designed its use, constituted its first cluster of residents, and set the terms for the community's expansion. Environmental commitments were made to open space and preservation of woodlands, organic agriculture, development of cottage industries, and an educational component. The land on which the community is located abuts a 55-acre nature preserve called Coy Glen, which is owned by Cornell University. EcoVillage set aside 50 of its 176 acres adjacent to Coy Glen as a permanent conservation easement managed by the Finger Lakes Land Trust. Projects for the future described on the organization's website are a compost-heated greenhouse, a you-pick organic berry farm, gray-water recycling, and an education center, among others. A nonprofit coordination and education arm of EcoVillage operates in conjunction with Cornell's Center for Religion, Ethics, and Social Policy (CRESP) to help foster sustainable community development. It built the community and now offers educational programs to convey the lessons of the project (Walker 2000). The community has garnered international attention, including a 1996 award for excellence in innovative housing from the National Association of Homebuilders (EcoVillage at Ithaca 2003).

Residents of the first EcoVillage neighborhood opted for compact, energy-efficient private units (a three-bedroom unit is thirteen hundred square feet), and a common house in which they gather for three meals a week. The common space includes play, craft, and meeting space; space for guests; eight offices; a laundry; and a teen room.

One of the challenges engaged by EcoVillage planners and residents was to create ecologically sound but affordable housing. Compact units, energy-saving building techniques, and shared site preparation helped contain costs. Initial costs were $70 per square foot, or $100 per square foot if common space were counted. Units cost $90,000 to $150,000 each before "extras," such as a carport, are added. The limited history of their resale has been that they maintain the value in real dollar terms. The new thirty-unit development is projected to cost $3.5 million, with higher cost individual units because of greater owner-builder emphasis on design features and amenities (Walker 2001). If the goal is met, each unit will cost $117,000, approximately the average price of an existing home sold in the Ithaca market in 2001.[6]

EcoVillage was planned as a community of 150 housing units. As the second cluster of 30 energy-efficient homes was planned, the site chosen for this new neighborhood was questioned for its possible impact on the adjoining nature preserve and for its emergency access and access for public water and sewer connections. Neighbors of the development who reside in the Longhouse cooperative urged EcoVillage residents to site the neighborhood a shorter distance down Rachel Carson Way, their access road connection to a state highway to Ithaca (Bishop 2001). Concerns were addressed, and EcoVillage is well on its way to completion of its second cluster of homes. It will be the first cohousing complex in the United States to build a second neighborhood (Liz Walker quoted in Bishop 2001).

Sorting out problems and differences of opinion is a regular activity for residents of this community. Getting the project framed in a way that people could feel good about making initial financial commitments to it, financing land acquisition and infrastructure investment, and overcoming a devastating fire that destroyed an early cluster of homes as it neared completion were just a few of the challenges that have been met. Expansion created the question of how new community members might be assessed for some of the start-up cost for its land, initial roads, and infrastructure. Since consensual decision making is a goal of this community, one resource needed by all its members is tolerance for long meetings and compromise. To residents these are hallmarks of building community.

6

Financial Services

A list of basic needs can get long before financial services are mentioned. However, in the world of electronic money management personal financial transactions must be facilitated at reasonable cost, and credit is sometimes essential. People need financial services, and community organizations need them as well. This chapter highlights institutions that provide both of these services in support of development. One such institution is a new credit union in a poor section of New York City that provides financial services for individuals. (A support organization for credit unions of this kind is discussed in chapter 10.) Others include a successful financial intermediary for development projects in Boston and a bank that serves cooperatives from its base in Washington, D.C.

People who have money take financial services for granted. Financial institutions bombard them with telephone calls, mailings, and television advertisements offering loans, credit cards, lines of credit, and incentives to move accounts to their institutions. People without resources ignore these come-ons for several reasons. They know that with an account balance below an amount that may seem unattainable to them—three thousand dollars is a common cutoff—the monthly fees and per-use fees associated with gaining mainstream financial services can be prohibitively high. In addition people without resources may live in poorer neighborhoods where banks do not have branches. If people are new to this country or to a steady job, they may have little understanding of how banking works, whether it is safe, or when it is advantageous.

The ability to write a check or use a credit or debit card simplifies life. The alternative is to convert a paycheck to cash (generally paying a fee to do so), carry cash or keep it at home (with attendant risks), and use money orders as check substitutes (at some cost per money order).

Renting somebody else's money costs the borrower interest, which all borrowers want to keep as low as possible. The best rates go to those with assets, but for those with few assets reasonable rates, and the loans themselves, are unlikely. If "it takes money to make money" it also takes some property (as collateral) to borrow at reasonable rates of interest. If decent financial services are unavailable, one alternative is to make use of the local loan shark. His (typically) or her services may be essential and the only alternative, but they tend to leave patrons poorer for the high rates charged. At the bottom of the market for small loans is the pawnbroker, who holds (and may sell) an asset until a loan is repaid. This service provides bridge financing for short-term needs but at costs that can run as high as 10 percent of the amount loaned per week. This is brutally predatory lending.

Even communities that have banks or bank branches may not be well served by them. A bank has to perform two operations to play a full role in fostering commerce and development in a community. One is to aggregate and safeguard savings and to make basic services such as checking and ATMs available for demand accounts. The other is to loan the aggregated savings out to those who qualify for loans. A bank may lend for borrower consumer purchases (which can help foster local sales) or for business loans (which can foster local business activities). The bank makes money on "the spread," the difference between the rate it has to pay for deposits and the higher rate at which it can lend the money, less its operating expenses. It can also make money as fees on other services it provides. One problem for poor communities is that there may be a lack of connection between the places where banks take in their deposits and those where they make their loans. If the community is considered a high-risk area in which to lend, the bank may funnel resources out of that community. Banks accused of redlining were presumed to be segmenting their mortgage markets in ways that prohibited lending in areas considered risky, even though they may have had retail branches there that took savings from those areas. This practice, which dates from the use of Federal Housing Administration (FHA) maps by banks through the latter half of the twentieth century,[1] was a major impetus for creation of the Community Reinvestment Act (CRA), which was enacted in 1977 and modified in 1995 (Federal Reserve Board 2002). This federal regulation charges banks with responsibility to contribute to meeting the credit needs of the communities in which they are chartered to do business, although it contains no specific criteria for performance.

Where banks do not provide services other safe and reasonable alternatives are possible. For immigrant groups from various parts of the world informal savings clubs form pools of money to which people contribute and from which they can borrow. For Koreans this takes the form of the *kye;* Latin Americans call such a credit institution a *tanda* or *sociedad.* These groups depend on a good deal of trust among members, and if something goes wrong there is no insurance and little in the way of official recourse. Another local alternative, often mentioned in company with pawnbrokers, is moneylenders known as "sharks" because of the rates they charge. They match their available funds with local needs for interest rates that typically range from 2 to 5 percent per week (Filkins 2001). This kind of lending tends to concentrate wealth in a few hands and drain it from those who borrow for all but the most high payoff uses of the borrowed funds.

Credit unions are a viable institutional response to the financial service needs of residents of poor communities. They are state and federally regulated nonprofit organizations that can provide a full range of services from simple savings and checking (share draft) accounts to mortgages and business loans. But as explained in chapter 2, historically credit unions have been chartered to serve employees of firms. A community with a large enough concentration of employees with a firm who wanted to start a credit union (perhaps a thousand or more members to make such a credit union viable) is probably not a poor community; credit unions have tended to be fixtures of stable working-class and middle-income communities. Creating the kind of credit union that can serve poor areas has been challenging.

People addressing development problems turned to credit unions throughout much of the twentieth century. Social service organizations such as the Henry Street Settlement House in New York created one in 1937, and religious organizations such as Mt. Olivet church did so in 1941, also in New York. In North Carolina, African Americans excluded from the banking system formed rural community credit unions. In the 1960s the Credit Union National Association (CUNA) provided seed money to initiate credit unions for residents of housing projects and poor neighborhoods in urban areas (Rosenthal 1999). Later in the 1960s credit union development for disadvantaged communities was linked to federal antipoverty programs through Community Action Agencies of the federal Office of Economic Opportunity (OEO). Some received federal funds, but most were simply given assistance in gaining charters and provided with office space. Most failed due to a mix of inadequate roots in the community, support structures, and training (Rosenthal 1999). The formation of the National Federation of Community Development Credit Unions (discussed as a support organization in chapter 10), addressed the needs of these organizations. The case that follows introduces the challenges of launching one.

Neighborhood Trust Federal Credit Union

New York City's booming economy through the 1990s was accompanied by population growth, much of it from immigrants. Despite media attention paid to the revival of Harlem, poverty persisted there, in other parts of Manhattan, and in the city's other four boroughs. The recession of 2001 and two fall disasters that year further depressed much of the city. The neighborhoods of Washington Heights and West Harlem stand in need of many services, some of them financial. Loan sharks (known as *prestamistas*, or moneylenders, in the heavily Spanish-speaking Washington Heights area), check cashers, and pawnshops were their principal providers (Forero 2000). Competing with them today are a community development credit union (CDCU) known as the Neighborhood Trust FCU and its parent nonprofit organization, Credit Where Credit Is Due (CWCID). CWCID and Neighborhood Trust were begun by Mark Levine, a former inner-city schoolteacher, by other schoolteachers who sought to strengthen the areas of the city in which they worked, and by area residents and church leaders. It opened in 1997 with a retail outlet in the Washington Heights bus terminal at West 178th Street under the Manhattan end of the George Washington Bridge. This location was a former ChemBank office that had been closed for approximately five years. The space is rented from the Port Authority of New York–New Jersey, a major landowner in the city. In 2000 Neighborhood Trust opened its second office in West Harlem, a largely African American neighborhood. By early 2002 the credit union had a staff of sixteen, deposits of over $6 million, and four thousand members. The nonprofit CWCID had a staff of six.

Launching this CDCU was a struggle, and the hard work is not over. Two tragedies in the fall of 2001 had a strong impact on the Dominican community it serves. Most obvious was the Trade Center attack, which eliminated jobs for many neighborhood residents who did much of the low-wage work in the financial district and Trade Center areas at the other end of Manhattan. The second, a short time later, was the crash of American Airlines flight 587 while departing from New York's JFK Airport for Santo Domingo. Most of its passengers were traveling to the Dominican Republic, and many of them lived in or had family in Washington Heights. These events and the recession of 2001 dampened economic activity among members of the credit union. Its revenue slipped, as did its capital ratio, and it came under closer supervision by the National Credit Union Administration. By 2002 its capital ratio had improved and it seemed on the road to renewed growth. During the difficult months the hours for business at the West Harlem branch were cut back dramatically. Positive steps in the 2001–2 period were receipt of a major federal community development financial institution (CDFI) grant in 2001 and establishment of the credit union as a U.S. Small Business Administration lender in 2002 (Zinkin 2002).

Why marry a credit union and a nonprofit? In the case of this pair the answers are fund-raising and education. The initial challenge (for this and most other CDCUs) involved starting a "bank" with no money. New credit unions in poor neighborhoods need benefactors, and their new members need to learn why and how to use a financial institution. CWCID designed and implemented a bilingual financial literacy curriculum that was intended to begin "empowering low-income residents in Upper Manhattan to take control over their financial lives" (Credit Where Credit Is Due 2003). One of its employees is a former schoolteacher who works full-time at this effort. It includes a four-session basic financial literacy workshop (over sixteen hundred had attended it by early 2001; the Entrepreneurial Training Program (eight sessions), which provides links to free legal counseling in Spanish or English and small grants for microenterprise start-ups; seniors and youth financial education; and homeownership education. Fund-raising for these projects requires CWCID staff time.

The board of directors of CWCID consists of several officers from major New York City banks, a public school teacher, and leaders of neighborhood organizations. Neighborhood Trust's board consists of Levine (who has moved to a new job in another nonprofit), Justine Zinkin (Levine's replacement as executive director of CWCID), CWCID's assistant director, the credit union's manager, its education coordinator, a business consultant, and a neighborhood resident member. The long-term aim is to have a credit union board that is composed of more members who do not have daily managerial responsibilities in the credit union.

CDCUs demonstrate that stable, useful financial institutions can exist in poor communities, but they need assistance until they make it to financial and managerial stability. Lending to low-income borrowers carries greater risk than lending to those with assets,[2] but successful CDCUs demonstrate that these organizations are able to gain stability, strength, and independence. A key measure of strength for credit unions is how much net capital they have relative to assets, since net capital serves as the cushion against occasional financial shocks.[3] For credit unions assets are primarily members' deposits and net capital is the equity of the credit union held in common by its members. Regulators look for a minimum net capital-to-asset rate of 7 percent, and CDCUs typically struggle to reach and hold this level of security until their deposits are in the neighborhood of $10 million.

A majority of Neighborhood Trust's members have never had a savings or checking account before, and some fear that having one will make them ineligible for what remains of public assistance. Banks available to them charge monthly fees of ten to thirty dollars if account balances drop below several thousand dollars. Neighborhood Trust charges one dollar a month if a member's account drops below one hundred dollars; otherwise checking services are free. Short-term personal loans of from five hundred to ten thousand dollars are available to members at regular market rates. Providing services at this scale requires that the credit union's operation be subsidized, and this is one key role played by the nonprofit CWCID.

Subsidies for the financial services provided by Neighborhood Trust come through CWCID from several sources. An initial $450,000 in grants came from foundations. Pledges of additional low-interest deposits came from Citibank, Chase-Manhattan, and Fuji Bank. The list of corporate and foundation supporters of CWCID contains over fifty organizations, including the Columbia-Presbyterian Hospital Neighborhood Fund; the charitable fund of Consolidated Edison, the major New York public utility provider; The Aspen Institute; and the Industrial Bank of Japan. Grants that go directly to the credit union add to its net capital account—the equivalent of the equity in a for-profit bank. Organizations of all kinds can also subsidize CDCUs with large deposits on which they are willing to accept low or no interest payments. Unlike conventional credit unions, CDCUs are able to accept deposits from nonmembers. This provides a means by which philanthropic organizations, major religious organizations, and others can put their liquid assets to work in CDCUs.

Approximately twenty of the fifty organizations on the 2001 CWCID supporter list were banks or bank foundations, and this highlights one outgrowth of Community Reinvestment Act (CRA) regulations. Banks can fulfill their obligations to low-income neighborhoods that they underserve by supporting institutions in those areas that do provide financial services. Rather than operating branches there that may not meet their profit goals and that they would have to staff with people who do not understand the neighborhoods well enough to compete well there, the banks can give money to nonprofits and take the tax deductions for the gifts against their incomes. Pleasing the CRA regulators in the Federal Reserve by this means provides some funds for services in poor neighborhoods and allows for the creation of innovative, service-oriented nonprofits there. Regulated banks thus provide poor neighborhoods with a small part of the social surplus they reap from their operations elsewhere.

Building a depositor and member base is vital to the success of the credit union and enables it to reach a scale that makes it viable without outside funding. In part Neighborhood Trust established itself by working through neighborhood churches to inform their members of the services available and by making the credit union a tuition payment location for a parochial school that serves area families. The credit union provides youth training and savings accounts for students in several neighborhood public schools. Helping members gain the confidence to conduct their business with the credit union by electronic direct deposit and ATMs is one of the next challenges, as now roughly 10 percent of the membership makes daily personal visits to one of the two offices. As Mark Levine pointed out, the start-up phase for a new credit union in a poor neighborhood is long and involved (Levine 2001).

Scale of operation is an ever-present topic of discussion within credit union circles. The banking industry is consolidating rapidly, and economies of scale are one of the forces driving this trend. Neighborhood Trust has grown quickly to a size roughly double the average deposit base for the nearly thirty CDCUs in New York City, but gaining efficiency in support, back-office accounting, and computer services is a pressing issue. Neighborhood Trust and several other CDCUs in the city have been discussing collaboration and sharing of services, bulk purchase of credit card services, and other ways to overcome some of the inherent disadvantages of their small scale of operations. Progress is being made in some areas, but responding to the impact on operations from the September 11 attack has been a recent priority (Zinkin 2002).

Those who created CWCID and Neighborhood Trust understood that key ingredients for development were missing in the neighborhoods they sought to help, and they acted to provide one of them. Financial services are catalysts for development on two fronts: helping individuals and households accumulate and manage their financial affairs with sound information and the best possible options; and providing seed money for new investment and entrepreneurial activity in the community. This aggregator of assets and intermediary in the financial life of the neighborhoods it serves got off to a good start. Its task now is to stabilize and grow.

Neighborhood Trust/Credit Where Credit Is Due and Good Development

This combination nonprofit and credit union was created to achieve many of the goals of this book's criteria for good development. CDCUs serve a market segment that is generally ignored by the typical businesses of this sector, banks. If successful, CDCUs help the communities they serve to prosper and their members as well. One of the seeming paradoxes of this activity is that if CDCUs succeed they will find themselves competing with more mainstream financial institutions that move into their then-more-prosperous communities and serve their then-more-prosperous members. This poaching or skimming of the cream from the market is normal (given the structure of the economy), and innovative credit unions will move on to serve new needs among the underserved—their purpose. This also provides another rationale for the banks' philanthropic handouts: if successful, CDCUs produce a new potential customer base for the banks.

Social Surplus Creation and Retention

Neighborhood Trust/CWCID attracts social surplus to the communities it serves and retains it there. The role these organizations play is compelling enough to charitable organizations, including those of mainstream financial institutions, that those charitable organizations provide funding for initial asset building where those funds have been absent. From this base more social surplus can be built in the community, where it can be put to work under the democratic control of directors elected by the members of the credit union.

Philanthropic donations and the subsidies provided by low-interest loans help a CDCU get launched. Its members' deposits then provide the foundation for its operation and the grounds on which it can slowly build its own surplus. The same processes that allow banks to be profitable are practiced by credit unions but with far slimmer margins. If successful the credit union gradually builds its net assets and uses them to foster other services for its members as well as outreach to others. The geographical roots of the process are fundamental—the surplus is a community-based asset for development.

In the institutional development of CDCUs there is constant tension between (a) the aim of the credit unions to provide their members with the lowest possible cost for their services, loans at the lowest possible interest rates when it is clear that risky conditions of low income and little in the way of assets for collateral exist, good return on members' deposits, and decent incomes to those who work in the credit unions; and (b) the need for credit unions to build the organizations' capital in order to assure their existence and ability to continue providing new ways of assisting the underserved. Can these competing needs be served? The record of CDCUs to date indicates that they can. CDCUs grow, as evidenced by Self-Help in Durham, North Carolina; Alternatives Federal Credit Union in Ithaca, New York; and the Santa Cruz Community Development Credit Union in Santa Cruz, California. Each of these CDCUs has served its community well, grown, and become stable institutions for development.

Job Creation

Job creation on the basis of CDCUs such as Neighborhood Trust takes two forms: jobs in the credit union (and in this case the nonprofit CWCID) and jobs stimulated by the lending and training done by the credit union. A small loan for an entrepreneurial start-up often creates only one job, and for Neighborhood Trust it is too early to know how many small beginnings will grow. Anecdotal evidence points to the desired outcome—firms that quickly employ several people with regular jobs. The ability of the credit union to engage successfully in business lending in the ten-to-thirty-dollar range and now to expand larger business loans with SBA procedures and backing auger well for contributions to job creation.

The number and nature of jobs created in the two organizations are clear. Sixteen people staff the credit union, and six work for the nonprofit. Pay ranges from approximately twenty thousand dollars to seventy-five thousand dollars per year with benefits. Entry jobs require solid basic education, bilingual speaking ability, basic math skills, the ability to work with details, and a willingness to respond well to a variety of people in face-to-face transactions. These are jobs that can lead to internal promotion, and on-the-job skill development and training are transportable to good jobs outside the credit union.

Environmental Sustainability

Evaluated in terms of environmental sustainability, Neighborhood Trust provides a service for which few negative environmental effects can be found. Office equipment and computer systems are energy intensive but no more so than for many other businesses. If members of Neighborhood Trust sought equivalent services elsewhere in the city they would more than likely require some form of transportation in order to reach a bank or credit union at which to conduct their business. Retail outlets in two neighborhoods provide services that diminish the transportation needs of the neighborhood residents.

Linkages, Spin-Offs, and Multipliers

By providing a key economic service in its neighborhoods this credit union creates a strong probability of solid linkages and spin-offs from its activities. Making local savings and some outside resources available to members as loans serves to foster consumer activity, and pooled savings can help launch new enterprises that generate jobs, income, and social surplus formation locally. Multipliers go up to the extent that more money circulates more times in the local economy, and local saving and lending aid this process. As with the discussion of multipliers in other cases, no claim can be made that a credit union offers advantages over a good local bank, but none from which contrasting evidence could be sought is in place in these neighborhoods.

Meeting Basic Needs

Basic needs are better met because of the existence of this credit union. Low-cost and safe financial services exist for over four thousand members and indirectly for their families. The money saved by the relatively low cost of these services provides funds that can be used to obtain other basic needs for those living on the economic edge in the communities served by this financial institution.

Neighborhood Trust and CWCID demonstrate the potential for third-sector provision of basic services when markets fail a community, and they demonstrate the tremendous effort required to make such a project work. The people who made this happen and who sustain it today know social entrepreneurship from the trenches.

Boston Community Capital

The average person is concerned with financial services in retail form—those provided by a bank or credit union. Organizations seeking to foster development through nonprofits and new commercial activity face the challenge of finding funding in larger amounts, and historically the challenge has been complicated by a dearth of sources. After 1979 co-ops gained the option of turning to the National Cooperative Bank. Nonprofits can turn to foundations, but grants are generally limited in their duration to periods of one to three years. For organizations that have an established revenue flow, facing loan repayments can be less daunting than life on "soft money" grants, although it can create other problems. The past decade has seen development of lenders for this specialized market—nonprofits to serve nonprofits with wholesale credit. Boston Community Capital (BCC) is an example of this new breed.

When BCC began in late 1984 as the Boston Community Loan Fund (BCLF) its purpose was limited to providing below-market interest rate loans for creation of affordable housing. Successful at this work for a decade, in 1994 it expanded its scope to community development lending in general. It formed three affiliated nonprofit corporations: the loan fund; a loan services provider for new businesses called Managed Assets Corporation; and Boston Community Venture Fund, a venture capital (equity) provider for small businesses in low-income communities. BCC's loan fund and its venture fund were certified as community development financial institutions shortly after passage of the Community Development and Financial Institutions Act of 1994. BCLF Inc., the holding company for the other nonprofits, was renamed Boston Community Capital in 1997 "to better reflect the full scope of operations" of its component parts (Boston Community Capital 1998). At that time the venture fund became manager for BCLF Ventures I, a for-profit limited-liability partnership. A second venture capital fund, Ventures II, has since been launched.

This community development lender began in the Boston area and now serves all of Massachusetts as a "financial intermediary." It marshals funds from donors, socially responsible lenders such as faith-based organizations and foundations, for-profit corporations, and government sources and puts them to use in communities where development has lagged. Much of its lending has been done for affordable housing, where its track record with over $40 million in loans since 1984 has a loss rate of one-third of 1 percent. This loss rate is the equal of commercial banks but in riskier lending than banks will typically consider. By 2001 BCC had financed over thirty-eight hundred units of affordable housing (Boston Community Capital 2001). Community organizations not engaged in housing are also borrowers; a list for 1998 includes loans to an agency doing public policy analysis on problems of teenage pregnancy and adolescent health, others to provide literacy outreach and violence prevention, and others to community gardens. In 1998 loan interest rates ranged from 6 to 9 percent with durations from two months to twenty-five years. Loans provided part of basic housing finance, working capital, or bridge loans until housing rehabilitation was completed.

One of BCC's most successful grassroots-level programs has been its One-to-Four Family Program, which targets buildings containing one to four housing units. This housing is common in the Boston area and is generally too expensive for a single family to renovate but too small to attract commercial developers. The One-to-Four Program works through neighborhood-based community development corporations to renovate buildings and make them available to first-time buyers. It stabilizes neighborhoods by helping to place in them people with a stake in their future, and it expands the stock of affordable housing. Beginning in 1995 BCLF loaned more than $5.7 million for this program in its first few years of operation and brought two area banks into the activity, leveraging its own funds in the process. The program created more than two hundred individual housing units by 1999 (Boston Community Capital 1999).

In 1998 BCC received a capital grant of $1 million from the CDFI Fund. Fleet Bank made a $1 million investment in the venture fund in the same year. A wide range of banks, foundations, and religious institutions provide capital for BCC; including individuals it counts over five hundred suppliers of capital for its operations (Boston Community Capital 2001). In lending or investing those funds BCC works directly with the state of Massachusetts, cities, housing associations, community development corporations, and community organizations. It is supported by the area Local Initiative Support Corporation (LISC), one of many nonprofits created by the Ford Foundation in 1979 to help foster community development.[4]

Boston Community Capital is modifying its strategy to move beyond the individual projects that were the mainstay of its early years and into neighborhood initiatives and commercial development on a larger scale. With a base of more than $40 million in assets and nearly two decades of experience, the organization has as its aim to make a larger impact on development in Massachusetts (Boston Community Capital 2000).

National Cooperative Bank

The National Cooperative Bank (NCB) was created by Congress in 1978 as the National Consumer Cooperative Bank; it was meant to provide financial services for the underserved cooperative sector. The result of extensive efforts by consumers, labor organizations, and cooperatives, it was nearly eliminated by the incoming Reagan administration (Gunn 1984, 58–60). To save the bank its new staff and supporters converted it in 1981 to a private financial institution owned by its cooperative customers. In the bank's first twenty years of operation it made over $6 billion in loans, and by 2001 it managed $3.6 billion in assets (National Cooperative Bank 2002). It has launched a subsidiary called the NCB National Savings Bank that can provide on-line retail financial services for individual and institutional accounts. The Savings Bank provides financing for cooperative apartment ownership, among other services.

Commercial lending to major cooperatives is the specialty of NCB. Its annual list "NCB Co-op 100," available through its website, is organized in the categories of agriculture, grocery, hardware and lumber, finance, and utility co-ops, provides a changing picture of the largest one hundred co-ops in the country. In addition to commercial lending NCB provides real estate lending for cooperative buildings and co-op housing mortgages, small (co-op) business lending, and the NCB Savings Bank retail services.

One of the key roles lost in early restructuring into the form NCB has taken for the past twenty years was its cooperative development and technical assistance mission. Today the bank concentrates development efforts in the area of housing and works as part of the Cooperative Housing Coalition to point the way to use of cooperative housing as a provider of affordable homes (National Cooperative Bank 1999). NCB also works with organizations such as the Cooperative Development Institute in Massachusetts and several university centers for cooperatives to encourage start-ups and growth of smaller cooperatives.

NCB sells many of its loans, such as mortgage-backed securities, on secondary financial markets. This expands the reach of the bank and makes more resources available to the cooperative sector. Its lending to smaller firms takes place in a number of ways, illustrated well by its ability to lend to independent hardware stores that are members of wholesale buying co-ops. Lines of credit, term loans, and real estate loans in amounts smaller than $1 million are provided through its NCB Priority Banking Center for these small- to medium-sized members.

One of the major contributions NCB makes to cooperatives is to work with other lenders in structuring needed packages of financing. On the small end of the lending scale it was one of three lenders for a building acquisition and renovation loan to Greenstar Cooperative food store in Ithaca, New York; on the larger end of the scale it was one of several lenders for the Lummi Nation assisted-living center in Washington State (National Cooperative Bank 1999, 8–9). NCB has been a long-term lender to the Alaska Native Corporations, provider of many services to Native American communities in Alaska.

Functioning as a financial cooperative, NCB is managed by a board of directors made up primarily of members elected by member co-ops.[5] Board members tend to be senior officers in organizations such as the Cornerstone Cooperatives in Atlanta, Georgia; the Council of New York Cooperatives and Condominiums; and the Arctic Slope Native Association. A patronage refund is made to members in years following successful operations, and to accelerate its equity building that dividend is generally distributed in the form of new stock to be held by members (National Cooperative Bank 1999, 10). Regional offices of the bank function in Alaska, California, Chicago, and New York, and the Savings Bank has retail operations in Washington, D.C., New York, and Hillsboro, Ohio.

NCB provides a vital part of the support necessary for development of cooperatives in the United States. While its strength has been servicing the largest of the organizations in the co-op sector and co-op housing needs, its presence enables other co-ops—retail, wholesale, housing, and workers' co-ops—to grow into the need for its services and then find services available from an organization that understands the unusual financial structure of this form of organization.

The examples of nonprofits providing financial services presented in this chapter only scratch the surface of a fast-growing area of development for development. Urban, rural, statewide, and regional organizations provide loan services, microenterprise loans, loans and grants for new businesses owned by women, funds that can be linked with public and for-profit funding, financial assistance for minority-owned businesses, and more. Venture capital funds provide new sources of equity funding. These organizations bring to nonprofit development efforts financial resources and sophisticated thinking and management techniques. Their ability to raise the level at which the members they serve function in financial matters is one of their major contributions.

7

Health Care

Nonprofit organizations have traditionally been at the center of health care in the United States, and for the nonprofit sector health care makes up approximately 60 percent (by far the largest source) of revenue (Salamon 1999, 77). While for-profit organizations are making inroads in some portions of this sector, most notably nursing home care, specialty treatment, and health insurance, it is still a sector largely based on nonprofit institutions. Hospital care is the largest single area of health care expenditure in the country and one in which nonprofits predominate (79).

The health care sector has seen rapid change in recent years. "Managed care," the country's uneasy compromise in health care funding and delivery that has shifted power to insurers and health maintenance organizations, has been accompanied by pressure to contain rapid health care cost increases. Changes have included steep declines in the number of public sector facilities, declines in the number of general hospitals, and growth in specialty care facilities, many of them in the private sector. Outpatient clinic and home health care aspects of the health sector have grown in both national expenditures and number of providers, and here again nonprofit and for-profit providers compete (Salamon 1999, 84–85). In the insurance arena in 1996, 26 percent of premiums were paid to nonprofits, many of them the remaining Blue Cross/Blue Shield organizations that had not converted to for-profit status.[1] Health maintenance organizations (HMOs) grew out of the Kaiser Permanente nonprofit and now provide 30 percent (the largest single components) of insurance in the United States (90).

At the level of national policy the early days of the Clinton administration saw the nation's last major debate on its health care system, although there are indications of renewed pressure among health care consumers (individuals and employers) to repair what can only be described as a crazy-quilt system. The mix of private for-profit, nonprofit, and public-sector institutions that provide care do so in a world with fast-changing high technology care; insurance and drug companies whose main objective is returning profit to their stockholders; consolidation in the industry; bureaucratization at the HMO, insurance, and governmental regulatory levels; and expensive liability insurance in the face of lawsuit settlements for mistakes in treatment. The United States is the world leader in the amount of its gross domestic product devoted to health care,[2] despite the fact that nearly forty million U.S. citizens have no access to paid care through an insurance plan or government program.

Compounding the difficulties of health care delivery is that, discounting government-provided Medicare and Medicaid, most people get HMO or insurance coverage through their employers. However, employers are not required to provide this coverage to their employees, and those seeking to minimize employment costs in labor markets where they can get sufficient job applicants without offering this benefit generally do not offer it. Some offer plans as options to be paid at employee expense, which for low-wage jobs is prohibitively expensive. The outcome is that many employed people and a large percentage of the unemployed have no insurance. They must pay for incidental doctor or hospital visits or do without. If they should need major care they may not be able to get it without paying in advance.

The idea of health insurance (applicable to health maintenance organizations as well) and the basis for the mutual insurance companies (some currently being privatized) is that the care of the sick or injured is paid for by the good fortune of the healthy. Since none of us knows which card we will be dealt and the costs of care for those getting a bad hand are extreme, it is worthwhile for us to pay to share the risk with others. When insurance becomes a profit-motivated business two contradictory results typically occur. First, the quest for profit may drive insurers to push management to run the health care companies more efficiently—eliminating wasteful practices that may be acceptable where the bottom line is not all. The second and negative outcomes of cost minimization may auger badly for provision of the service to those who most need it. The insurance companies may pressure providers with the goals of greater work output, and they may sort clients and deny coverage of services. Management will be drawn to look for ways of refining the pool of those insured to the healthiest—denying access to or coverage for those with poor histories or preexisting conditions. The quest for profit may lead to denying coverage in rural areas (where low density of population increases per capita cost of delivery) or in neighborhoods where patterns of behavior can be seen to increase the risk of disease or injury.

When employers pick up the tab for the main costs of care or insurance their interests in minimizing costs may also mean compromises in care. In the familiar pattern of for-profit ventures, mergers and acquisitions may promise economies of scale but in the end eliminate options in the market-place and eventually eliminate the competition that was supposed to contain profits to normal levels of market return on investment.

It is beyond the scope of this book and the expertise of the author to profess a way out of the morass of the present system. Rather the focus is on innovative third-sector organizations that deliver health care and provide insurance for it. In this traditional stronghold of nonprofit providers numerous innovative organizations stand out, but only a few can be profiled here. The first case presented is worker-owned Cooperative Home Care Associates, based in the South Bronx in New York City. It was created to help people from a low-income urban area find decent employment. The second is the large regional health maintenance organization Group Health Cooperative, based in Seattle, Washington. It is the largest health care cooperative in the country and hence the country's largest consumer-governed health care organization.[3] The third case is that of a nonprofit start-up insurer in Ithaca, New York, the Ithaca Health Fund. This organization is bucking the trend of demutualization; it has been launched with full commitment to nonprofit status and basic (noncatastrophic), low-overhead service to its members.

Cooperative Home Care Associates

This cooperative's roots lie in a model of worker ownership developed by the Boston-based Industrial Cooperative Association (now the ICA Group) two decades ago, a model partly inspired by the Mondragon co-ops in Spain. Cooperative Home Care Associates (CHCA) has two goals: to provide its employees (associates) with quality jobs and to provide quality home care to its clients. It is based in an urban area of persistently high unemployment and has played a vital role in helping move people (primarily women of color) from public assistance to stable work. In the process CHCA has served as a learning center from which several other firms have been spawned, and it has developed a nonprofit institute designed to influence public policy on long-term-care issues.

Paraprofessional home care is a service whose time has come, at least if the signals are an aging population, high cost of institutional care, and many people's desire to stay in their own homes as long as possible. Home care agencies are typically licensed by state governments, and they exist as both for-profit and nonprofit organizations. CHCA was founded in 1985 and currently employs nearly seven hundred providers who move from home to home to deliver basic direct-care services to the elderly, ill, or handicapped. What sets CHCA apart is a commitment to provide full-time work, defined as over thirty hours a week of billable time (in 2002 CHCA employees were averaging thirty-five hours per week); careful selection of its associates; and the best training possible to enable each to become certified "home health aides" under federal Medicare and New York State regulation. Associates who have been with CHCA for three months can become worker-owners of the firm and participate directly in its governance through involvement with a worker council, an assembly, or the board of directors. It is not uncommon for an employee of CHCA to begin acquiring an ownership stake in the firm within months of having been on public assistance. In 2001 CHCA generated $16 million in sales, and the net worth of the organization at the end of that year was $2 million (Dawson 2002).

A key figure in the history of CHCA is Rick Surpin, who today is board chair of the organization. He helped conceive of the organization and its goals partly from his prior experience as director of the Center for Community Economic Development of the Community Service Society of New York City (Dawson and Kreiner 1993, 5). Through the work of Surpin; Peggy Powell, who began as the education specialist for CHCA; and Steve Dawson of ICA the new firm made it through start-up years with financial assistance from several charitable organizations and loan funds. It was profitable by 1987 (and has remained so), and by 1990 it employed 160. A strategic planning process pointed to the need for growth in order to spread administrative costs over a larger income, but the growth in need for aides had temporarily peaked and funding for training was limited. By 1991 growth was back on the agenda, and it continued through the 1990s to a then-planned level of approximately five hundred paraprofessionals. Employee turnover bedevils the industry for several reasons, but the CHCA approach to training, adequate amounts of work, decent pay and benefits, and employee ownership have meant a steady decline in annual turnover. Today the turnover rate at CHCA is half the average rate for the industry.

By the early 1990s, 80 percent of those eligible to be owners (employed for over three months) had become worker-owners by paying a fifty-dollar initial investment each on the one-thousand-dollar membership fee. Company policy is that the rest of the fee is deducted from a worker-owner's salary on a weekly basis over five years. Dividends are distributed to owner-members based on the number of hours worked in the accounting period, but in a system similar to that of Mondragon not all the amount distributed to them is paid out; a significant part of it is invested in the firm in their names. The first allocation from profits (surplus from operations) is typically 50 percent that is added to the company's capitalization. The remaining 50 percent is allocated to worker-owners, but not all of it is distributed. The amount distributed varies, but typically the board of directors will allocate 40 percent of the remaining 50 percent to worker-owners' accounts in the firm and distribute 60 percent of it (30 percent of the firm's total profits) in cash. Individual dividends in the early years were a few hundred dollars per year, and they have remained in the range of two hundred to six hundred dollars because of members' desire to maximize current wages and benefits.

Another commitment defined this firm from the start: it was to be operated democratically. Many of its employees had minimal formal education and no experience in running a firm. Education was essential for both delivery of services and competent decision making on the part of participants. As an early history of the company made clear, its core business strategy had to succeed on two fronts at once: in the marketplace and in satisfying the "wants and needs of the employee-owners" (Dawson and Kreiner 1993, 28). Building and maintaining a participative work environment required designing a legal structure and system that would facilitate participative governance, and it meant devoting considerable training resources to education and skills building for participation. At the beginning the majority of the organization's board members had trustee status, and they were gradually replaced as employee-owners began to elect their own board members. Today owner-members make up a 75 percent majority of the board.

The survival and expansion of this organization are remarkable because of the commitment of the co-op to worker ownership and to organizational democracy, and also because of the industrial conditions within which the organization has grown. Home health aides provide an essential service, but their remuneration and working conditions are not conducive to a career. Minimum-wage, part-time work typifies the industry, and payment rates are set by Medicare and Medicaid and private-sector insurers looking to minimize costs. Home health care workers usually move from home to home at their own expense on unpaid time. Their work resembles the "domestic work" of past decades, and the workforce is largely women of color. CHCA provides one path of escape from the worst conditions of this work; the more traditional alternative is unionization. In a break-through case for low-income workers in Los Angeles County the Service Employees International Union (SEIU) was elected to represent seventy-four thousand home care workers in early 1999 (Malveaux 2000). This holds the potential for a significant gain in a field of work that is generally less remunerative than that of parking lot attendants. Recently the New York Local 1199 of SEIU approached CHCA to discuss affiliation; the two organizations aim to work together to influence all-important public policies on home health care.

Tight labor markets of the late 1990s brought national press stories of the shortage of home care aides (Rimer 2000). CHCA had been attuned to national policy issues for most of its history: policy drove reimbursement rates that then limited pay and benefits to aides. Recognizing the need to affect policy and to investigate means to replicate the success of the company in the South Bronx, CHCA formed a parallel nonprofit organization in 1991 called the Paraprofessional Healthcare Institute (PHI). With support from the Charles Stewart Mott, Ford, Annie E. Casey, Ms., and other foundations PHI enabled the separation of policy advocacy and consulting from the profit-oriented operating environment of the co-op.

PHI has helped create successful home health care co-ops in Philadelphia and New Hampshire and supported training initiatives in Detroit and Arkansas. It was also instrumental in launching a co-op in Boston, which subsequently failed. In the late 1990s Medicare payments for home care were cut nearly 50 percent and Medicaid spending in Massachusetts was cut by 8 percent. With aides earning less than eight dollars an hour for part-time work and the availability of other opportunities prior to the downturn of mid-2000, Cooperative Home Care of Boston closed its doors and arranged for many of its aides to carry on their work with client families through the Women's Education and Industrial Union (Dawson 2000).

On the policy front PHI has pursued a sectoral strategy of uniting different organizations to work for policies that would allow more favorable and stable conditions for those working in home health care (Inserra et al. 2002). The institute has allied with workers, consumers, and providers throughout the country to form the Direct Care Alliance (DCA). DCA aims to improve job quality for direct-care workers and thus to improve the supply of this service in the economy. The group has participated in congressional hearings on the trends affecting the direct-care workforce in long-term care (Direct Care Alliance 2000). By seeking to improve labor market conditions for care workers PHI and CHCA are a team seeking to improve the job prospects of working women at the same time that they hope to improve the availability of essential services for an aging population.

Cooperative Home Care Associates and the Paraprofessional Healthcare Institute represent very different third-sector organizations even though they were begun with the same basic ideas and ideals. CHCA is a cooperatively structured and democratically run organization that seeks to provide stable employment to its members. PHI is more traditionally third sector, although it has CHCA members and its own worker members on its board. As a nonprofit it receives foundation grants to research organization development and regional and national policy in the direct-care industry. Working out of an area that remains emblematic of urban decay in the United States, both have had a clear impact on one aspect of health care.

Cooperative Home Care Associates and the Criteria for Good Development

Social Surplus Creation and Retention

The process of building social surplus has been slow but steady for CHCA. The fact that its operations have generated a surplus each year since 1987 provided the basis for accumulation. CHCA built on initial grants from funding agencies that recognized the need it was designed to serve and had faith that this form of organization could meet its objectives. Supporters also had to be confident that the people involved knew what they were doing and could be trusted to persevere through the start-up years of the co-op. Low-wage work provides little on which to build an organization's capital base, but the commitment that members made to place half of the organization's surplus into its equity account and retain another portion in the co-op in the form of individual accounts is a proven model: it is essentially the source for the equity financing of more than one hundred industrial cooperatives by Mondragon. The difference is that industrial work typically has far higher value-added from which to build than does such poorly paid service-sector work.

Job Creation

Creation of jobs has been a primary objective at CHCA, and the number of jobs created in the organization is impressive. The aim for the co-op now is to keep growing to a staff of one thousand and then evaluate further growth. To the question of whether these are good jobs there is no easy answer. That they provide an essential service is clear, and the fact that they provide skills quickly to people who typically had few when they joined the organization is positive as well. With a current average pay rate of $8.15 per hour plus benefits (most notably health insurance and paid vacation) these jobs could not be said to pay well, but compared to no job and meager public assistance they can be seen as a positive start. Working thirty-five hours a week would bring less than fifteen thousand dollars per year. Given that many workers and worker-owners in this co-op support families this remains poverty-level income, although it is approximately 20 percent higher compensation than that received for comparable jobs in New York City. (Dawson and Surpin 2002)

The affiliation of CHCA with Local 1199 of SEIU was intended to provide a likely means of addressing this compensation problem. The union is unfamiliar with the special nature of this worker-owned company: there is no employer to bargain with other than those whom the union represents. However, the target of their common cause is the state and federal regulatory agencies that set the pay levels for this work (Dawson and Surpin 2002).

Environmental Sustainability

The work of CHCA is environmentally sustainable. At the level of human ecology it is vital. For the natural environment there is little harm created except that the workers have to travel within the city in order to do their work. Use of an automobile would be prohibitively expensive, and parking would often be impossible; public transportation is the obvious means by which this travel gets done.

Linkages and Multipliers

The multipliers created by CHCA have a direct impact in the relatively poor areas of metropolitan New York in which members of the organization live. Payment to them typically comes from outside the area but gets spent in the community, potentially raising multipliers. *Linkages* are more tenuous since beyond medical supplies there are not many material inputs to the work and its end-service goes to the person at home.

Meeting Basic Needs

A basic human need is met by this third-sector organization. Home care helps keep people from being institutionalized and helps keep the nation's health bill down. For individuals being served it provides a means by which to continue independent living, and for their family members and friends it provides temporary relief from care duties and some worry.

CHCA has been a brave urban experiment that has worked. The problems faced by the people doing this work are largely those of a nation that cannot commit to decent health care for all. The people who pay the price are those who need the care and many of those who provide it.

Group Health Cooperative

Group Health Cooperative (GHC), the major Washington State health care provider, gained a reputation as an innovator in health care with its inception in 1947. Then the idea of prepaid group medical coverage was relatively new. According to the history of the co-op GHC was begun by "union members, farmers, and people from other cooperatives" who had a vision of a progressive way to organize care. It began with the purchase of an existing Seattle clinic that included a small hospital, and today it includes two hospitals, thirty primary-care or family medical centers, five special care units, and affiliation with forty-eight other providers of care (Group Health Cooperative 2003).

GHC serves an enrollment of nearly six hundred thousand people. Currently one in ten Washington State residents receive their health care from GHC. People enrolled in GHC plans reside across the state of Washington and in two counties of northern Idaho. With a total staff of over ten thousand GHC is Washington State's fourth largest employer (Group Health Cooperative 2003).

In 1997 Group Health affiliated with Kaiser Permanente, a pioneer health maintenance organization founded in 1945 and the largest nonprofit provider in the country. Affiliation requires sharing some health care practices, maintaining reciprocity for members of the two plans, sharing some purchasing, and working together in marketing in the western United States and nationally (Group Health Cooperative 2003). Other parts of GHC include a subsidiary that markets health plans as alternatives and additions to GHC's regular plans; the Group Health Community Foundation, which supports educational programs in the region; and the Center for Health Studies and the MacColl Institute for Healthcare Innovation, which conduct medical and health care research.

GHC's notoriety stems largely from three characteristics: its co-op structure, its long-standing focus on preventive care, and its ability to compete with larger national for-profit insurers. Consumers/patients in the system can choose to become voting members of the cooperative at no cost and join over forty thousand others who have a voice in running the co-op. The numbers are large and the organization complex, but members elect the eleven-person consumer board of trustees, make and change bylaws for the organization, and shape co-op policies. As is the case with other cooperatives the members own and (indirectly) run this health care and insurance provider. Extensive information about the operations of GHC is available to members and the public at large. The most recent annual report of operations is available to them in print or on the GHC website, which provides up-to-date information on financial results, aggregated costs, and allocation of surpluses from operations.

Preventive medicine *should* make sense to a provider/insurer. Keeping members from getting sick and diagnosing and treating their illnesses early keep members healthier and costs down. At GHC care policy is set by the board of trustees, whose members are elected by, made up of, and represent the organization's users or consumers. This board provides a system that focuses care on groups in the population that may be affected by certain chronic conditions; engages in close case management for high-risk patients; emphasizes the benefits of immunization; directs attention to trouble areas such as diabetes, breast care, and depression; and operates with a sophisticated clinical information system. GHC has been a leader in children's health (including a pioneer in encouraging the use of helmets for bicyclists) and smoker cessation programs. Beginning over thirty years ago GHC provided its enrollees with free twenty-four-hour telephone access to consulting nurses.

Quality of services delivered by a provider such as GHC is difficult to measure. One means of evaluation is provided by the National Committee for Quality Assurance (NCQA), which maintains the Health Plan Employer Data & Information Set (HEDIS). Group Health used HEDIS criteria to establish a "report card" system that was made available to GHC members and subscribers beginning in 1992. Accreditation committees report regularly on the quality of care provided by health care dispensers, and NCQA gives Group Health's commercial and Medicare plans the committee's top rating of "excellent." Professional qualifications are evaluated in part by board certification of physicians, and by this measure Group Health staff is board certified at levels from 86 to 92 percent, well above the national average of 60 percent. A measure of organizational effectiveness is the ratio of administrative expense involved in delivering services, and on this criterion GHC ranked fourth lowest of twenty plans in the state of Washington in 2001 (Group Health Cooperative 2003).

Putting into perspective the ability of GHC to succeed requires a brief detour into some of the intricacies of the crazy quilt mentioned above and recent trends in health care in this country. This also highlights some of the constraints that make GHC behave like its competitors. Most obvious is national consolidation among for-profit HMO providers, typified by AETNA with coverage of twenty-nine million Americans (over 10 percent of the population) and United Health Care with over fifteen million under coverage. Regional levels of concentration can be higher; in eastern Washington, for instance, Premera controls over 60 percent of the market for insurance (Gollhofer 2000).

Because of competition in this system, to appeal to employers insurers have to offer lower-cost packages of insurance—what could be called partial coverage. One common way of doing this is to offer plans that include a high deductible (unpaid portion) for use of services. While this keeps the cost of a plan lower it also serves to discourage use of care. If this eliminated only unnecessary uses it would be fine, but it can also discourage basic preventive care—meaning higher costs (in health and dollars) later. To capture economies of scale at a level to assure competitive pricing GHC has to sell coverage to large numbers, but to do so the co-op is pressured to minimize coverage. Markets have a way of encouraging the lowest common denominator in costs of input, but in the case of health care low (short-term) costs of inputs means compromising people's lives. It would be naive to suggest that care/cost trade-offs are not part of people's life decisions, but with the current national health care policy in this country insurers and employers have the dominant voices in these decisions.

Cooperatives do not have to distribute profits to stockholders, but neither can they operate at a loss. GHC lost money on operations in the late 1990s and had to move aggressively to eliminate those operations in which expenses outstripped revenue. One result was that the co-op pared back some money-losing projects in rural eastern Washington and Idaho. In 2002 the cooperative found itself on the verge of a strike by sixteen hundred staffers over wages and benefits. Members of Local 8 of the Office and Professional Employees International Union authorized a strike vote, but a contract was reached that left both parties satisfied (Nyhan 2002). As another cost-saving plan Group Health announced in summer 2002 that it would sell or fundamentally reorganize Eastside, a member hospital located near the Microsoft headquarters. In general Seattle hospitals, including those belonging to Group Health, had run at low capacity utilization for years. The move was based on the decision of the co-op to get out of the inpatient care aspect of health care, contract for those services, and concentrate on delivery through the extensive clinic system of GHC (Perry 2002).

This overview of the rigors of the competitive world in which GHC operates would not be complete without addressing for-profit behavior at another level. Conversion of mutual (cooperative) insurance plans (for health care insurance or other forms of insurance) is rationalized on the basis of the need to be able to raise large amounts of capital. Capital markets will provide the capital if there is the promise of solid return on investment or profit from operations. This exchange is conditioned on the assumption that the greater efficiency of the for-profit operation inspires the cost-savings that provide the profits for investors. Providers are supposedly kept under control by accepted business practice and legal constraints, government regulation if it applies, and competition. If competition wanes because of a trend to oligopoly or monopoly in markets, the remaining large firms can begin to play by their own rules—unless closely regulated.

Cooperatives such as GHC can compete in this world if they have sufficient volume of business to more or less match costs with others, operate efficiently (here they may be able to take a longer perspective because of a relatively stable member base or staff base), and pay a lower return to capital because they reward members' funds at lower rates than capital markets may provide for investments of similar risk. This is the position of GHC today. The co-op could also, of course, attempt to pay staff less money. The

role of Group Health Cooperative as a significant regional provider of
health care gives the co-op advantages, but the shifting sands of the industry, especially to national-scale operations and tightly constrained packages
of coverage made to appeal to employers, will force the organization to continue to be a nimble innovator in order to survive and maintain its progressive reputation.

Organizing to provide general insurance on a cooperative basis has a long
history in the United States, but mixing insurance and health care delivery
is largely a post–World War II phenomenon. Group Health stands out because it brings together consumer co-op, health maintenance organization,
mutual insurer, and provider/clinic/pharmacist/hospital in one organization. The impact the co-op has on economic development and quality of life
in the Seattle region and other parts of the Northwest is significant, and
GHC would get high marks in terms of the good development criteria used
for the major cases of this book.

Ithaca Health Fund

The Ithaca Health Fund (IHF) began operations in 1997 and made its first
payment for member treatment in 1998. The organization was created by
Paul Glover, Ithaca activist and founder of Ithaca Hours local currency
(www.ithacahours.org). IHF is an informal insurance plan, but it is meant
to serve other objectives as well. One is to keep costs down by negotiating
discount prices for services, including alternative and nonmainstream
forms of medical services. Another is to provide payment to a local group
of providers, strengthening them and keeping health care and insurance expenditures circulating in the local economy.

In the realm of insurance IHF is a bare-bones system at rock-bottom cost
to its members. Designed for the uninsured (which IHF estimates to be one-
third of the population of the county it serves), its basic cost is $100 a year
for adults, $75 a year for a spouse or partner of a member, and $50 a year
for a child. Members get immediate coverage for acute care such as broken
bones (up to $2,500), emergency stitches (up to $800), and ambulance rides
(up to $400) (Ithaca Health Fund 2003a). Some members use the fund as a
supplement to high-deductible insurance. Delayed coverage is available for
procedures such as dental root canals. There is no deductible; all costs up to
the maximum are paid. A description of the program likens it to an Amish-
style safety net (Ithaca Health Fund 2003b).

In 2002 IHF served over five hundred members. As of early December of that year it had $148,000 in assets, and it had paid out $17,000 during the first eleven months of the year. The fund had received over $34,000 in foundation grants and individual donations and earned $9,600 in interest income (Ithaca Health Fund 2002a). Pooling of payments to IHF provides basic insurance for many needs, leverage for members in negotiating forms of care that they agree they want, and discounts with local providers. IHF has 120 member health care providers (ranging from physicians to massage therapists) who each pay from $30 to $100 annually to be listed with the fund (Ithaca Health Fund n.d., 1, 4).

Ithaca Health Fund keeps rates low partly because of volunteer labor—there are no paid administrators. The fund is run by a member-elected board of twelve and will make payments for health services received anywhere in the world. If IHF can grow successfully the fund hopes to hire its own dental hygienists for members' annual cleanings and checkups and eventually to staff its own full-service dental clinic. Full of ambition, the organization aims eventually to influence national health policy—not for a government-run single payer system but for local and regional plans "owned directly by citizens" (Ithaca Health Fund n.d., 4).

The Ithaca Health Fund operates under the IRS 501(c)(3) status of Ithaca's Southside Community Center. The fund is seeking its own tax-exempt status and faces an important hurdle as it seeks recognition in the New York State health insurance regulatory system. Before IHF can apply for certification the fund must amass assets of half a million dollars. At its current rate of growth reaching this goal will take several more years.

Each of the cases profiled highlights the third sector's continued presence in providing health care and insurance in the United States. Equally significant, each points to an important role for organizations of this sector in innovation. In a segment of the economy delivering (or failing to deliver) a human need as basic as health care this is an important positive externality. Solutions to some current health care quandaries may be found in the experiences of these third-sector providers.

8

The Arts

I t is no secret that arts organizations can help stimulate development. The Guggenheim in Bilboa, Spain, drew attention to the redevelopment of a depressed city in Basque Spain and visitor spending to fuel the development. In the United States downtown San Jose's revitalization has been enhanced by the San Jose Repertory Theater, and Newark's Center for the Performing Arts is expected to play a similar role in that city's depressed center. Some of these developments involve major new building, and some are part of complex historical preservation-based redevelopment efforts. None works on its own. All do best as part of complex webs of arts-related small businesses such as galleries, music clubs and restaurants, parks, and coffeehouses. Good public transportation helps keep them from being surrounded by bleak parking lots or garages, and if people do not live near them they are as desolate for much of the day as office areas are at night. Lessons from common gentrification problems and the sterility of past "urban development" have to be carefully factored into their planning.

Arts organizations are generally nonprofits for the usual reason: no profit. They require major funding and only rarely return sufficient monetary reward to make them justifiable on that basis. They deliver other returns deemed essential to life and to social and cultural reproduction. The historical formula has been that high art followed money, whether from the wealthy patrons of medieval Italy or from families on high rungs of the social ladder of New York City. In bourgeois society one mark of rising above the crass world of making and spending a fortune was to associate with high culture and sometimes leave a name (Guggenheim, Whitney) on it. Art was an ornament to wealth and power, but today culture is a power and generator of wealth in its own right.

Several biases are already apparent in this story. One is the urban context. Cities reflect the accumulation of capital, and the intense exchange of ideas and stimulation provided by urban life feed the development of art. The presumption has been that art developed with the city or because of the urban development. When art is used for redevelopment this part of the story is open to question. Another bias is that art does not happen in rural settings, although quick reflection recognizes rural enclaves of art, as in artist "colonies" and well-known artists who escape to work (write, sculpt, paint) in quiet rural locations. The products of their work may be sold in urban galleries, hung in urban museums, or staged in urban theaters, but the original production does not necessarily take place in an urban context. Yet another bias is that much of the reporting on arts-driven development highlights the grand projects and the wealthiest of nonprofit museums while skipping the galleries, playhouses, and coffeehouse scenes that are also arts driven, with smaller nonprofits playing key roles.

Art is produced (whether or not there is an enduring tangible product) and then it is printed, displayed or staged, and sold or lent for public and private consumption. Nonprofit organizations have important roles in the production and enjoyment of whatever society chooses to call art. Art is also many things: high or low, depending on the education and awareness needed to enjoy it; popular, folk, or elite, given its intended audience and how it is received; and media too numerous to mention. This chapter explores several ways in which nonprofit organizations have contributed to the arts and to community development and revitalization. The cases highlighted have to do with production and display in urban and rural settings. They are a sample of the dynamic activity within this sector, a comprehensive picture of which would require book-length treatment.

MASS MoCA

The acronym MASS MoCA (Massachusetts Museum of Contemporary Art) is itself almost a work of art—whether seen in huge polished metal letters illuminated against the nighttime sky across the top of one of the museum's buildings or heard flowing off the tongue as an appreciative visitor tells her friends not to miss it. In its short life this museum has established itself as one of the nation's premier staging places for contemporary art of all kinds, including painting, sculpture, and other tangible forms as well as music, dance, and performance art. There are several unlikely elements in the story of the creation of this museum, which opened in 1999. They include its location, its physical space, and its vitality.

MASS MoCA is located in North Adams, Massachusetts, 140 miles from Boston, the state's cultural, financial, and political center. North Adams is a small city of approximately sixteen thousand residents; it is not easy to get to; and it had been depressed for decades. Big money from a wealthy donor did not bestow an arts treasure on North Adams. Hard work by several key players, a mix of state and private funding, a mayor with foresight, and risk-taking all around made it happen. As it did, this small city began to come back to life.

North Adams is in mountainous Berkshire County, just below Vermont in northwestern Massachusetts. For much of the twentieth century the area's economy was driven by a mix of rural agricultural activity, summer and some winter tourism, and manufacturing. The manufacturing centers of Pittsfield and North Adams have suffered the same fate experienced by other rust-belt areas of the country; the decline of North Adams accelerated with the closing of Sprague Electric Company's facility there. Sprague had once employed over four thousand area residents when the city's population was nearer eighteen thousand. By the time the company moved out in 1985 the workforce was considerably smaller (John Heon in Trainer 2000, 10). Sprague made capacitors (small electrical components that store electrical charges) in its sprawling downtown complex of twenty-seven brick nineteenth-century buildings, which had been used for textile printing before Sprague took over. With Sprague's departure the buildings sat empty, and the city had little reason for hope that the bottom of its economic decline had been reached. Employment in North Adams had dropped from eighty-three hundred in 1983 to sixty-nine hundred in 1996, and livable houses were for sale at prices well below the national average (Massachusetts Division of Employment and Training 2001). The city ranked next to last in per capita income among Massachusetts cities in 1990 and received more state aid per capita than any other city in the state (Barrett 2001).

Into this depressing setting several key people and factors came together to create a vision, or what some were inclined to label a hallucination. One important factor was the presence of Williams College six miles to the west of North Adams in Williamstown. The college is a center of learning, culture, and people with connections and money—or access to money. Thomas Krens, then director, and other curators of the Williams College Museum of Art were looking for display space for newer and larger artwork than Williams could house. At the same time John Barrett III, self-proclaimed "blue-collar mayor of a blue-collar town" (Barrett 2001), was trying to find tenants for the Sprague space. The physical space impressed everyone who saw it, both for the beauty of the buildings and courtyards and for their need for repair.[1] Krens and two young Williams alumni, Joseph Thompson and Michael Govan, along with Barrett and local business leaders pitched the idea of a museum to then-governor Michael Dukakis. Dukakis liked the idea for its job-creating potential and helped to get approval of state funds for the project. The funding took years to materialize and a decade of perseverance was needed before the museum opened, but fifteen years from the time Sprague departed, those old buildings were again creating value for the local economy.

Funding to leverage state money came from several sources. Local businesspeople were coaxed into "tithing" from their profits for a fund to be used if state funding were garnered. In total 650 pledges were made for a fund totaling over $1 million, with many business owners devoting considerable volunteer work for the project as well. Museum advocates gained promises for art loans from top sources that included the Saatchi collection in London, the Sonnabend collection, and the Guggenheim in New York (Krens became its director in 1988). Private philanthropic donations provided funds for a feasibility study. Money from the state of Massachusetts was approved in the form of a 1987 bond issue for $35 million, but then-governor Dukakis shifted focus from state issues to his 1988 campaign for the presidency; in 1991 the new governor, William Weld, was skeptical of the job-creating potential of the project, so he froze distribution of the funds. Persuasion and private commitments of $8 million in donations eventually won Weld over, and in 1995 the state released the first $18.6 million for the project.

The years between the conception of the project and the start of work brought changes in plans. The original feasibility study submitted to the state was nearly two inches thick and called for a restaurant and hotel on the site as well as day care and retail space. The list of those contributing to the study read like a Who's Who of architecture: Skidmore, Owings & Merrill; Venturi, Rauch and Scott Brown, Inc.; Frank O. Gehry & Associates, Inc.; and more. As time enabled closer planning for the operation of the museum, use of extra space for commercial offices and industrial leasing became a higher priority. The computer animation company Kleiser-Walczak was an early tenant, and its presence suggested that more high-tech tenants could follow. For the museum the long delay in getting started provided time to rethink the mix of art that would be displayed. Founding director Joseph Thompson added significantly more performing art than was originally envisioned. This change brought two courtyard stages and a 650-seat theater to the project and, more importantly, identified the museum with music, dance, and theater, longtime staples of Berkshire County cultural tourism.

Within months of its opening MASS MoCA had garnered praise in media from the *Boston Globe* and the *New York Times* to *Time, Artforum,* and somewhat later *Smithsonian* magazine. In 2000 the museum won a National Preservation Honor Award from the National Trust for Historic Preservation. The opening had been organized as a national event and a celebration for the town and the people—mostly women—who used to work in its buildings for Sprague. In the first year of operation 120,000 visitors viewed the adventurous contemporary art or attended performances at MASS MoCA. Nineteen galleries, one as large as a football field, occupy only part of the complex; there is plenty of space for expansion on the thirteen-acre site. Some of the character of what visitors are about to encounter is announced at the courtyard entrance to the museum, where six sizable blaze maple trees grow upside down suspended in air in an installation by Australian artist Natalie Jeremijenko. The buildings now in use have been revitalized but not restored. There are elements of old paint on some of the brickwork, clear indications of where walls once connected, and exposed structural elements, electrical conduits, and air ducts. Refurbished windows provide extensive natural lighting. "Found architecture" might be the best term for the approach of architects Simeon Bruner and Henry Moss to the space—and for the outcome of two years of work by teams of workers.

The museum, billed as a "supercollider for the arts," is more than just gallery and performance space. From the beginning the intention was to provide fabrication space for the arts and to use some of the complex's 780,000 square feet (with only about half used for the museum) for new businesses. Marketing of mixed-use commercial space began to attract the high-tech start-ups that Mayor Barrett had in mind from the beginning of the project. Again a Williams College connection was important. Two students there approached Dick Sabot, a faculty member, with the idea of creating a company to supply internet users with software for creating Web sites. Together they launched Tripod. In 1998 Tripod was sold to the search engine company Lycos for almost $60 million, and Sabot moved on to found

Eziba, a catalog and on-line seller of imported and folk art, crafts, and interior decorating items that is located in MASS MoCA space. A dot.com village of sorts had emerged around MASS MoCA and nearby blocks of the city, creating approximately 320 jobs in eight firms by early 2001 (Barrett 2001; Thompson 2001).[2] In 2002 the museum undertook development of another 70,000 square feet of commercial real estate, which will house a new state court, law offices, and additional retail and office space.

The total operating budget of MASS MoCA in 2000 was $3.4 million, and typically half of the operating costs of the museum have to be raised annually from donors (Thompson 2001). Creation of an endowment to provide income is considered an essential next step for the museum. Such a fund would help overcome the difficulties of raising operating funds each year, especially years when big donors are not feeling flush.

Museum and high-tech jobs are different than factory jobs, and North Adams is still in transition from the manufacturing town it was thirty years ago to a new mix of tourism, arts, and silicon village. In 2002 MASS MoCA had a staff of sixty-four full-time equivalent positions, an additional thirty summer staff members, and a payroll of $1.6 million. Museum activity and to a certain extent employment are seasonal, with the summer half of the year busy and the winter half quiet. Linkages to schools and a mix of cultural activities keep locals engaged with the facility in the winter, and director Joseph Thompson estimates that 25 percent of visits are from local residents. The museum attracts fifteen thousand to twenty thousand "destination" visitors per year and many others who are in the Berkshires for the mix of attractions there. The museum is marketed, in part, as one of a growing web of culture providers, all nonprofits, in the region. The others, including the Clark Art Institute in Williamstown (undertaking major expansion), Jacob's Pillow Dance Festival, and Tanglewood's summer concert series, help make the Berkshires popular for tourists and culturally rich for residents.

High-tech jobs in North Adams are largely filled by young new employees. They make much higher pay than did the factory workers of the old economy, but of course they require expensive educations. Most are imports to North Adams, and many exhibit the migratory characteristics of the young in this new sector. Local landlords have been slow to create the kind of housing they want—not older homes to buy and fix up but relatively sophisticated townhouses, for instance—but otherwise they are high-income consumers of rental housing, restaurant meals, and automobiles. One indicator of the nature and salary level of this new employment was a job for an experienced Web-page designer for a new e-commerce company that paid seventy thousand dollars per year. MASS MoCA lost its own design intern to that far-better-paying first-sector position.

For now the other area of economic growth for North Adams lies in serving visitors to the museum. Guest facilities in the town have been limited to a Holiday Inn that has failed several times. A local entrepreneur (and Williamstown resident) brought it back to life by incorporating commercial, office, and health club space. The facility is within easy walking distance of the museum. Several bed-and-breakfast inns have also opened in the town. A new fifty-four-room hotel, The Porches Inn at MASS MoCA, has been fashioned from a row of five semi-abandoned, nearly identical mill-workers' duplex houses just across a branch of the Hoosic River from the museum complex. This addition to the tourist infrastructure of North Adams is operated by a successful Berkshire-area inn and serves a more upscale clientele than the Holiday Inn serves. The city encouraged the project by purchasing some run-down commercial property between the inn buildings and the museum and converting the land to a small park beside the river. MASS MoCA served as the project's construction coordinator. The owner of the new inn is a Williams trustee and senior executive in a major brokerage firm in New York. This is unusual for North Adams—more likely in upscale Williamstown—and the city is new territory for the well-heeled cultural tourist. Some consider the hospitality industry jobs a mixed blessing, since they involve low wage service work. The jobs in renovating and connecting the buildings that make up the inn generated good work for North Adams tradespeople. On the day the author observed construction of the inn, signs on all the trucks listed North Adams as the home base of electricians, carpenters, and plumbing and heating contractors working there. Much of the $8 million work on the mill renovation was done by local tradespeople as well. These jobs are for a limited time period, of course. They will have to be sustained by continued growth and development in the region.

Main Street in North Adams is a strange monument to the history of urban renewal. On one side it is relatively new, mall-like, and visually indistinguishable from revitalization efforts of the past few decades all over the country. A fast-food restaurant and K-Mart are tucked behind it in a large parking area. Facing this commercial sprawl is a block and a half of nineteenth-century buildings with attractive storefronts and a theater in need of restoration. Mayor Barrett speaks with barely concealed disdain for the slow response time of a few local landlords who control much of the area and seem content to sit back and collect low rent for builders that could be enhanced. Indeed, they might think that hanging on in North Adams has finally paid off, as downtown commercial property that rented (or was vacant) at four to five dollars per square foot in 1994–95 rented for eleven to twelve dollars a square foot in 2000. In the deepest phase of the North Adams depression more than 60 percent of commercial property was vacant, and by early 2001 vacancies were below 30 percent. New commercial activity brings with it major improvements in the local tax base and new resources for the city to use in fostering further development.

Mayor John Barrett has worked for a long time for the revitalization of North Adams. Before the idea of MASS MoCA he borrowed money to refurbish downtown areas and repair city streets. When the North Adams YMCA was in trouble Barrett worked to enable the city to take over its building, lease the facility back to the "Y" at favorable rates, and build a much-needed new elementary school around its recreational space. Barrett is famous for commenting that he would not walk across the street to see the art in MASS MoCA. He worked for the museum for years because he saw it as a stimulant to development, but his concern has long been to build a more diverse economy around it. His criticism of local entrepreneurs seems to stem from his own entrepreneurial inclinations. They have served North Adams well thus far, and his constituents have signaled their approval by keeping him in office for an unusually long period of time. As of late 2002 he was the longest serving mayor in Massachusetts.

There is a regional aspect to the aspirations of North Adams to encourage high-tech jobs, as they require appropriate infrastructure in the form of efficient telecommunications capacity. Berkshire County was isolated enough that the nearest major provider of services was in Albany, New York, forty-five miles to the west. The county, the Berkshire Regional Planning Commission, and the Massachusetts Technology Collaborative, a state-chartered semi-public entity, worked together to develop an environment that would attract several private-sector firms to provide services aimed at high-tech business needs in the region (National Association of Counties 2001). High-quality and relatively low-cost wired and wireless technologies are now available. What might have been a long-term cart-or-horse-first stalemate (demonstrate the demand and then business will install the technologies or install the technologies so the region could attract new high-tech businesses) was forestalled by coordinated county, regional, and state action.

In August 2000 MASS MoCA received a combination grant and loan from the U.S. Department of Housing and Urban Development intended to strengthen the urban-redevelopment role of the museum. The $2 million grant and $3.2 million low-interest, Massachusetts State–supported loans will enable the renovation of an additional seventy thousand square feet of commercial space with high-bandwidth telecommunications capacity. MASS MoCA continues its multiple missions: encouraging preservation and change, staging visual and performing arts, providing educational and community-based programming, and leveraging new job creation.[3] This third-sector development story began with an empty factory complex and was propelled by people with vision, perseverance, and a knack for attracting resources to an innovative project. A similar project is about to open in Beacon, New York (http://www.diabeacon.org) as this book goes to press.

MASS MoCA and Good Development

It is early to assess the contribution MASS MoCA has made to development in North Adams against the criteria for good development outlined in chapter 3. At the time of this writing the museum had been operating for three years, and differentiating the contributions of its development phase from its normal operations is difficult. The following assessment will attempt to project ahead through the near-term planning horizon to estimate the likely impact of this nonprofit on the local and regional economy.

Social Surplus Creation and Retention

MASS MoCA has served as a major magnet for attracting social surplus to North Adams. Resources for creation of the museum include the $16 million in donations from private individuals and foundations, most of which would have otherwise been unavailable to the community. Funds from the state of Massachusetts, $25.6 million to date, were available to pay for renovation because of this project. This is social surplus that would have gone to other uses, and probably not to North Adams, without the museum. The $1 million raised from local donations by individuals and businesses might have been directed elsewhere or used for personal consumption if it had not been "invested" in the project. Business donations could have been used for new investment and job creation, although the slumping local economy did not provide an encouraging environment for that.

MASS MoCA generates social surplus in several ways, and it uses the money to pay for a part of its operating costs. Net revenue from sales at the museum shop is an obvious small source, while the rent from renovated space leased to businesses is more substantial. As space is renovated and if new business clients keep materializing, rental revenues should diminish the amount of annual subsidy needed for operating costs of MASS MoCA. At present a major source of this subsidy is donations from outside the community, including from foundation grants and members of the board of directors of the museum. Local first-sector owners of commercial and industrial space compete with the museum in leasing space, but thus far the new development touched off by the museum has stimulated the economy enough to benefit them as well.

Job Creation

Job creation has been spurred directly and indirectly by the museum project. Direct job creation was substantial through the physical rehabilitation of museum space and continues today as additional buildings are readied for commercial clients. The operation of the museum provides regular employment for over sixty full-time equivalent positions and more in the summer. The $1.6 million paid to staff members flows directly into the economies of North Adams and surrounding towns as new spending that spurs development.

Indirect job creation stimulated by MASS MoCA has been substantial. Tens of thousands of new visitors to the area spend money each year for accommodations, food, and retail purchases. The high-tech and dot.com jobs created in North Adams are related to the museum both in the sense that the museum helped make North Adams a more interesting place to live—a place where a "silicon village" was possible—and in that the museum helped recruit the firms to the town by creating and marketing the unusually attractive space in a stimulating environment. MASS MoCA provides a center for creative activity that is valued by its tenants. These new jobs helped diversify the local labor market, and much of the income these businesses provide is spent in the community.

Comparing employment and income figures provides little leverage with which to isolate and measure the impact of a nonprofit that has been in operation only since mid-1999. General data suggest positive changes in a period of weak economic performance for the nation as a whole. As would be expected, the largest gains in employment occurred in construction and services. From an unemployment rate 87 percent above that of the state in 1990, in 2001 unemployment in North Adams was 4.2 percent compared to 3.7 percent for the state, or 14 percent above the Massachusetts rate (Massachusetts Division of Employment and Training 2003).

Environmental Sustainability

How does MASS MoCA stack up by measures of environmental sustainability? The answer is, quite well. Chances are good that MASS MoCA will be operating in twenty to thirty years without threatening the local or regional ecology. Its operation is dramatically "cleaner" than most industrial activity, and it has major incentives to keep operating costs low by using energy, largely for heating in the winter, wisely. The environmental impact of transportation is less severe than when four thousand employees were going to work in this small city tucked in a valley, and new traffic has been welcomed—for now. The traffic will continue to provide a challenge to local planners who aim to keep streets safe for residents; as the museum succeeds in attracting visitors it contributes to problems caused by automobile and bus transportation. Revitalizing passenger service on the rail line through town and linking regional cultural destinations using bus or light rail alternatives to the automobile are means by which environmental problems caused by transporting visitors and staff might be mitigated.

Linkages, Spin-Offs, and Multipliers

MASS MoCA has aggressively sought linkages for development as it has evolved. An original intent for the project was to use it to jump-start a sluggish economy, and Mayor Barrett's focus on this objective has been sustained. North Adams is situated in beautiful physical surroundings and is well situated, if somewhat isolated, in the northeastern region of the country, but it was a depressed and depressing place to visit or to contemplate as home or a possible business location. MASS MoCA and the mayor's other initiatives have changed the feel of the place, and these changes have enhanced the ability of the city to attract significant business start-ups. Credit is due as well to the regional planning effort that sped development of sophisticated telecommunications linkages. The new inn is both a linkage and a spin-off, the latter in that it is the project of a person with connections to the museum and the museum staff has supervised its construction. Multipliers are strong for the kinds of activity that have gone into the reconstruction of the museum property and the relatively self-contained nature of North Adams. Careful analysis of multipliers from spending by visitors to the museum will have to consider the city, its economic links with Williamstown, and the place of both in the economy of north Berkshire County.

Meeting Basic Needs

While food, shelter, and medical care come to mind first as basic needs, education, entertainment, and cultural and aesthetic needs exist as well. MASS MoCA makes a strong contribution in these areas for local residents as well as for visitors. The museum is regularly used for community meetings, weddings, and as a place to socialize, indicating that its role for the community goes beyond generating tourist visits. The ability to meet these needs in North Adams is an important part of making the town a magnet for new enterprises and new jobs.

One key decision in revising plans for the museum in its long predevelopment phase was to expand its role in the performing arts. This shifted the interaction of local residents from occasional visits to see what was new to ongoing interaction with the facility. Theater, music of all kinds, performance art, dance parties, and even culinary art are featured on a regular basis and priced at levels that enable working people to enjoy these attractions. Of the ten thousand people attending the museum's opening, it is estimated that eighty-five hundred were from the area and many had worked in the mill for Sprague Electric. Local and regional residents can think of MASS MoCA as their cultural center as well as a national outpost for the contemporary arts. This new community asset serves needs for cultural enrichment and entertainment.

In sum, MASS MoCA deserves high marks for the contributions it makes to development. It is a striking example of how development can be stimulated by a nonprofit cultural organization, and it should continue to contribute to other forms of development for the economy of North Adams and northern Berkshire County in Massachusetts.

Greenpoint Manufacturing and Design Center

Nonprofits provide most of the space in which art is performed or displayed, and they can also play a key role in shaping where art is produced.

New York City provides an energizing environment for the arts but challenges the artist to find space in which to work. Gradual redevelopment of lower Manhattan has driven up rental rates there and displaced the artists and craftspeople who used the loft space once built there for long-departed industries. For some of those displaced, the Brooklyn waterfront now provides a worksite because of a nonprofit initiative to convert run-down or abandoned factory buildings to use for small-scale manufacturers, designers, and artists.

The Greenpoint Manufacturing and Design Center (GMDC) occupies a complex of nineteenth-century brick buildings that once housed the Chelsea Fibre Mills. With a main building six stories high and seven others containing a total of four hundred thousand square feet of space, the center is home to sixty-five businesses, including antique restorers, glass blowers, sculptors, wood-carvers, and photographers, to name a representative sample. They tend to occupy the upper floors of the main building, with light manufacturing below. All are tenants of GMDC, a nonprofit founded in 1992 by David Sweeny and others and now run by Sweeny and twelve other staff members and maintenance personnel. Situated on Newtown Creek between Brooklyn and Queens, GMDC is associated with the North Brooklyn Development Corporation for the education programs GMDC runs.

GMDC is a rarity—a nonprofit real estate development company. The company has bought and revitalized five properties in the Greenpoint and Harrison areas of Brooklyn. In these buildings some tenants share services such as office space, marketing, and even some machinery. At the original site sophisticated manufacturing equipment for woodworking is leased to tenants and to other producers in the neighborhood. GMDC also provides the focal point for an entry-level woodworking trade school that serves forty students per year. Working with the local board of education the center provides five to ten apprenticeships in construction trades for area youths. Like MASS MoCA, the Greenpoint Center has won an award from the National Trust for Historic Preservation for renovation of its factory buildings, and the center has won numerous other awards for "urban excellence" and "economic ingenuity" (Greenpoint Manufacturing and Design Center 2001). Some of the buildings were once owned by the City of New York and considered prime candidates for demolition. GMDC raised over $5 million for the cleanup of asbestos and toxic waste, renovation, and fire safety equipment for the first buildings. Money came from private and public sources, and future tenants contributed sweat equity. That Greenpoint property opened in 1994 with only a tenth of its space rented, and today there is a waiting list for future tenants. Five hundred people are employed by the center and its tenants. From the first building GMDC renovated, the city netted $135,000 in annual property taxes—this from part of a city-owned complex that had once stood vacant because of past tax delinquency (Prud'homme 1999).

The history of GMDC is complex. When the city owned the buildings of the first cluster it rented space there to artists and craftspeople on a short-term basis. Part was closed for code violations, and the city had been unable to sell it. Because tenants were unhappy with the condition of the buildings and the city was unwilling to fix them up, the Woodworking Center Equity Corporation was created to negotiate better leases and repair the most obvious problems. Headed by an abstract painter named Dennis Niswander, this group invested themselves in the buildings by sweat equity and created the culture through which GMDC was formed. Shortly after formation of GMDC in 1992 many of the woodworkers in the complex staged a protest on the steps of City Hall because city building inspectors had shut down the elevators, making the upper floors of the building difficult to use. In the process the city was fining itself (Prud'homme 1999; Sweeny 2002). Another year of frustrating dealings with the city, during which GMDC managed but did not officially lease the complex, led the non-profit to write a development plan for the property with itself as owner. The city sold the building to the nonprofit for $1.00. After spending $750,000 on environmental cleanup and committing another $1 million for safety improvements on the property, the city considered this a good deal. The city had carried the property on its books as an estimated $14 million liability for additional work needed before it could be sold to private developers (Prud'homme 1999).

By the end of the decade GMDC was operating in the black. Its operating budget of approximately $1 million came from rent and allowed the company to provide full maintenance of the complex. Funding for the renovation came from public and private grants totaling nearly $4 million combined with approximately $3 million from revenues over a four-year period. The total was about half that estimated by the city for renovation. Rent for tenants, including a seventy-employee woodworking business that occupies nearly two floors of the main building, were four to five dollars per square foot in 1999, less than half the cost of comparable space in Manhattan.

For this development project the cross-fertilization of ideas and business skills, artisanal industrial focus, and shared infrastructure are fundamental to its success.[4] It has become a center for woodworking in the city, and from the nonprofit a new for-profit joint venture with a Brooklyn furniture designer has begun. If the venture is successful the for-profit income will return to the nonprofit, essentially subsidizing rental rates for artists, craftspeople, and tenants of small businesses.

As a real estate developer GMDC both occupies a niche and works for what would be considered meager returns by market standards. Its niche is to redevelop older buildings that the market shuns in favor of mid-twentieth-century or newer properties. The general mission and nonprofit status of GMDC allow the company to work with older buildings and take on problems such as hazardous waste removal by fund-raising for the resources to solve them. A rate-of-return on investment calculation for GMDC would produce a figure of 2.5–3.0 percent, hardly enticing to profit-seeking capital (Sweeny 2002).

A tenant of one of the first buildings has been quoted as saying the project is "half-communism, half-capitalism, and it works out pretty good" (Prud'homme 1999, 1). David Sweeny has described the nonprofit's board of directors as "four hippy woodworkers; four gray suits from the worlds of finance, architecture, and law; and me" (Quoted in Prud'homme 1999, 8). The outcome of this amalgam is development for the arts community in New York, development for North Brooklyn, and a model that can inspire other initiatives to be built with their own unique combinations of people, places, skills, and circumstances.

New Orleans Warehouse District

The redevelopment of the warehouse district of New Orleans is an example of arts retailers helping to bring a depressed area back to life. This process can be derided as boutique development, in which retailers cater to a relatively wealthy clientele seeking the new or unusual, and often coincides with gentrification. A familiar and large-scale example of such development in the United States has taken place over recent decades in lower Manhattan. There the migration of artists and arts retailers from Greenwich Village to Soho, then to Tribeca, then to Chelsea has accompanied enhancement of neighborhoods but also rising costs of living that make life there too expensive for many residents, including some who led the redevelopment.

The warehouse area of New Orleans extends northward from the Mississippi, with Lafayette Park and St. Charles Street roughly in its center.[5]

The warehouses and mills of the original district served the cotton and sugar industries and river traffic of the nineteenth century, and then they fell into disrepair. Many visitors to New Orleans know the French Quarter, to the northeast across Canal Street from the warehouse district, or the Convention Center area, which separates the original warehouse area from the reason for its being, the Mississippi River. Local residents and visitors alike are now being drawn to this formerly forsaken part of the city.

Recent development of the National D-Day Museum on the district's southwest edge has proven beneficial as a draw for visitors, a success story that counters some of the economic failure of the 1984 Louisiana World Exposition (World's Fair) nearby. Other museums in the area are the Contemporary Arts Center founded in 1976 and the new Ogden Museum of Southern Art of the University of New Orleans. Working space for artists has been made available by conversion of a former furniture store and warehouse into a complex of workshops and display space for their art.

While the rejuvenation of the warehouse district has been described as driven by arts projects (Blumenthal 2000), the history of its rebirth predates the current gallery glamour there. At the heart of the district is the Preservation Resource Center (PRC), a dynamic nonprofit organization that has been based in three different buildings in the district since its inception in 1974. Staffed by nineteen full- and part-time professionals, this organization works to preserve historical architecture in over a dozen neighborhoods in New Orleans. PRC operated with an annual budget of approximately $1.5 million in 1999, derived primarily in the form of grants from public and nonprofit sources.

Rather than simply aiming to preserve buildings, PRC seeks to "expand . . . the constituency that understands the economic, cultural, and aesthetic importance of historic preservation" (Preservation Resource Center of New Orleans 2003). Most fundamentally Patricia Gay, director and longtime staff member of the organization, and her staff recognize that historical preservation works best as the reconstruction of community. Viable communities require housing, commercial services, recreation, and a special glue that helps to define each community (Moe and Wilkie 1997). The PRC staff coaxes businesses back into areas they have left; helps residents to understand, purchase, renovate, and celebrate homes of historical importance; and helps revive the infrastructure that enables the neighborhood to work (Gay and Bruno 2001). The center works closely with city, state, and national government and organizations, homeowners and small-business people, and major developers in efforts to preserve the French, Spanish, African, and Caribbean heritage of New Orleans. It was PRC work that brought the warehouse district to people's attention and stimulated its renovation and redevelopment. One outgrowth of the process was creation of an environment in which the arts can flourish. For visitors to the city the district provides a welcome counterpoint to the perpetual party atmosphere of the nearby French Quarter.

Historic preservation and the arts are naturally intertwined because a part of what is to be preserved is the best of the past—its arts and crafts as experienced in everyday life. For New Orleans and the region, in housing alone this means highlighting and preserving the uniqueness of the creole cottage, the shotgun house, and various styles of townhouses. Most remaining examples of these structures are not to be preserved as museums but as contemporary homes in what have to be neighborhoods in which people want to live. This means that the neighborhoods and housing must preserve opportunities for low-income residents but not for them alone. Residents with disposable income are needed to provide the incentive for business owners to supply the basic amenities of life nearby. As people with some means return, job creation in the neighborhoods can accelerate.

Public transportation is essential in this mix because large numbers of automobiles fit poorly into neighborhoods designed for earlier modes of transportation and many residents still have to get to work elsewhere. Historic preservation is expensive, and redeveloping neighborhoods while preserving the best of their historical buildings and amenities involves constant danger of elitism. Art was involved in what is to be preserved, and art can play a role today in helping to avoid exclusion in the process of preservation. The Preservation Resource Center staff seems to be aware that to be successful the organization must reinforce this balance.

The arts contribute to interesting and well-rounded lives, and the organizations that sustain the arts can contribute to development as well. From steel bands to opera companies, nonprofits play a vital role in this important part of people's lives.

9

Other Basic Needs

Previous chapters highlight a variety of third-sector organizations that meet needs in housing, food, health care, and other key areas. This chapter shows single examples of organizations by which some other basic needs are met through third-sector initiatives. More cases could be added for each need, but the previous chapters provide abundant evidence of the variety of innovative third-sector institutions that meet basic needs for goods and services within the same area.

The most obvious need missing from those chapters is water. While water supply has generally been a public-sector concern, it can be supplied by nonprofit corporations as well. The water system of the poor border town of Progreso, Texas, is a case in point (Gunn and Gunn 1991, 87–90). The *acequias* (channels) of New Mexico provide an example of water association management of largely crop irrigation water (Crawford 1988). Public-sector failures and aggressive private, for-profit initiatives are increasingly making water a market commodity and water system management a service of the for-profit sector (Barlow and Clarke 2002). This is a world where organizations of all three sectors will be involved in distributing water. However, the public-sector and nonprofit citizens' organizations will have to take more decisive action if water resources are to be protected and to assure that profiteering will not cut people off from this basic need.

Child Care: Childspace Daycare Center and Management Group, Philadelphia

Child-care workers have faced difficult working conditions and limited tangible rewards throughout the transitional years to extensive use of child care in this country. Other parts of the world, most notably European countries, have made more substantial commitments to quality child care. In the United States it is treated either as a benefit that may be available through places of work or as a service secured through friends or relatives, neighborhoods, or religious organizations. That child care is a basic need is a fact of life as the number of households with two working parents or single parents with children continues to expand.[1] Yet provision of child care is fraught with difficulties related to cost, quality, availability, dependability, and safety. If public entities or employers were required to provide the service, a clearer national system of provision and regulation might have emerged. But since there are few uniform means for its provision (somewhat as in health insurance), many forms of delivery have materialized, few of which seem to satisfy the parents who are responsible for obtaining it or the workers who provide it.

Adversity in the field of child care has bred a (desperate?) quest for improved ways to deliver this service. One innovative result of this search is Childspace Cooperative, begun in Philadelphia in 1988. It delivers quality care for approximately two hundred children and parents in three locations and quality work environments and remuneration for a staff of thirty-five providers. In addition the cooperative has served as a model for similar centers and a conduit for making child care affordable for parents of moderate income.

Childspace Management Group (CMG) is a worker-owned cooperative. In the child-care industry consumer-owned and worker-owned co-ops are both prevalent, although the consumer-owned form is more common. CMG is comprised of sixteen of the thirty-five providers, and these sixteen elect the organization's board of directors. Eight parents (consumers) also serve on the board but in an advisory and oversight role (Nonprofit Pathfinder 2003). The Childspace Daycare Center is the nonprofit provider that contracts with the cooperative to provide services. Its workers can become members of the Management Group (the co-op) after a year with the organization by paying $250 (payable over a year) for a share. In a typical co-op arrangement the owner-members receive a partial distribution of any surplus based on the hours of work (patronage); and in the pattern of the Mondragon co-ops a part of their surplus is accumulated in individual internal accounts that are payable to them over five years if they leave the co-op.

Fundamental to Childspace is that quality care goes hand in hand with quality jobs. The organization provides staff with flexible hours, a voice in running their own firm, and wages and benefits that are better than the norm; wages are approximately 10 percent higher than the norm in Philadelphia, and the co-op provides unusual benefits for the industry of health coverage with 10 percent copay, sick leave and vacation time, and child-care benefits (Walljasper 1998). These employment conditions have helped Childspace overcome the industry pattern of high turnover and low pay.

Reaching beyond its own staff as an advocate for child-care workers in general, Childspace and related groups have organized Individual Development Accounts (IDAs) available for all Philadelphia child-care workers whose incomes are less than two times the federal poverty level (Grassroots Economic Organizing 2001). Matching grants help these workers save through IDAs for home ownership, schooling, or investment in their own businesses.

Quality child care is not inexpensive, and one worry as this organization began operating was that its cliental would be upper-income rather than a cross section of the three neighborhoods where it is located. In 1998 Childspace charged from $639 to $812 per month for full-time care, and Pennsylvania's subsidies for low-income family day care were well below that rate (Walljasper 1998, 17–18). Grants and income from providing rental space for Childspace's other advocacy organizations help to subsidize the care for lower-income users of the centers.

Foundations such as Annie E. Casey, Charles Stewart Mott, Ms., and the Catholic Campaign for Human Development have been financial supporters of Childspace, and they have hopes that other communities will learn from this successful experiment. Foundation support and technical assistance from experienced organizations such as the ICA Group and the National Cooperative Bank have helped Childspace gain insight from other cooperative experiences. The Childspace Replication Project has made lessons of the Childspace model available to others, collaborates with unions and child-care advocacy organizations on means to improve employment in the field, and has helped create centers in several cities across the country (Grassroots Economic Organizing 2001, 4–5).

One of the keys to creating good jobs is to build career ladders within the child-care centers. These ladders give people opportunities to apply new education and training, advance in their work, and broaden their horizons. Development of means within Childspace to assist replication of that model has helped serve this purpose, as has advocacy work for child care and child-care workers. For Childspace staff these initiatives have provided new opportunities that have reinforced their experience in running their own enterprise—itself a growth experience.

Energy: Electric Cooperatives

Few areas of the third sector provide a development history as rich or matter as much in many daily lives as do rural electric cooperatives. While their early history included small co-ops created between 1914 and 1930 and inspiration from Canada's Ontario Hydro Electric (National Rural Electric Cooperative Association 1990, 12–15), their central role was established by passage of the Rural Electrification Act of 1936. This initiative aimed to improve the quality of rural life and provide cheap power for economic growth. It was linked, of course, to some of the largest public works projects of the New Deal. The roles of the public and third sectors were controversial even in this period, as the for-profit sector sought to assure that profitable markets would not be encumbered by "subsidized" entities (Brigham 1998). The subsidy for electric co-ops came in the form of the low-cost loans[2] that the newly created Rural Electric Administration made available to rural providers—including private for-profit companies. The other advantage the co-ops had was that people were willing to provide them with no-cost easements for installation of their lines; for-profit companies usually had to pay for this use of people's land. In addition use of federal loans required complying with stringent construction and maintenance standards, which some for-profit firms preferred not to meet.

Today rural electric cooperatives provide power to approximately 12 percent of households in the United States and bill 9 percent of the power sold. They have built and maintain 43 percent of the miles of transmission line in the country covering three-quarters of the nation's land mass. The group's 930 co-ops control $76 billion in assets that have primarily to do with transmission of power but include 64 generating and transmitting suppliers (National Rural Electric Cooperative Association 2002).

Rural electric cooperatives are a classic example of a third-sector response to market failure. Density of population provides economies of scale in power transmission, making urban and suburban markets the heart of most for-profit systems; rural areas were neglected by for-profit providers. From a public policy perspective it was hoped that more rapid spread of electricity to rural America would help end the Depression. In the years since, rural distribution has remained an area of co-op industry while co-op generation of power has, like public generation and transmission, been relatively less common.[3]

Electric co-ops are governed by their consumers through member-elected boards of directors, and they are designed to provide power to their members at cost. They are incorporated at the state level and are often organized into state-based associations. In addition to rural homes and farms they serve businesses, governments, and other nonprofits such as hospitals. Some are now engaged in delivering services such as water, sewer, and technical assistance for small business development. According to the figures of their National Rural Electric Cooperative Association electric co-ops in the United States employ sixty thousand people and pay over $700 million in state and local taxes (National Rural Electric Cooperative Association 2002, 1).

This branch of the third sector is more linked to government than most others are. The original Rural Electric Administration of the U.S. Department of Agriculture (USDA) has become part of the USDA's Rural Utilities Service (RUS), which addresses assistance to development of other services such as telecommunications and water and sewer development. Through the Rural Electrification Act and now the Rural Utilities Service the federal government is the majority lender to nearly 750 rural electric systems in the country (United States Department of Agriculture 2000). One example of the kinds of projects supported today by federal funds is a nearly $5 million loan to the Navajo Tribal Utility Authority for financing off-grid renewable energy systems in rural tribal territory in Arizona, New Mexico, and Utah. Where the cost of provision of electric service by conventional lines is prohibitive, photovoltaic facilities will provide renewable energy that enables remote rural living with basic electrical amenities such as lighting and radio and television. This loan was what RUS classifies as a "hardship loan," available for service provision to low-income households or sufferers of an unavoidable hardship such as a natural disaster (2).

Another example of a recent loan under the RUS program was one for $26 million to the Withlacoochee River Electric Cooperative, Inc., in Dade City, Florida. The loan was made in 2000 to help finance installation of new line, connect additional consumers, and upgrade equipment. Because of the co-op's location on the hurricane-prone west coast of Florida, part of the loan also financed installation of new emergency generating capacity to provide electricity for hospitals, water pumping, and key government facilities (United States Department of Agriculture 2000, 4).

Regular government loans through this program are made at rates below those that the private capital market would charge, and therefore it can be argued that taxpayers are subsidizing provision of electric services to people in rural areas through the rate differential or through assuming the risk of the loans. Other government services (better highways, airports) are provided, of course, for urban and suburban residents.[4] Electric co-ops operate at cost (with reserves for growth and contingencies), eliminating the profit potential in delivering this service. They exist largely because profit-motivated capital holders have traditionally not wanted to invest in transmission facilities to rural areas. For-profit investment has been the norm in generating power and more recently in expanding the market for its distribution, the primary activity of the now-infamous Enron Corporation. Today deregulation (and debates over re-regulation) and restructuring continue throughout the energy industry. Through these changes electric cooperatives have provided a steady source of electricity supply for rural consumers as well as organizations designed to look out for their interests.

There is a recent urban counterpart to this rural co-op history, and Hartford, New York City, and Chicago provide examples of it. In Hartford, Connecticut Energy Cooperative provides for a full range of energy-related needs, including a certified green-source form of electricity, fuel oil, and telephone service (Cliburn 2000). In New York City, 1st Rochdale Co-op Group began in 1997 and sold its first electricity in 1999. In addition to electricity the co-op now sells fuel oil and natural gas (through its Twin Pines Fuels subsidiary) and renewable energy services. Rochdale Co-op is developing telecommunications (direct TV and Internet) services as well. Its area of operation is the city of New York and Westchester County to the north. This high-density market includes the nation's largest concentration of housing cooperatives, a market that 1st Rochdale serves extensively. The Chicago-based Community Energy Cooperative has a different mission: it exists to help consumers in Chicago manage demand for electric power. The co-op does this by improving service reliability and reducing pollution. Its revenue comes in part from payment from ComEd, the local for-profit utility, for demand reductions Community Energy Cooperative helps achieve (Cliburn 2000).

Cooperatives serve as one line of defense against the ongoing concentration of energy production into the hands of megafirms. Their declining cost with large scale of production makes them economically rational but has also meant, in the past at least, that they were tightly regulated. Attempts to split distribution from production have created new ways to manipulate that distribution to monopoly advantage, as illustrated in the Enron case. Real breakthroughs in energy await production through renewable energy sources such as wind, solar power, and hydrogen. Nonprofits such as Rocky Mountain Institute support research for this future and educate people to the potential benefits of renewable and decentralized energy systems.

Telecommunications: Public Television and More

If the changing market conditions of electric generation and transmission provide an unsettled environment for consumers, for many that environment remains more stable than the world of telecommunications: the general term for telephone, radio and television, and computer-based Internet access services. Third-sector organizations have a role in this fluid world.

The familiar world of public television is not really public. Although created in its present form by the Public Broadcasting Act of 1967, the organization designated to provide the broadcast service is the Corporation for Public Broadcasting (CPB), a private nonprofit. The purpose of CPB is to promote public telecommunications services in television, radio, and online.[5] Public television is not a new idea; the first public station was launched in the United States in Houston in 1953 as an educational television station (Association of Public Television Stations 2003). Today CPB invests in more than 1,000 local radio and television stations and their programming. The 177 public television license holders in the United States and its territories operate 356 stations, with the majority of them operated by nonprofit community organizations and colleges and universities. A minority are truly public and controlled by local government (7 of 177 licensees with 7 stations) or state governments (20 of the 177 licensees with 126 stations) (2). The 1999 funding for public television derived primarily (57 percent) from private donations by individuals and businesses, while approximately 20 percent was from state and local government and 11–12 percent from CPB's appropriation from Congress. Business donations of 13–14 percent get the most public mention in what increasingly sounds like advertising on conventional for-profit stations—leading to a quip about the acronym standing for Petroleum Broadcasting Corporation rather than

Public Broadcasting Corporation. Public television stations are operated under license granted by the Federal Communications Commission (FCC). The Public Broadcasting System is a nonprofit membership organization that exists to coordinate program acquisition, distribution, and promotion (Association of Public Television Stations 2003).

A typical example of an independent nonprofit television station is the Minneapolis Telecommunications Network (MTN). However, its roots derive from public regulation of the cable delivery industry. MTN was created by the city government of Minneapolis in 1983 because of the arrival of cable in Minneapolis. Minnesota State law required cable operators (franchised by local government) to provide operating and capital equipment funds and channel space for public use. The current cable operator in Minneapolis is the giant AOL Time Warner. MTN operates its own production and editing space but also has playback facilities in the AOL Time Warner building (Minneapolis Telecommunications Network 2002, 1).

MTN is run by a professional staff under the control of a board appointed by the Minneapolis City Council and mayor with one ex officio member each from the city of Minneapolis, the Minneapolis Public Schools, and AOL Time Warner. MTN operates three public access channels of programming. Taking its role of public access television seriously, MTN initiated an Internet service in the mid-1990s. Its goal was to offer Internet dial-up access to members and web-hosting for nonprofits. MTN built a substantial business, which it sold to a large Internet service provider (ISP) in 2000. Reasons for the sale were "changes in the market place, increased competition and the struggle of staying current with rapidly changing technology" (Minneapolis Telecommunications Network 2002). This description of rapid changes in the industry from the station's website characterizes transitions challenging many public stations and the fluid world of the Internet and web-based communication. MTN will face other hurdles in the future, including expiration of its building lease in a few years and the challenge of franchise renewal in 2004. New digital technologies require investment in expensive equipment. The fund-raising efforts of public broadcasting are legendary; and typical of nonprofits, membership funding provides the largest single category of money: 23 percent nationally (Association of Public Television Stations 2003). Directors of gifts and development at these stations have their work cut out for them meeting the financial resource needs of their employers.

Minneapolis Television Network describes itself as a "vibrant community gathering place." The station runs continual classes to impart media literacy and provides public-access channels with programming in native languages for many immigrant groups and programs for gays and lesbians and religious groups, among others. One of the strongest assets of MTN is "a grass roots [sic] membership base made up of citizens who believe in public access television" (Minneapolis Telecommunications Network 2002, 2). For the citizens of Minneapolis and the nation, maintaining that access for television and other telecommunications is a very big challenge.

Large metropolitan markets with high-income residents such as Minneapolis (including Saint Paul) offer cable television providers their best chances to build a strong bottom line. Cable delivery of television signals provides advertisers access to consumers in their homes and elsewhere, and the cable industry has consolidated rapidly into an oligopoly dominated by AOL Time Warner, AT&T, and a few others. Access to largely commercial-free public television programming in such a system is made possible by public-access requirements. Until and unless other technologies (e.g., satellite and dish delivery systems) provide sufficient competitive challenge most customers will get access from cable, and most areas have one cable company. Access through that cable to Internet service is the question of the moment and one linked to attempts to maintain some semblance of the early promise of an open Internet. At the time of this writing the battle rages over whether Internet service under broadband cable provision will be subject to legal regulation requiring open and diverse sources or be proprietary products of the major cable companies. Those arguing to preserve the open access and diversity of the Internet and World Wide Web liken the need for openness to the situation that allows public broadcasting access through the cable television facilities of for-profit companies (e.g., MTN and the AOL Time Warner arrangement in Minneapolis). Cable companies have worked hard to avoid this regulation of what they consider to be a unique new service and market. Proponents of open access fear that if cable providers are unregulated the owners of broadband lines will direct their own programming and advertising through them, stalling the diversity and innovation that have been such parts of the Internet and the Web to date.

In March 2002 the FCC ruled to give the broadband providers what they had sought: the ability to avoid providing line access to competing ISPs. Thus the major means by which most consumers will receive high-speed service (through cable and proprietary wireless systems) will be commercially driven oligopolies (and local monopolies) that can exclude alternative sources of these services, including those provided by nonprofits (Benner 2002). The open access of the Internet will end, threatening its contribution to civil society. In light of the FCC ruling traditional phone companies (now four "Baby Bells" rather than the original eight) are looking for relief from the requirement that they must maintain open access for digital subscriber line (DSL) providers. Commercial interests seem to have the regulators' attention, and smaller independent and nonprofit producers may find themselves without access to an audience. If so, the promise of a high-speed digital form of communication and information sharing both helpful to and partly composed of nonprofit organizations will be clouded (Center for Digital Democracy 2002). Advocates for "parity" between access to DSL service over phone lines and that access through broadband cable networks may find the parity working in reverse of their intent, with the phone companies freed of the regulation that cable companies seem to have avoided.

The rush to commercialize an already oligopolized young industry has produced arguments for what is being termed a "digital commons," an arena in which nonprofit cultural and civic communications can take place (Center for Digital Democracy 2002). How such a noncommercial space could be maintained is one of the key questions facing the nonprofit world. It calls forth the need for an alternative delivery system, but the capital investment needed to make this happen given available technology would be prohibitive. The ability to raise a large amount of capital for use in projects of this sort is the hallmark of the AOL Time Warners of the world or of national governments.

For now the uneasy compromise of government regulation in the public interest based on licensing of the nation's twenty-first-century equivalent of "airwaves" (cable space and the airways from satellites to antennae) seems the most likely means to maintaining open and diverse electronic media. Hopefully technological breakthroughs that favor public access and many diverse players will again shake up a world now increasingly dominated by commercial interests.

Education: Mainstream and Unusual Providers

The educational segment is one of the nonprofit world's largest. Attention within it usually centers on major universities (counterparts to large state institutions) and colleges. At the primary and secondary school levels private nonprofits have maintained a minority presence, although recent Supreme Court decisions on use of taxpayer-funded voucher systems may encourage expansion by this service provider. Controversy that led to the court's ruling had to do with public money going to schools sponsored by religious nonprofits and related questions of the separation of church and state.

Private nonprofit universities and colleges can be powerful institutions of accumulation (the 2002 endowment of Harvard University was reported to be $17.6 billion after a recent loss of $88 million [Healy 2002]). They can be vital but sometimes dominant employers in the communities in which they exist. They and their students (temporary residents) are users of local services provided by the public sector but often not funded by taxes on the property owned by educational institutions. Payment of a negotiated annual fee for services sometimes substitutes for tax revenue. Media attention has recently highlighted ways in which universities can seem to work against the interests of some in their communities (e.g., fighting against wage increases for service staff at Harvard and Yale) in the hope of pleasing others (e.g., parents who pay tuition). Stung by criticism of cost increases that outstrip inflation, college and university administrators can be quick to squeeze those at the bottom of their pay scales, and they can be as anti-union as are most for-profit employers.

Colleges and universities can be engines of local development as they expand operations, and they sometimes enter into a broader development role as a matter of policy aimed at helping the communities in which they are located overcome adversity. Two colleges well known for this proactive approach are Trinity in Hartford and Union in Schenectady. Done right, most importantly with the educational institutions working in partnership with other local interests rather than as arrogant local powers, these efforts can produce benefits for the community and at the same time help create a more attractive atmosphere for students and staff of the educational institutions. That outcome, of course, helps assure the colleges' ability to attract students and staff and enhance their future.

Educational institutions take many forms, and two nonprofits less well known than Ivy League universities highlight the innovative and activist side of educational nonprofits. One in this mold is the Highlander Research and Education Center in New Market, Tennessee. This nonprofit began its work in 1932 and has remained committed to popular education for people in the southeastern United States. The center concentrates on training activists in the labor, civil rights, environmental, prison reform, women's, migrant workers', and related movements. Early years at the institution were influenced by key figures, such as Miles Horton, who had influence on Rosa Parks, Jane Addams, Eleanor Roosevelt, and Pete Seeger.[6] Highlander has long been associated with strategies for advancing civil rights and is credited with reinforcing this major grassroots activism of the past half century.

The target of unsuccessful efforts to shut it down in the McCarthy years, Highlander today thrives as a training and conference center, an incubator of organizing strategies, and a research center for social change. Its sprawling "campus" of remade buildings sits on the edge of the Smokey Mountains, and it is rural in feeling but sophisticated in outreach and program. Many Highlander classes and educational materials are bilingual or available in English and Spanish versions, and the center continues to emphasize the role of cultural expression—music, dance, theater—in its work.

The operations of Highlander take place within an operating budget of approximately $1.2 million. Foundations and institutional support provide approximately 50 percent of that amount, individual contributions another 25 percent, and other sources and income from an endowment of roughly $2 million provide the rest (Highlander Research and Education Center 2002, 13–14).

The Manchester Crafts Guild/Bidwell Training Center (MCG/BTC) provides another example of a nontraditional nonprofit educator. Located in a neighborhood of industrial buildings in Pittsburgh, Pennsylvania, MCG/BTC provides job training for the disadvantaged, including adults who have never been employed, and training in arts and craft areas of ceramic arts, photography, and music. The craft guild and the training center began as separate organizations in 1968 and subsequently merged in 1972 when William Strickland, successful founder of the Manchester Craftsmen's Guild, was asked to help save a failing Bidwell Training Center, which had been founded by Presbyterian ministers as a vocational training program. Today both centers are housed in an immaculately maintained facility built in 1986 at a cost of $7 million (Heskett et al. 2000, 2), and they operate with an annual budget of over $5 million. The physical plant contains art and recording studios, training classrooms, labs, and commercial kitchens—all with state-of-the-art equipment; in addition there is a 350-seat auditorium for jazz concerts. MCG produces its own jazz CD series (with one Grammy so far) marketed by Telarc (Showrank 2001).

A recent version of the MCG mission statement summarizes the guild's approach to education as using "the arts as an educational devise that captures the student's attention and keeps it focused on a post-secondary education or vocation that allows for growth and promotion" (quoted in Freeman et al. 2000, 3). MCG operates after-school programs for area high school students, providing training for approximately 350 students at a time in drawing and painting, photography and digital imaging, and ceramics. Through foundation support MCG runs an arts collaborative with the Pittsburgh city schools that has expanded to include middle schools along with high schools. In these classes "life skills," a loaded term that covers a myriad of personal forms of expression and dress, are tackled on a one-on-one basis between arts instructors and their students.

The Bidwell Training Center is more vocationally and employer oriented than MCG. BTC works with referrals from social service organizations to get young adults (typically in their twenties and early thirties) through general equivalency diploma (GED) educations and then vocational skills training. Programs are aimed at specific skills that local employers need and that the employers (e.g., Pittsburgh Medical Center, H. J. Heinz, Bayer Corporation) help design. Equipment and software at Bidwell are kept up-to-date by donors and interested employers, which helps assure students a smooth transition between, for instance, the lab at Bidwell and the lab at Bayer (Showrank 2001). State and federal funding as well as employer and foundation grants help pay for these programs, although students often do bear some of their costs and financial aid is available. Courses are generally taken over a short period of time (twenty to thirty-eight weeks), although there is a full-year associate degree program for chemical lab technicians. Most courses are job oriented. Job placements for students in 1999 ranged from 75 to 100 percent, with pay at that time from $8.23 to $10 per hour (Heskett et al. 2000, 7). Chemical lab technicians placed in 2001 were earning approximately $30,000 a year with full benefits. Class sizes are linked to employers' needs projections for the end of a class cycle. In 2001 students who had to begin with the GED course and who had no other source of income could begin work as "lock box operators" processing credit card slips; they worked flexible hours for $7.00 an hour and no benefits (Showrank 2001).

MCG and BTC share a board of directors, but plans are being discussed to separate them. MCG/BTC is still strongly influenced by Strickland, its president and CEO. Successful except for a failed attempt to enter into the food-service business, the organization is pursuing new projects as diverse as urban agriculture and a for-profit consulting business to assist social entrepreneurship.

MCG/BTC has received national attention for its work, accolades from a broad range of public officials, and extensive foundation and Pittsburgh employer support. The organization has served as a model for "affiliates," to which it provides consulting services, in formation in the San Francisco, San Jose, and Saint Louis areas.

Other human needs provided by nonprofits that could be addressed include print news and opinion (e.g., the Associated Press and the *Nation*), book publishing (e.g., the New Press), and faith-based community-building and teaching (mosques, temples, churches, and their educational organizations and charities). In many of these activities the nonprofits either compete directly with for-profit counterparts or fill in where profit does not seem likely enough or high enough to attract investment. The means to meeting needs change over time as technological and organizational innovation open new possible areas of activity. Needs are redefined as well, and new wants are created. Political and policy choices alter the terrain of what is possible. Some of those choices and the implications that arise from using third-sector institutions to stimulate development are addressed in following chapters.

Support Organizations

The organizations profiled in this book are in many ways unique results of sacrifice, shared entrepreneurial skill, and tenacity. Many began in relative isolation from the institutional webs that make it easier for more conventional organizations to concentrate on their business, knowing that other activities essential to their existence are taking place. For ordinary businesses this web includes the banks, industry organizations, chambers of commerce, training and educational programs, lobbying organizations, think tanks, and professional associations that make their operations easier. Third-sector organizations need the same support, and part of the building process of the late twentieth century involved work to develop it. In some cases their history is older, part of the institutional development of organizations such as labor unions or philanthropic organizations in the United States. The sample of support organizations that follows provides insight into the roles they play.

Community Development Corporations:
Coastal Enterprises, Inc.

Community Development Corporations (CDCs) were introduced in chapters 1 and 2. Part of the third sector, they also function as support organizations for new enterprises of the first and third sectors and as partners with second-sector institutions. Coastal Enterprises, Inc. (CEI) of Wiscasset, Maine, is what might be called a "diversified" CDC for two reasons: it addresses development in a larger geographic area than many CDCs do; and it provides several services in order to foster development.

CDCs began in the 1960s as urban and rural entities often concerned with furnishing needs to people in defined neighborhoods of cities or in particular rural counties. CEI was one of the leaders in translating lessons from that early development activity into a broader rural setting. The initial work of the company was in Lincoln County on the coast of Maine, and CEI gradually expanded programs throughout the state. Where many CDCs have focused on one area of need, such as job training or housing, Coastal Enterprises has from the start addressed a range of development needs from jobs to business growth and later venture capital.

CEI was launched in 1977, and the current president, Ron Phillips, was its founder. The idea around which the organization seems to have been built is that development can be enhanced and accelerated by creative use of resources from all three sectors. CEI works directly with small businesses to strengthen their development; has implemented innovative training programs that use public funds to encourage workforce development and assist business (Pierre Clavel and Karen Westmont in Giloth 1998, 19); and has participated in delivery of over $300 million ($80 million in direct lending or equity and $225 million in partnership lending with mostly Maine banks) in economic development financing to more than twelve hundred business, housing, and social service recipients (Coastal Enterprises, Inc. 2000, 1). CEI is a nonprofit organization willing to work with and for for-profit firms as long as the development their joint effort creates means better lives for low-income residents in Maine and does so in a sustainable way. Sustainable development is more than a feel-good phrase at CEI, whose staff has devoted considerable time and resources to figuring out how to include explicit environmental goals into the projects the organization supports.[1] As a nonprofit community development corporation CEI is governed by a volunteer board of fifteen Maine residents with interests and skills in social and economic development.

Community development corporations take many forms and engage in a variety of activities, but Coastal Enterprises is larger and more extended in its work than most. This results from its multifaceted view of what development is and what is required to achieve it. Funding to keep a large staff at work and offices functioning comes from major foundation grants and contract work for several federal agencies. From the inception of the company CEI made clear efforts to get the necessary recognition and licensing to function as a Small Business Administration local development corporation, a U.S. Treasury community development financial institution, and a certified financial packager for the state of Maine (Coastal Enterprises, Inc. 2003, 1).

CEI has concentrated much work in the areas of development finance, housing, jobs, training, and new agriculture. It has launched five major sources of debt and equity capital for use in Maine, provided technical assistance to over ten thousand businesses, and helped create or sustain over eleven thousand jobs (Coastal Enterprises, Inc. 2003, 1). The coastal area of Maine is largely rural but benefits from summer resident and tourist activity that provides a base for development and tax revenue. Central, western, and far northern Maine are more rural and poor, with continued dependence on the timber industry in many regions. Small to medium-sized cities in Maine such as Lewiston and Auburn have been assisted by CEI in making the transition from old industries to new ventures. CEI has also been a pioneer in agriculture with a sustainable fisheries project and a farm project funded by the U.S. Environmental Protection Agency to encourage more environment-friendly farming (Coastal Enterprises, Inc. n.d.).

One of the more audacious initiatives of the organization was successful development of a venture capital fund as a for-profit subsidiary of the nonprofit CEI. CEI Ventures was created to help finance new businesses throughout the state. Based in the commercial center of Portland, Maine, CEI Ventures invested its first fund of $5.5 million in companies in Maine that employed over twenty-two hundred people, two companies in New Hampshire, and one company in western Massachusetts. The companies created approximately two hundred new jobs that paid average starting wages of fourteen dollars per hour; 98 percent carried health insurance, approximately one-third went to low-income individuals, and twenty-six jobs went to people leaving public assistance (Henshaw and Kaplan 2001). Coastal Ventures II LLC, the second fund created by CEI, was launched in 2001 and raised and invested $20 million. A third venture capital fund was launched in 2002. The linkages between the venture capital funds and the mission of CEI are several: CEI sometimes finds good start-up companies that need more equity financing, and CEI's venture funds can provide it. Providing equity capital, however, binds the firm to CEI's commitments to provide good jobs, target low-income people for those jobs, train their workforces, and behave in environmentally sustainable ways. By bringing an additional ownership stake to start-up businesses CEI Ventures can open the door to added debt financing through the lenders with whom CEI has built working relationships.

CEI is itself a bit of a growth industry. Over eighty company staff members worked in Wiscasset and eight regional offices around the state in 2001. CEI recognized a need for a voice for the kind of development the company championed in Maine state policy making and launched a research-and-development/public-policy group within the organization with a staff of over ten people. This group works within the framework of the "three e's" that CEI set for sustainable development: economy, environment, and equity (Dickstein 2001). For the Ford Foundation the research-and-development/public-policy group, which has extensive research capability, is doing a major longitudinal study tracking the impact of participation in CEI-financed firms by low-income individuals in Maine (Coastal Enterprises, Inc. 2000, 16).

Labor: King County Labor Council, AFL-CIO

Labor coalitions and councils are staples of support for union activities in cities across the country. They provide for coordination and support among union locals for organizing, lobbying or other action on issues facing the local labor movement, worker health and safety programs, and general solidarity. Affiliated unions elect delegates to represent them on councils, and the boards then set the agendas of those councils. Delegates to a council typically elect council officers, trustees, and sometimes staff.

Labor unions are nonprofit membership organizations that provide means by which workers who have been able to choose union representation bargain with employers collectively. Unions typically enter into contracts that spell out terms and conditions of employment with employers for three years and sometimes longer. The process of gaining union representation and the general labor relations process are regulated by the National Labor Relations Board created by the Wagner Act (National Labor Relations Act) of 1935. Labor councils or coalitions are urban or regional corollaries to the national/international AFL-CIO, also a nonprofit member organization.

Seattle, which is within King County, Washington, has a long-held reputation as a union city. Unions have played important roles in the socioeconomic history of the city, from its docks to major employers such as Boeing.

The King County Labor Council, headed by Nancy Young, has board members from unions such as Machinists and Aerospace Workers, Stagehands, Inlandboatmen's, and Food and Commercial Workers. Its trustees are from unions such as Ironworkers, Musicians, Office and Professional Workers, and Service Employees International Union (SEIU). At-large board members come from the Coalition of Labor Union Women, Pride at Work, and the A. Philip Randolph Institute. The council includes 157 local unions and an additional 18 organizations as affiliates, and it "represents 139,000 working men and women" (King County Labor Council 2003b).

Projects of the council include assistance for its affiliates in their attempts to expand membership; supporting the Changing to Organize program of the AFL-CIO; mobilizing members in support of strikes; championing local public-sector governance choices that are good for union members; educating the public about union issues; and working with employers and public officials for what the council labels "worker-friendly economic growth" (King County Labor Council 2003a). Worker-friendly jobs are those that involve job ladders, pay living wages, and provide safe working conditions.

The King County Labor Council was a key participant in what became known as the Duwamish Coalition in King County (City of Seattle 2001). Composed of representatives of labor, Native American tribes with rights in the area, major employers, and the local public sector, the coalition sought to revitalize Washington State's most industrially concentrated area, a corridor surrounding the Duwamish River. The river is a spawning ground for salmon, and environmental cleanup was as much a part of the coalition's efforts as were preservation and expansion of industrial jobs. The King County Airfield (Boeing Field) and port facilities on the river were important parts of the area as well. The council was created by an act of the Metropolitan King County Council. Coalition task forces defined and mapped several important projects for the corridor and subsequently turned over work on them to public and other representative agencies. The Duwamish Coalition is considered a success both for identifying and beginning work on problems in the area and for the way in which labor, environmental groups, Native American tribes, and public- and private-sector organizations worked together toward coalition goals.

The Labor Council helped organize demonstrations against World Trade Organization (WTO) meetings in Seattle in 1999. Members played key roles in trying to keep the demonstrations peaceful and in reaching out to environmental and younger anti-WTO demonstrators with resources, solidarity, and years of experience in organizing public demonstrations.[2] To whatever degree that cooperation still endures, it had its start on the streets of Seattle with leadership and participation by the council.

Labor coalitions and councils are often dominated by building trades locals, which have a reputation for being conservative strategically (more development is good for jobs) and politically and for limited union democracy. The King County Labor Council has been more progressive than most in its diversity and its commitment to democratic representation and practice. Just as workers generally need a union in their struggle for just conditions of employment, so unions need each other to improve their chances of success. Nonprofits such as the King County Labor Council provide effective support to their many local union affiliates.

Capital: National Federation of Community Development Credit Unions

Earlier in this book the case of Neighborhood Trust Federal Credit Union/Credit Where Credit Is Due illustrated the role of community development credit unions (CDCUs) in development. Credit unions exist, as banks do, in a complex web of related institutions, some providing support and some regulation. Support organizations are particularly important to institutions that are unusual in the economy; if they are not unusual it is safe to say that society is already providing the elements for their reproduction. Banks are the common analogue to credit unions, and their support is provided by associations representing banks of different sizes, functions, and chartering levels that provide training for their staff; by the world of advertising that routinely places the idea of banks and their services in front of a customer base; by formal educational programs such as undergraduate and graduate business training that prepare a management cadre for the banking industry; by a federal reserve system that regulates and services banks—the list could go on. Mainstream credit unions have a similar infrastructure for reproduction but at a much smaller scale. They gain a major boost from their employer base and employers' incentives to contribute to creation and operation of the credit unions. Members of this "field of membership" are generally employed, have regular incomes, and possess some degree of money management skills based on years of employment.

CDCUs are typically started under conditions quite different from those under which banks or conventional credit unions are begun. CDCUs begin in neighborhoods where people have little in the way of financial resources, potential members are unfamiliar with what a conventional credit union is, new members have potentially irregular job opportunities, and there is no stable employer to sponsor them. While some of the organizations that support conventional credit unions helped CDCUs get started, the unique needs of people in these neighborhoods warrant a "dedicated" organization. The National Federation of Community Development Credit Unions was created for this purpose.

The organization was founded in 1974 at a Madison, Wisconsin, meeting of representatives of sixty-five credit unions from across the country. The word *development* was included in the name because the National Federation of Community Development Credit Unions, which will be referred to as the National Federation, was designed to help build organizations that would play key roles in development. This nonprofit is sustained by funding from the established and successful members it serves, private philanthropy, government grants, and income earned from its role as a CDFI intermediary channeling capital from regional and national sources to local credit unions.

The start-up years for the federation were tenuous, and like the beginnings of many nonprofits they required volunteer efforts. The work centered around convincing regulators and lawmakers that the needs of CDCUs were unique and arguing for funds to be used as loans and grants that would enable groups to meet qualifications for federal assistance through the Community Development Revolving Loan Program for credit unions established by the federal government in 1979. Progress made in the Carter years gave way to retrenchment during the Reagan administration. By late 1982 federal funding through the Community Services Administration (CSA) was eliminated. Since CSA was the federation's major source of funds, the federation closed its office, terminated its staff of thirteen, and was kept alive by voluntary labor in space provided within the home of former technical assistance director of the federation Clifford Rosenthal.[3] What was needed was a source of funds that was not dependent on which party held power in Washington. Those still involved with the federation began work on a capitalization fund for CDCUs derived from private-sector "social investors" such as religious organizations and foundations. Rosenthal and the federation board began to raise money, and by 1983 the organization was alive again with a staff of two: Rosenthal and Annie Vamper, a former National Credit Union Administration (NCUA) staff member and credit union manager from the Southeast. By 1984 the federation had established a new working office, and in 1992 it moved to its current home in the Association Center for nonprofits on Wall Street. Today the National Federation has a staff of eighteen serving more than two hundred member CDCUs that have more than seven hundred thousand members. CDCUs serve predominantly African American, Asian, Latino/Latina, and Native American populations. The National Federation membership is a mix of approximately two-thirds urban credit unions and one-third rural credit unions; approximately 40 percent are faith-based. In 2000 the average assets of member credit unions were about $9.4 million, and their median assets were close to $1.4 million (National Federation of Community Development Credit Unions 2002). The National Federation serves small financial institutions in an age of the megabank.

Technical assistance and training are essential for people with the thought of creating a new credit union to serve a low-income community. People who begin on this path may well lack the skills that banks would simply go into labor markets and hire people to provide. Building organizations with these skills is part of the development process and requires on-the-job training. By providing a staff that can advise and train through the start-up phase of a CDCU and providing financial assistance to help leverage other funding, the National Federation plays a vital role in guiding CDCUs to self-sufficiency.

The National Federation operates in the interest of its member credit unions, and as a nonprofit it is governed by a board of directors elected by those member credit unions. The federation offers technical assistance to groups interested in launching a CDCU and lobbies for federal regulatory and funding assistance to make that creation possible. For instance, the Community Development Financial Institutions Fund (CDFI Fund), administered by the U.S. Department of the Treasury, has provided grants and loans to credit unions and other qualifying CDFIs since 1996. The National Federation argued for a recent addition to that program that targets some of its funding to smaller institutions that would otherwise have a difficult time competing with more established, well-staffed organizations more likely to provide sophisticated grant proposals. The Small and Emerging CDFI Assistance Program (SECA) launched in late 2000 offers grants of up to $200,000 to institutions with less than $5 million in assets. Grants, if won, yield capital for the institutions and can also be used to pay for the kind of technical assistance the National Federation provides. SECA funds can go to a wide range of community development lenders, including microenterprise funds, loan funds, and even start-up banks (NFCDCU 2000). Unfortunately the future of the U.S. Treasury CDFI program is uncertain under the administration of George W. Bush. To alleviate poverty federal policy may be returning to nothing but the market, families and faith-based groups, and more narrowly circumscribed "self-help."

Replication is a term that is on the minds of many who struggle to get new nonprofits or cooperatives started, stabilized, and serving people's needs. This awkward but useful term reflects movement in two directions: the first success might reproduce itself in other communities (e.g., the Southshore Bank expansion model); or the original organization might help educate others to do the same thing in their communities. Many successful third-sector organizations help others to do what they have done with less sacrifice and pain and to learn from their start-up mistakes. Support organizations such as the National Federation institutionalize these scattered efforts by aggregating educational, capital, and consulting resources for use throughout the country (or world) and helping to stabilize the gains made by the pioneering organizations. If newly created organizations are worth reproducing, support organizations such as the National Federation provide means to transfer knowledge and build new organizational capacity quickly and efficiently.

Faith-Based Federations: Lutheran Services, United Jewish Communities, and Catholic Charities

Faith-based organizations make up the major institutional presence in the third sector. The work they do is immeasurable, especially for the sense of well-being shared religion brings to people. Spiritual affiliation and shared belief provide one of the strongest forms of community that people experience. More easily measurable is much of the other good work that religious organizations do: in education, social services, charitable and emergency relief work, nursing home care and hospitalization, and more. This work is paid for by donations to religious organizations, income from endowments, and funding by government or other third-party providers.

Local communities of faith are joined in nationally and internationally based organizations in all major religions of the world. In the United States major religious organizations raise funds for more or less decentralized nonprofit service providers, and they have a place among the largest of the nonprofits. In the 2001 annual listing of the *NonProfit Times* top one hundred nonprofits in terms of income (the nonprofit world's *Fortune Magazine*'s Fortune 500), major federations of religious service organizations held the first, fourth, and fifth positions (*NonProfit Times* 2002, 1).[4] The top income earner was Lutheran Services in America, a "national system of health and human service providers" (Lutheran Services in America 2003), with $7.7 billion in 2001 income (*NonProfit Times* 2002, 1). Saint Paul– and Baltimore-based Lutheran Services generated the majority of its income for work performed, receiving payment from the government and insurance companies for program services. Other major sources of income were approximately $1.7 billion in donations and $90 million in investment income.

Lutheran Services in America functions with a staff of 138,000 and 130,000 volunteers (Lutheran Services in America 2003). The organization brings together the 280 human service organizations of the Evangelical Lutheran Church in America and the Lutheran Church–Missouri Synod to provide for needs as diverse as hospice care, prison ministries, and alcohol and substance abuse programs. Income that Lutheran Services in America received from government sources reflects the impact of the federal "Charitable Choice" initiative of 1996, which enhanced the ability of religious organizations to be contract providers of services to federal programs, for example Temporary Assistance to Needy Families and Community Service Block Grants, that were replacing the former welfare system (Lutheran Services in America 2003).[5]

Catholic Charities USA ranked fourth among the big nonprofits in 2001, and much like Lutheran Services it provides a host of community services through a paid staff and volunteers. In 2001 more than two-thirds of the nearly $2.6 billion income of the organization came from government payment for services and close to $390 million in donations was raised by the group (*NonProfit Times* 2002, 1). Based in Alexandria, Virginia, Catholic Charities describes itself as a membership organization for church agencies that provides them with training, resources, and technical assistance (Catholic Charities USA 2003). The international sister organization to Catholic Charities USA is Catholic Relief Services.

With income in 2001 of $2.2 billion, United Jewish Communities (UJC) was the fifth-largest nonprofit on the *NonProfit Times* list for 2002. The sources of that income differ from those of Lutheran Services and Catholic Charities in that while UJC serves 189 federated and 400 independent Jewish communities around the country with social services (United Jewish Communities 2002), it does so without government payment for those services. UJC's 2001 income derived from approximately $2.1 billion in contributions, and $133 million in investment income from a substantial endowment (*NonProfit Times* 2002, 1).

The federation character of United Jewish Communities enables it to serve needs of Jews in the United States and to join with two partners for international work. A major source of contact between young people and students in the United States and Israel, UJC has roots in development of the Jews of Boston in 1895, which evolved into the Combined Jewish Philanthropies (United Jewish Communities 2002). The orientation of the organization was domestic until the 1930s, when international programs were added because of escalating trouble for Jews in Europe.

In order to receive government payment for services delivered religious nonprofits have to provide services to people regardless of their faith, race, or age. Lutheran Services and Catholic Charities do that; United Jewish Communities does not. UJC has a commitment to help Jews and hence is not a contract provider of services to government and other third-party payers, but donors to the organization clearly provide strong support.

Supporting Information: GuideStar and the Idealist

Support by and for nonprofits comes in many forms, and two of the most unusual are GuideStar, an on-line and free source of information on philanthropic and nonprofit organizations, and the Idealist, a website devoted to jobs and volunteer work in nonprofits. While both are recent developments, they already play important roles in bringing financial and human resources to nonprofits.

GuideStar is the name of the information service founded in 1996 by Arthur "Buzz" Schmidt and operated by Philanthropic Research, a nonprofit based in Williamsburg, Virginia. It provides web-based summary information on 850,000 nonprofits, including their most recently reported available financial data. Approximately 250,000 nonprofit 501(c)(3) organizations, not including religious groups with 501(c)(3) status, are required to report financial data annually to the Internal Revenue System. GuideStar makes this completed IRS Form 990 available to the public on-line. This is an invaluable source of information—especially for potential donors to these organizations. The fact that it serves to create a higher degree of confidence in many third-sector organizations is grounds for counting GuideStar as a support organization. GuideStar lists as its goal "to revolutionize philanthropy and nonprofit practices with information" (GuideStar 2003a).

The contents of a typical GuideStar report include a summary of the organization's mission and programs, its goals and results, its senior staff, press releases about it, and access to the IRS Form 990. While data is sometimes missing from the Form 990, the report generally provides detailed financial summaries, lists of assets and debts, most senior administrative salaries, and compensation to consultants. GuideStar aims to do three things for nonprofits and philanthropies and for those who support them: 1) donors can follow the progress of organizations toward their goals; 2) nonprofits can compare themselves to similar organizations; and 3) duplicate reporting to government and philanthropies can be reduced (GuideStar 2003a). Users (individuals or organizations) can each pay one thousand dollars annually to become members of GuideStar and contract for more detailed analyses and comparative reports. GuideStar is a 501(c)(3) nonprofit started and supported by approximately a dozen foundations that can clearly benefit from its services. Basic information on nonprofits is available to anybody with access to the Internet.

The Idealist website is the creation of Action Without Borders, an organization founded as the Contact Center Network by Ami Dar, who won the Stern Family Fund 2000 Public Interest Pioneer award for this work. The Idealist website, at www.idealist.org, was created in 1996 and is international in scope. It lists information provided by 27,000 nonprofit organizations in 153 countries. Those listings provide organizational profiles, paid job opportunities and the volunteer needs for the organizations, and contact information. Located in New York City, Action Without Borders employs more than a dozen staff members. The website for the organization was the recent recipient of the Webby Community Award for Excellence. Foundation grants sustain Action Without Borders.

Philanthropic Organizations: Progressive Foundations

There is extensive literature on philanthropic foundations partly because their role in society is controversial and partly because new foundations have been formed at an accelerating rate in recent decades.[6] While philanthropic foundations were not directly involved in the work described in preceding chapters, they often support that work. Without this support many of the concrete examples and cases described would not have been possible.

Philanthropic organizations are funding intermediaries and repositories of social surplus. They are devices by which the wealthy can institutionalize their money for the purposes of supporting their chosen causes well into the future. If small, these organizations are generally run directly by succeeding generations of the family; if large, those descendants often hire staff to deal with potential recipients of grants, evaluate their work, and maintain foundation investments. The missions and causes served by foundations run the gamut of the progressive and regressive, the idiosyncratic and the idealistic. For the organizations described in this book support has generally come from foundations known for commitments to various forms of social change and citizen empowerment. They include, among others, the Annie E. Casey Foundation, the Ford Foundation, the Charles Stewart Mott Foundation, and the John D. and Catherine T. MacArthur Foundation.

Foundations give away money in the hope of influencing public policy and social development. Most do not do research or write position papers in-house but instead buy these services from people in other third-sector organizations such as universities and research institutes. Just as conservative foundations have supported think tanks such as the Heritage Foundation and Cato Institute to develop ideas useful for public policy makers, so too have the more progressive foundations nurtured broad-based research organizations such as the Aspen Institute and Woodstock Institute and industry-specific policy research organizations such as the Paraprofessional Healthcare Institute (discussed in chapter 7). Foundations willing to fund organizations working to develop new solutions to problems, for instance cooperative child care, may fund them directly but may also do so through an intermediary that can monitor progress in the organization and assess results. Foundations supporting progressive third-sector initiatives in the 1990s funded "capacity building," the development of the skills necessary to enable new organizations to function well. With more of that capacity in place a newer concern is to address the ability to reproduce a successful new venture—to enable the human and monetary investments in it to multiply.

Support for third-sector innovation comes from the second sector as well. Taking the financial sector as an example, public-sector regulations such as the Community Reinvestment Act have reinforced whatever interest banks (from the first sector) had in "investing" in community development credit unions. The National Cooperative Bank (profiled in chapter 6) began as a governmental entity. The currently embattled CDFI fund of the U.S. Treasury has provided essential support for a new generation of financial institutions that serve low- and moderate-income citizens. These organizations mirror, at much smaller scale, institutions that provide routine support to the private, for-profit sector in this country. If the third sector is to be more than the cleanup team for problems caused by or left unattended by the profit-driven market economy and minimal state social programs, then more supporting infrastructure will be essential to its growth.

Public Policy for Third-Sector Development

The diversity of the third sector as it has been defined in this book means that its policy considerations have a broad range, and specific policy recommendations will not address all parts of the sector. Beginning with nonprofit organizations and then moving to cooperatives and credit unions, this chapter provides an overview of some key issues affecting important components of the third sector. This summary is conditioned by the focus on the potential of third-sector institutions to play positive roles in development.

Nonprofits, Subsidies, and Taxes

One of the hallmarks of the nonprofit sector is that its public-serving institutions operate with funding that derives, often in large part, from donations. They are subsidized by private and public funds. Because organizations of this type produce public goods and services, they are exempt from taxes on their incomes and on the properties they hold that are used directly for their missions. The money given to an important group of these public-serving institutions by individuals and corporations is also exempt from income tax for the donors. Both features involve complex policy questions.

The proliferation of nonprofit organizations in the United States could be the result of the fact that U.S. citizens have historically resisted a strong government presence in social matters or the fact that in this heterogeneous country people could not agree on what public goods and services should be provided to a disparate population. Rather than developing as a nation with extensive provision of public goods, which in the past century the United States could have readily afforded, people have opted for indirect subsidies through tax advantages for organizations that provide quasi-public goods and services and tax incentives for donors to support these organizations.

Donations to nonprofits can take many forms, including donations to political parties, contributions to religious organizations, annual checks written by households to support their favorite charities, and major grants from corporate charities, foundations, and occasionally governmental sources. For individuals the major public policy incentive to encourage this giving is that for 501(c)(3) nonprofits donations are deductible from income before taxable income is determined. There is, however, clear class bias in this incentive. The deduction is worth more to those in higher tax brackets, skewing donations to organizations and political groups favored by high-income citizens.

A change to a federal tax *credit* could produce greater and more representative public support for those nonprofits desired by the public at large and enhance the ability of many nonprofits to raise money for their work. Advocates suggest a figure of up to $250 that all taxpayers could simply deduct from the taxes they owed. Evidence of contributions could be provided along with other tax documentation. The money would flow directly from donors to the recipient organizations rather than through the government.[1] This would diminish the incentive for nonprofits to polish their ability to win federal grants and would stimulate provision of local public goods and services and local innovation in their delivery. A tax credit of this kind could apply to political parties and organizations as well, dramatically changing the campaign finance process. William Greider has suggested that the tax credit for political donations could be limited to active voters, creating incentive to get more people of moderate means engaged and to the polls (Greider 2000a).

Seeking funds for their work, nonprofits have increasingly turned to profit-motivated activities for their revenue (Weisbrod 1998). Nonprofits engaged in commercial activity unrelated to their missions as nonprofits are subject to federal, and generally state, unrelated business income tax (UBIT). This is reported on the IRS form 990-T, which is not made available for public scrutiny as is the Form 990. In theory the tax on unrelated business activity helps to equalize conditions between commercial activity designed to provide funds for a nonprofit's mission and for-profit traditional business engaged in the same activity (James 1998). Difficulties occur in practice, however, because the nonprofit is often able to shift some of its expenses to the for-profit subsidiary's books, thus minimizing any reported profit and the taxes on it. To the extent it exists, this is a legitimate area of complaint by business about unfair competition from nonprofits, and it can only be addressed by closer monitoring of the accounting practices of nonprofits that have for-profit subsidiaries or by outlawing this combination. Since the ability to raise funds for their good work is enhanced by profit derived from commercial activity, prohibition of this practice is not an easy choice. Closer monitoring of the activity by the Internal Revenue Service is desirable but unlikely given the funding constraints and other work this agency faces.[2] People's understanding of the scope of the problem would be enhanced with more careful information gathering, which could be possible by use of a revised Form 990-T (James 1998).

Given the purpose of public-service nonprofits, the turn to commercial activities raises questions about a diluting of their mission, sometimes referred to as "mission drift." The problem is that the resource demands and organizational dynamics needed to succeed at a commercial venture might weaken the managerial resources available for the organization's primary mission. This can raise difficult policy choices for the boards of directors of nonprofits, who have the responsibility to assure that the organizations serve their intended missions. Their assessment of whether or not to take the road of for-profit ventures must include attention to where the internal resources will come from to build the new venture, how the potentially different cultures of the two parts of the organization will fit together, and whether the incentive and compensation structures of the two organizations might clash, among other issues.

Philanthropic organizations are nonprofits, and their grants are vitally important to many other nonprofits. They exist to distribute private fortunes, but current IRS regulation enables them to pay out as little as 5 percent of their assets per year—an amount they can easily make, on average, on investments. The 5 percent includes their (sometimes lavish) operating expenses. This slow rate of distribution can allow for their own growth and development, but to what end? If the purpose of philanthropies is to do public good with funds that were privately accumulated and spared from taxes, the question of time frame looms large. Reform of the nonprofit status of philanthropic organizations could encourage them to distribute their assets more rapidly and complete the giving they were intended for without perpetuating themselves indefinitely. Policy changes could shorten the life cycles of philanthropies and increase the flow of funds from them. Those changes would have to be designed while considering related issues such as whether the recent rapid creation of philanthropic foundations is a trend that will continue and what the net effect of diminished (or abolished) estate taxes will be on the formation of philanthropic organizations.

The role of philanthropic organizations in the United States provides an example, for better and worse, of the outcome and impact of citizens' reliance on nonprofit organizations rather than government. More progressive tax rates, even simply a return to the rates of the 1950s and 1960s, would better serve to fund public provision of basic goods and services for those most in need. A "safety net" that worked, or that provided for a substantial threshold of the basic material elements of a decent life, would diminish the need for foundation funding and the work of many public-service nonprofits. More steeply progressive taxation would at the same time, of course, make it more difficult to amass the large estates from which many of these foundations derive. While more progressive personal income tax rates are decried for the dampening effect they are claimed to have on incentives for personal wealth seeking, thereby dampening new enterprise formation and economic growth, the comparatively robust economic performance of the "golden era" for the U.S. economy (roughly 1947 to 1973) was produced along with more steeply progressive taxation. This suggests that the link between lower tax rates and economic performance is not as simple as recent rationales for lower tax rates for high-income individuals would have people believe.

Another "incentive" issue in this argument has to do with the question of who might be willing to do dead-end jobs for low wages if there were better public provision of basic housing, food, and health care. Europe has its "guest workers," and the United States has its working poor citizens and "illegal aliens." Since some portion (determined how?) of the working poor deserves help, people count on liberal foundations to design and fund programs to deliver it, and the foundations become a highly selective, private, and undemocratic substitute for better national policy. Foundations encourage nonprofits to dance to their tune since the foundations have the money. Government assistance programs become bureaucratized, but is large institutional philanthropy a better alternative? The hope at present is that the innovation fostered by the foundations and nonprofits will enable citizens to design a better, more universal, and democratically controlled means of providing everybody in this wealthy society the basics of life.

New policy is needed for nonprofits, but it would be intertwined with tough policy choices for the first and second sectors as well. The emphasis for the past two decades has been on strengthening the market and first sector, constraining the second sector, and counting on nonprofits to ameliorate some of the damage. New public policy for the third sector will be better made if it is accompanied by consideration of why people are counting on the third sector to meet particular needs. Much of the literature on traditional nonprofits appropriately emphasizes the variety of its organizational forms, revenue sources, production technologies, and other variables. One-size-fits-all reforms would be difficult to conceive and implement, and the unintended consequences of sweeping policy changes could be severe. The newness of academic research on this sector, the difficulty of extracting data from the IRS 990 that would be appropriate to their study, the lack of data availability from the IRS 990-T,[3] and the intertwined relationship of giving patterns with changes in personal and business income tax policy— all these factors make research and well-designed reform essential to this arena.

Cooperatives present a particular arena within the third sector for careful public-policy formulation. Some forms of cooperatives, particularly housing co-ops and agricultural producer co-ops, have well-developed policy and legal frameworks. The same is not true for workers' co-ops, which have only become an alternative legal form in a majority of states within the United States in the past twenty years.[4] Insecure as odd constructs even in Oregon where they have been a recognized legal form for most of the twentieth century, the plywood cooperatives there were deeply affected by actions of the U.S. Internal Revenue Service and the Anti-Trust Division of the Justice Department. In the IRS case the co-ops were accused of paying owner-members wages that were higher than normal in the industry in order to lower taxable income to the co-op. Demonstration of the higher productivity of the co-ops compared to conventional firms in the industry won the case for the co-ops (Gunn 1984, 99–108; Berman 1967). Antitrust action was brought against the co-ops because they shared production data among themselves; conventional firms in the industry argued that this could give the co-ops unfair competitive advantage. Working to avoid the appearance of any action in restraint of trade, the co-ops gave up the opportunity to work together to enhance development of their unusual business model (Gunn 1984, 99–108).

Chapter 2 summarizes how credit unions have recently felt the heat of their banking industry competitors who argued that they had expanded beyond the membership constraints imposed when they were formalized by federal action in 1933. In the late 1990s the banking industry claimed that the policy constraining credit unions' field of membership (those eligible to join an individual credit union) was interpreted too loosely by the regulators. Banking associations sued the government to make it enforce the regulation more strictly. The courts agreed that the federal regulator was not interpreting the law strictly enough. It took new legislation from Congress to enable credit unions to serve a broader field of membership.

The basis for the restricted field of membership for credit unions (financial cooperatives owned by their members) was that as nonprofit member service organizations they had unfair business advantages relative to for-profit banks. Most notably they avoided the expense of paying taxes on their earnings,[5] and banks claimed that this enabled them to offer their members lower fees for their accounts and transactions. The banks feared encroachment into their profitable activities by these cooperative membership organizations. In terms of scale of operation, access to capital, the ability to move operations to any corner of the world or type of lending that looks profitable (and scale of donations to lawmakers), banks have the advantage. They surely will continue to work hard for public policies that constrain the activities of credit unions. This pressure must be resisted in the interest of preserving member-serving and member-controlled financial institutions.

Public policy has, of course, provided for-profit businesses with subsidies of their own. Nonprofits that engage in commercial activities typically pay federal and state income tax on any profit they earn, and they typically pay real estate tax to local governments. Traditional businesses are masters at avoiding local property taxes by playing one community against another in order to secure tax abatements (Anderson and Wassmer 2000). In addition businesses are subsidized to export their products; they can use accelerated forms of depreciation to lower taxes; in agriculture they are paid not to produce; corporate costs for take-over activities and mergers are deductible for tax purposes; and numerous other forms of "corporate welfare" exist. The advantages that accrue to membership organizations such as cooperatives and credit unions are minor in comparison.

Capital

The use of third-sector initiatives for providing goods and services is fundamentally constrained by the market-oriented, profit-driven character of the U.S. economy. Capital markets inherently limit the resources available for activities that do not pay the going return on investment. The risk-and-return relationship is the guiding force of capital markets, and that leaves (inherently risky) innovative new providers that cannot promise high financial returns out of the market. Pools of funds for financing nonprofit providers are formed by the government, by the foundations described above, and by other nonprofits with assets and social consciences, such as religious organizations. Grants, low-cost loans, and sweat equity provide the start-up capital for most third-sector organizations.

Cooperatives and credit unions can typically generate enough surplus to capitalize their own expansion gradually. Help to get them started can take the form of technical assistance or financing that assists the start-up period, as government lending did for rural electric co-ops. One of the problems facing co-ops has been to find for-profit lenders who are willing to play this role and who understand the unusual form of organization. The 1978 policy initiative that led to formation of the National Consumer Cooperative Bank (NCCB) was a federal attempt to address this need. The rationale was that cooperatives, if launched successfully, would create jobs and economic development. Even in its form constrained by early attempts to abolish it, the policy initiative has been a boon to the development of a wide variety of cooperatives in the United States.

In a pattern that mirrors some aspects of the NCCB history but for community development finance, a federal initiative in 1994 created a funding source for community development financial institutions (CDFIs) and related financial intermediaries (those who lend to CDFIs). Congress created the Community Development Financial Institutions Fund as a government corporation within the U.S. Department of the Treasury. Its purpose is "to expand the availability of credit, investment capital, and financial services in distressed urban and rural communities" (United States Department of the Treasury 2003). From its inception to 2002 the fund had made over $500 million in awards to CDFIs. The CDFI Fund lends to a restricted group of financing entities with a primary mission of community development; it also lends to those that offer related development services such as technical assistance, that are not public (governmental) agencies, and that serve an eligible target market (United States Department of the Treasury 2003). In an attempt to spur local entrepreneurship the CDFI Fund added an initiative for new markets and community renewal in 2000.

Much as the NCCB was targeted for elimination by the Reagan administration in the early 1980s, the CDFI Fund seems to be a target for elimination by the George W. Bush administration. Resources for the CDFI Fund have been cut back but, at the time of this writing, not eliminated. Whether this source of start-up capitalization for and lending to community-based and member-owned financial institutions can be preserved in the U.S. Treasury with adequate funding for its mission or revitalized in an alternative form remains to be seen.

Not much of value gets accomplished without resources, but private capital markets measure value strictly in financial terms. If social and human values are to be served, the sources of finance capital for them must be found. Foundations and religious and charitable organizations can provide some of this capital, but provision from tax revenue seems justifiable as well. Tax revenues should be used, with controls and open access, for development assistance loans and grants with big potential payoffs in job creation and local economic stimulus. It is appropriate for member-serving organizations whose members have adequate incomes to pay market rates for the capital they use. But where these organizations serve low-income or needy populations some public subsidy in providing access to capital seems a minimal substitute for the more egalitarian society that would make this particular form of intervention unnecessary.

Religious Providers of Government-Funded Services

It would be difficult to conclude a discussion of public policy toward nonprofits at present without taking account of George W. Bush's White House initiative to expand the ability of religious nonprofits to be contract providers of government services. Shortly after taking office President Bush used the process of executive order to establish a White House Office of Faith-Based and Community Initiatives and faith-based centers in five federal departments: Justice, Labor, Education, Health and Human Services (HHS), and Housing and Urban Development (HUD) (Lutheran Services in America 2001). To those who see the separation of church and state as an important defining principle of this nation, this action was seen as frightening, pandering to the religious right, or both. The first mission of the five centers was to study how government programs could be made more accessible to faith-based organizations. The aim seemed to be to find ways to increase accessibility through modification of the regulatory process, something that could be accomplished by further executive-branch action or through a more Republican Congress. Frustrated by the inability to pass legislation for this change in late 2002, President Bush used an executive order to make it happen. Nonprofit organizations that discriminate in staffing against those not of their faith or against those whose lifestyles they dislike are now eligible for federal contracts.

President Bush's initiative builds on the Charitable Choice program created by Congress and signed into law by President Clinton in 1996. That program enabled direct government funding to religious organizations for provision of services in Welfare-to-Work programs and aid to needy families. It was expanded in 2000 to include substance abuse and mental health services programs. The early 2001 Bush initiative expanded the range of services provided by religious organizations further to include housing, job training, child care, crime prevention, and other programs. To date little funding has existed to fuel the Bush version of these programs.

In the world of nonprofit organizations the most likely change that the Bush faith-based expansion of federally funded social services would create is shifting the flow of federal contract funds more substantially to religious nonprofits. This will increase competition between religious organizations for "a piece of the action." The questions that accompany this shift are many, and they include whether these organizations will benefit as service providers by expanding their religious constituencies and whether religious constraints against certain practices such as abortion will grow in public-service provision. The Charitable Choice programs already allowed faith-based providers to hire staff with a religious screen, enabling them to hire only those already of the faith to provide services. All of these practices were explicitly outlawed if the services were provided by government or under contract through nonreligious nonprofits. The "controls" in the faith-based provision of government-funded services are that the providers must serve everyone, regardless of their faith, and that the providers cannot use government funds to conduct religious services or proselytize. Enforcement of the controls seems difficult at best. For instance, what pot of money will pay for the religious poster that decorates the wall of the office in which services are provided? Does it proselytize?

Proponents of these faith-based initiatives welcome leadership from the White House toward their goals, seeing them as providing "a level playing field" (Lutheran Services in America 2002, 2). Opponents see this as a means of distorting the role of nonprofits back to the early days of the sector's domination by religious organizations as well as undermining the principle of constitutional separation. The July 2002 Supreme Court ruling that opened the door for use of tax-funded school vouchers for students attending religious schools is another step in this direction. The limit provided by the Supreme Court was consistent with the Charitable Choice provision: that recipients of educational vouchers or government-funded social services have a choice of providers. In education the considerable wealth of major religious organizations enables them to subsidize religious education. Rather than a level playing field, this one will be tilted in favor of the religious providers.[6] The choice principle fits the market precepts behind the incentive to create school vouchers to begin with, when they were seen as providing an alternative to public schools. The same vision seems to have been behind the White House initiatives. Competition and choice are considered good even when organizations from all three sectors will be competing for a limited pool of revenues. The net result is a trend toward privatization of what has, for many reasons, been a public good in the United States.

Public policies limit some activities and encourage others, and the policies do not fall from the sky. Community development activists who hope to influence the legal, regulatory, and financial environments that shape their tools, strategies, and organizations need to be players in trying to influence legislation in ways favorable to their efforts. Organizations that argue in favor of third-sector-based community development initiatives include the National Community Reinvestment Coalition (NCRC), working on issues related to the Community Reinvestment Act and predatory lending; the Consumers Union on general consumer protection legislation; the National Cooperative Business Association (NCBA) for cooperatives in general; and many more. Private corporations have what are often larger, better funded equivalents. Lobbying is part of the process of trying to affect public policy. In their ability to mobilize voters citizen-based organizations have an advantage that occasionally overcomes the power of the corporate lobby, as happened in the case of the credit union field of membership battle described above and in chapter 2. It is reassuring to note that at times potential votes, not campaign contributions, influence policy outcomes.

Dealing with public policy means dealing with reform of the present system. The process is messy and the outcomes often disappointing. In determining what reforms are worth the effort a guiding principle is to work for those reforms that make for egalitarian outcomes and that make the next progressive reform easier to attain. Such a guide to policy opens the question of why and how third-sector activity for development can help shape the future. That is the subject of the concluding chapter.

12

Developing a Future

The alternative institutions of accumulation described in this book are alternative because they stand apart from for-profit corporations in their reasons for existing and their potential to be more open and democratic. Concluding arguments explore the potential role of nonprofits in developing a more vibrant democracy and expand on local-global relationships.

Few would argue against the proposition that capitalism has been a powerful engine of economic growth. Among its positive attributes the pace of its development of material means of existence—the means of production—stands out. However, its more contentious features remain the addictive nature of individualized capital accumulation, the power associated with this wealth, and the ability to aggregate massive wealth through the modern (undemocratic) corporate form of enterprise. These intertwined factors have been fundamental to changing the material conditions of people's existence and to the more efficient (and accelerating—another matter) use of resources through rapid technological change. Capital has been accumulated, new technologies have been funded, human productivity has risen, and real material consumption—of health care and education as well as televisions and automobiles—has expanded.

Negative outcomes and nonoutcomes of this process are well known. Most obviously negative is the impact of increased production and consumption on the environment, particularly in the form of global warming.

Optimists think that technological fixes for environmental problems will be found before the planet is choked and flooded. Pessimists see people as on the road to Armageddon. Those in the middle hope that people will see the error of their ways and work for more environmentally benign ways of living on the earth. Another obvious negative outcome is uneven development. The nonoutcome of development is literally the lack of it, both in absolute and relative terms. Pockets of poverty (fundamental evidence of the absence of development) exist in the wealthiest of countries; mass poverty exists on the poorest of continents. Nonprofit organizations in their do-good form and cooperatives in their self-help form have long been used in the attempt to mop up this poverty, but rarely have they been used to start groups or regions on a distinct path to development.[1] This book shows that third-sector organizations can be more than Band-Aids. As alternative institutions of accumulation these organizations can contribute not only to charity work but also to building both capital (material) and human elements of development.

Other Facets of Development

Development has numerous definitions, each of them emphasizing different mixes of outcomes. The third sector has become an important part of multiple visions of how to improve life, or develop, in the United States. This section of the chapter surveys several versions of development strategies involving nonprofits and indicates how they might be enhanced by greater emphasis on alternative institutions of accumulation.

In the history of nonprofit institutions in the United States their most obvious role has been the "heart of a heartless world."[2] More than a century before the nation was created, a key document in the development of the third sector, John Winthrop's 1630 *A Model of Christian Charity* (Winthrop in Hammack 1998, 20–27), emphasized this role. In a speech given before his group of Pilgrims reached North America, which is best known for the metaphor "for we shall be as a city upon a hill," Winthrop addressed his community as a body knit together by love (23). The religious roots of this rationale for nonprofit associations spread beyond religious organizations and survive today in discussions of the role of service clubs in bonding communities together. To this author's reading, this tradition of Christian morality infuses *Habits of the Heart*, the well-known book by sociologist

Robert Bellah and his associates (Bellah et al. 1985). While the main argument of the book overlaps with the literature on civil society (to be discussed below), there is a religious aura of community reflected in *Habits of the Heart* and in its title. As David Hammack argues in the introduction to the text of John Winthrop's speech (Hammack 1998, 19), the charity work of the New World religious order, and later of many community organizations and foundations, extended beyond the noblesse oblige of the Middle Ages with a new basis in brotherly and sisterly love. It is still alive today, serving as counterforce to the extreme individualism of U.S. society.

By now it is apparent that the arguments of this book are not grounded in religious community sentiments of love, noble as these sentiments often are. Rather the emphasis has been on obtaining resources for development and building on them. The closest this argument comes to the spiritual is its endorsement of solidarity among and with the disadvantaged in society: those who have experienced the least benefits of development.

A literature on "civil society" has grown rapidly in recent years, and it addresses what is often perceived as a decline in the means for and kinds of engagement citizens experience in their lives. The United States has been considered an exemplar in the use of "intellectual and moral associations," to use the often-quoted words of de Tocqueville. With the fall of the strong state "communist" systems in Eastern Europe concern for how to generate this nongovernmental, nonemployer fabric (or in Winthrop's words, "ligaments") of everyday life took center stage. Those who routinely pointed to the U.S. example found themselves having to consider its decline. Robert Putnam's prominent essay "Bowling Alone: America's Declining Social Capital" (1995) explained this concern and summarized some of the evidence for it. The issue was considered important because the "quality of public life and performance of social institutions" are "powerfully influenced by norms and networks of civic engagement" (66). Putnam's survey of empirical evidence for the health of institutions and norms of civic engagement in the United States (and elsewhere) indicated declines almost across the board. Much of his discussion focused on "social capital," a term representing "social organization such as networks, norms, and social trust that facilitate coordination and cooperation for mutual benefit" (67). In Putnam's words, "networks of civic engagement embody past success at collaboration, which can serve as a template for future collaboration." An important result should be an enhancement of participants' sense of self in a way that emphasizes "we" or group outcomes rather than "I" and focuses on a "taste" for collective benefits (67). This emphasis on community and capacity building in Putnam's article (and subsequent book) is reflected in the cases included in chapters 4 through 10 of this book. However, this author has argued that building this capacity requires access to the more fungible form of capital as well—access denied those in poorer communities literally by definition. Putnam and others writing on civil society highlight the usual reasons for declining social interaction (the impact of television and computer-based forms of communication, longer work hours for households and the rise in the number of women working full-time outside the home, the decline of labor unions, among others) but often fail to make linkages to inequality and uneven development. The middle-class and professional-managerial patterns and institutions those writers find eroding have working-class and poor-citizen counterparts, but for the poor they often work simply to sustain the excluded rather than create a robust social capital that can be exercised as part of a more prosperous life.

The cases presented in this book suggest that civic engagement, which all of the organizations profiled here reflect at least to some degree and many illustrate intensively, can be generated even under difficult material conditions. Their chances of being sustained, however, require resources along with the tenacity and work that have made them possible.

Another literature with which the organizations portrayed in this study share connections is writing on communitarianism. One of the prominent early authors on the subject was Mary Ann Glendon, whose *Rights Talk: The Impoverishment of Political Discourse* (1991) decried the difficulty of finding common ground for action in a world of political discourse that emphasized personal liberty and individual rights. Amitai Etzioni's *The Spirit of Community: The Reinvention of American Society* (1993) brought clearer definition to communitarianism and attempted to reclaim an emphasis on family and community from the religious right. The book addressed the imbalance in political discourse caused by the emphasis on rights by stressing the responsibilities of citizens. Little attention was paid to how actual organizations might reproduce the desired qualities in citizens, and this dearth of attention for community-based institutions was addressed, in part, in a later volume (Etzioni 1995). Samples of the writings of those who work under the communitarian banner can be found on the website of the Civic Practices Network (www.cpn.org).

True to its name, communitarian literature seeks to moderate people's cultural emphasis on the individual, fundamental to both classical and modern liberalism, with renewed attention to the importance of community in influencing development. This is its strength—as long as the definition of community avoids re-creating old hierarchies of race, gender, or other invidious forms of distinction. The weakness of writings on communitarianism lies in their reticence to address the economic inequalities distinguishing communities and related power inequalities.[3] Yes, cultivating good citizens who can function well to enhance nurturing communities is vital. But so too is the question of how to do this when people are struggling to protect and feed their children in an impoverished neighborhood. Entitlement politics was a means of making do, of trying to pry more scraps from a meager welfare system. It should be no surprise that it failed to breed the kind of positive political discourse, problem-solving orientation, and common-ground-seeking behavior that the communitarians sensibly seek.

The patterns of behavior communitarians seek to promote are apparent in the development of the organizations profiled in this book and in the effects of those organizations on those who participate in them. But these organizations are about more than discourse; they are about delivering the basic material needs of a better life. One positive outcome of this engagement, whether from (to take two examples) cooperatively running a mobile home park or participating in management of a home-health-care company, is that the moral-good citizenship gains that communitarians emphasize and material development gains can be achieved together. Rural residents who left the isolation of their modest homes to join together to improve the physical conditions of their communities and urban women who moved from the "entitlements" of welfare to gain jobs and voices in their own companies have accomplished the communitarian objective and more. These gains make clear that at the community (residential or work) level change can enhance social and economic well-being. It remains to be seen how, or if, this can be translated into broader political and economic action.

The last literature to be highlighted for its connections to the arguments and cases presented here has to do with social entrepreneurship. To quote one of the leading voices in this field, J. Gregory Dees of the Stanford Graduate School of Business, social entrepreneurship "combines the passion of a social mission with an image of business-like discipline, innovation, and determination commonly associated with the high-tech pioneers of Silicon Valley" (Dees 1998). Dees's writing has drawn attention to the kinds of initiatives this book highlights. He sensibly distinguishes social entrepreneurship from simply running a business in a socially responsible way, and he uses historical and contemporary definitions of *entrepreneurship* to make the term mean more than simply starting a business or buying a franchise. Dees draws on the work of Peter Drucker to argue that entrepreneurship has to do with opportunity and with reaching beyond what is obviously possible to create new social value (3–6).

Peter Drucker too is closely associated with the idea of social entrepreneurship. He has written extensively on business management and social change and also on the need for improvement in the management of nonprofits. His ideas are spread through the Drucker Institute, which among other activities gives annual awards to nonprofits believed to be innovative and efficient. One of Drucker's concerns is that the third sector should be better able to absorb what he thinks will be major displacement from first-sector jobs caused by technological and organizational change (Drucker 1994). He is also concerned about social stability should this displaced population not be kept occupied in meaningful ways. Third-sector organizations will serve voluntary memberships to "create human health and well-being" and to "create citizenship" (76). The description portrays a nonprofit sector in its traditional role of cleanup, with little mention of a role for government. Absent is much discussion of where the resources will come from to enable development of the large array of organizations that Drucker believes will be needed.

An important feature of the innovative organizational developments discussed in this book is captured by the concept of social entrepreneurship. The concept often recognizes market failings and highlights ways social entrepreneurship can address these failings. The arguments in this book part company with the concept as it leads to the presumption by writers on social entrepreneurship that as the private sector creates market value its largesse will provide the resources needed by the third sector. Will this happen voluntarily? It seems unlikely under the best of circumstances for business, especially in periods when stockholders are not happy with the performance of their portfolios. To this author's thinking, a major portion of these resources will have to be supplied through the powers of government, at all levels, to tax, and another part will come from the third sector's ability to generate its own financial resources.

Religious morality, civil society, communitarianism, and social entrepreneurship, as discussed in the literature, are important components of a development process that could help reshape the political, social, and economic landscape of this country. However, inequality stands in the way of the development they seek, and inequality has to do with material resources, power, and real opportunity.

Resources, Development, and Democracy

At their best the third-sector organizations highlighted in this book point to models that can be emulated in other areas of the economy. They demonstrate new means of making development possible through organizational innovation that can enhance material life and democracy. However, they will have to provide inspiration for larger-scale applications and changes if the problem of uneven development is to be addressed at a meaningful level.

Alternative institutions of accumulation provide the potential for participants in society to have more voice for common causes. However, dissent is a part of this process, and so too is a chance to opt out or join another venture. Third-sector institutions do not have the guaranteed citizen rights of the public sector, but they have the potential for practice of more of those rights and greater democracy than do for-profit corporations and businesses. The first sector ranks last on any reasonable scale of democratic practice. Ultimately businesses in this sector are governed by stockholders who acquire voting rights along with their investments. For-profit corporations are dominated by top management, a group adept at controlling information flows and compensation in its own interest. For the vast majority of people working in corporations or smaller businesses most of their rights as citizens are checked at the office or factory door. They spend their working hours in an autocracy—the opposite of a democracy.

Can the third sector do better than this for democracy? The answer is maybe. Similar abuses of management occur in third-sector organizations, and even though board members legally in control of them do not have to buy their way in,[4] they are sometimes captives of management or a charismatic leader. Nonprofits that seek to do so can function more democratically in terms of basic policy decisions than for-profit corporations can. Those intent on creating democratic participation among staff and workers can do so more freely as well, as stockholders seeking nothing but higher short-term returns on their investments are not present to pull the plug on such innovations. Nonprofit organizations still must retain basic financial health. Organizational democracy requires the same kinds of regulation, rules of the game, and enforcement that are needed in the broader practice of this governance process. Conceptualized in terms of democracy, third-sector organizations are perhaps best described as on a middle ground between the public second sector, within which the nation's constitution provides basic rights for citizens (in theory, at least), and the first sector, in which those rights are most severely curtailed.

Within the third sector the historical example provided by cooperatives offers an important lesson in how to create an organization that can deliver goods, services, and material well-being and yet operate under basic democratic principles. The principles embraced by co-ops (voluntary and open membership; democratic member control on the basis of one person, one vote; limited return on any capital provided; surplus returned to members on the basis of patronage; concern for education and community) (see chap. 2, note 4) call for basic elements of procedural democracy and egalitarian distribution of the benefits provided by the organization. Cooperative members often must buy their way in, as stockholders do in for-profit corporations, but the fee is generally modest and payable over time or out of earnings. Members have full and equal voting rights rather than votes based on the number of shares owned as in a conventional firm.

The co-op example could be used to encourage expanded democratic practice in all third-sector organizations. Special privileges given to nonprofits, such as preferential tax treatment, provide leverage for mandating more democratic standards of operation. Mandates could require that a significant minority or a majority of nonprofits' boards of directors be elected by the organizations' constituents: the communities the organizations exist to serve. Fuller reporting of decision-making and financial information to the community served could be made the norm. Member-serving organizations could be required to report and document how they have considered the well-being of the communities in which they are located as they serve the interests of their members.

Years of free-market rhetoric have convinced many Americans that government regulation in any form is evil, but minimal reflection leads to the realization that regulation is one of the essential functions of government. For businesses regulation often works in favor of the industries it regulates, in part because historically much of it has been written by industry insiders (Kolko 1968), a tendency for which there should be better controls when creating all forms of regulation. More generally regulation tends to clarify law, provide standardized definitions of status, and assure national uniformity of enforcement of basic issues affecting an industry. Regulation sets and enforces the ground rules for all three sectors of the economy. Keeping the third sector independent remains an important goal, but important too is seeing to it that the third sector pays attention to democratic practice and community and that it does no harm.

It is premature to propose a regulatory body for nonprofit organizations, but given their growing scope and scale it is time to study more deliberately the potential gains and pitfalls of closer national governmental oversight and norms for the sector. The chicken-or-egg dilemma results in the fact that there is at present no agency to do this work. A logical starting point is either a governmental commission/panel or a new and independent nonprofit funded to do this work. Time and resources would be essential for either entity to research, debate, and propose any new regulatory framework for the nonprofit portion of the sector. The cooperative and credit union portions of the third sector should be included in this discussion for the examples they provide and because of the similarities between their member-serving functions and those of many traditional nonprofits.

Given the best possible future for the third sector, defined for this book as multiplying the kinds of organizations portrayed in the preceding case chapters, what difference would result for development? First, such a future could provide more new organizations targeted to solve specific problems in communities left behind in the development process. Given the basic policy recommendation for providing material resources for this work, new organizations would face a less difficult task of gaining start-up funding. Second, this future would continue a process of innovation in how to achieve the goal of wiping out what people define as poverty, or lack of development in human, social, and material terms. Third, when these organizations are successful they will contribute to this goal. When they fail, lessons can be derived from the failure for application to new initiatives. Fourth, the process would provide new lessons for its participants in how to work together and how to develop skills for the practice of democracy. Not all of the lessons would derive from positive outcomes, but this would mirror lessons in life. People learn from mistakes, and sometimes second-best solutions are the best that can be attained.

Gaining Momentum for Change

Many of the organizations discussed in this book are locally grounded, and the focus of each is on solving problems or creating opportunities within a defined community or geographic area. Yet as illustrated by many of the cases in preceding chapters, this work is tied to national and global politics. The discussion of public policy in chapter 11 addresses the need for resources by third-sector organizations, among other issues. But even creating a more substantial flow of resources to help generate more innovative third-sector organizations and models cannot be accomplished without a political mandate. Organizing to achieve that mandate is the challenge, and that involves the question of how these organizations fit into any new and coherent program for change in the United States.

Discussion of politics related to the third sector quickly calls attention to the conundrum of trying to affect a national and global system through local action. While decentralization is good, isolation is not. Somehow the work of these organizations must be linked or, at minimum, better understood in scope and meaning if their efforts are to be integrated into a political movement for change. Being part of such a movement can help assure access to resources—material, informational, and inspirational—for the third sector. Clearer presence of third-sector strategies that go beyond aid can suggest new solutions to old problems in development. There is at present no clear model for this action; there is merely what might be called suggestions of one.

For wealthy industrial countries over the past half-century political organization (and organizing) was largely premised on the social democratic model. More radical alternatives that existed out of the mainstream arguably provided the ideas for social democratic reforms. Today the social democratic model is being challenged and radical alternatives are largely absent. In Western Europe social democracy suffers from decades of compromise necessary to run capitalism, albeit in a modestly humane form. In the United States a much more timid form of the model found electoral expression largely through the Democratic Party, a shaky and highly compromised vehicle for social change, especially in recent decades. Given the difficulties of third-party politics in this country, the Democratic Party was the default vehicle for progressive forces. Neoliberalism has pulled what existed of this party's progressive modern liberal agenda back closer to classical liberal commitments to markets and a minimalist state (minimal except for the maximal military and, after September 11, 2001, police and security functions). Organized labor was one of the forces that could (and did sometimes) push the Democratic Party in progressive directions, but today labor is struggling to regroup from the onslaught of neoliberalism and the forces of globalization. In the often bizarre world of politics in the United States organized labor is often portrayed by the Right as a "special interest group."

Capital is not. Unions represent organized labor and indirectly many more workers. The U.S. Chamber of Congress and the Business Round Table represent whom exactly?

Given this less than encouraging picture, the temptation to concentrate energy for change at the local level can reinforce avoidance of national electoral politics. Given the affinity between big business and the Democratic Leadership Council (DLC)–dominated Democratic Party, those who are turned off by the drive for profit and the competitive market model often protest their international application in the form of globalization and turn to solving local problems. For this group the old moderate leftist or progressive agenda—equality, social control over corporations, progressive taxation, using the state for progressive ends—seems a distant goal or simply unattainable. Even when that agenda worked in the past, the results suffered just enough from the dead weight of bureaucracy and the arrogance of power that it became suspect. Voting for Green Party candidates provides an alternative that could promote change. Working to elect progressive independent people of color, women, and men is another alternative, but because it costs so much to run for national office this is most commonly exercised at the local level. Localized strategies often fail to address or suggest action for the large and difficult issues such as who really controls national and global politics, except perhaps as street protests against the suspect group's next major meeting of the WTO or Group of 8 leaders.

Anticapitalist protest may or may not help bring others to the cause, but at least it reveals that people around the world are angry about and resistant to many aspects of the current spread of market-driven global capitalism. If the seeming free rein of capital is to be stopped or constrained, the task is to transform the anger into an anticapitalist movement of the kind that social democracy never was. Social democracy was about living with capitalism and using its wealth-generating capability to make it more humane. With the fall of the centralized and party-dominated socialist regimes over a decade ago and the problems of contemporary social democracy, there is need to work toward new means of material reproduction. The process has barely begun. The third sector offers lessons and examples, especially in its alternative institutions of accumulation.

Nobody knows what future an anticapitalist politics, if successful, could create. If influences from progressive third-sector organizations and the environmental, civil rights, women's, and global anticapitalist movements are combined, attributes that would seem to be a part of that future could be sketched. They include an emphasis on opportunities for local initiatives within a context of nationally or internationally assured thresholds of acceptable conditions of life and behavior; far stronger commitments to equality nationally and globally; democratic rights and processes expanded in all spheres of life—home, work, and civil society; help for those left out of the rewards of development; and greater social control of capital. Third-sector institutions can play constructive roles in bringing about these changes, and at their best they would fit into a new world created by them. Organizations in the third sector can help answer the question, Which way is forward?

Notes

Chapter I

1. The term *fourth sector* is sometimes employed, but it has various meanings. For some it is used to identify a segment for cooperatives; for others it points to a "household" sector. The term will not be used in this book.

2. For instance, the energy crunch faced by residents of the state of California helped revive interest in municipal electric provision—functioning well in the state capital of Sacramento, among other places in the United States.

3. Mainstream economics contains implicit recognition of this characteristic of capitalism in its marginal analysis of the employer's hiring decision. Radical political economy makes the characteristic explicit and central. See any conventional microeconomics text for the mainstream analysis; for the radical view a good summary is provided by Foley (1986).

4. The field of economics uses the term *market failure* for a set of inefficiencies that fall short of its theoretical ideal of the market model. Of the five generally recognized sources of market failure (imperfect competition, externalities, imperfect information, public goods, and missing markets) the last is the form of market failure to which most of the third-sector initiatives described in this book respond.

Chapter 2

1. de Toqueville's *Democracy in America* contains essays on the role of voluntary associations in American politics and on their role in civil society. They can be found in David C. Hammack 1998 (141–53) or in the original (de Toqueville 2000).

2. The nonprofit status of the NYSE may end soon. For several years legal and financial changes have taken place to move the exchange into the for-profit corporate world, to sell equity shares in its business and facilitate their exchange, and to expand the NYSE's revenue-producing potential. Privatization may return home.

3. For example, Sweden has a population of approximately nine million and co-op membership of six million (Swedish Cooperative Centre 1997).

4. The original Rochdale principles have been distilled by the International Co-operative Alliance into seven. They are voluntary and open membership; one-member, one-vote democratic control; limited interest to be paid to share capital; surplus earnings returned to members on the basis of their patronage; an emphasis on member education for cooperation; cooperation among cooperatives; and concern for community (Isbister 1994, 24–25; International Co-operative Alliance 2003).

5. The same could be said for Newman's Own, the for-profit corporation that exists to give its earnings to charities. It is an unusual example of private entrepreneurship for public good.

6. See Gunn 1984, 118–22, for a discussion of the use of hired labor in the U.S. plywood cooperatives.

7. Workers' co-ops are treated as small businesses by the IRS; they pay taxes on the firm's earnings.

8. See Salamon 1999, 18 n. 6 for the history of the definition of public purpose organizations in English law.

Chapter 3

1. For summaries in an international context see Dawson 2001 and Wheelock and Oughton 2001.

2. In 2001 nearly thirteen million children in the United States (17.6 percent of the children in the population) lived in "food insecure" households (Center on Hunger and Poverty 2002).

3. Sources for data on wealth distribution in the United States include the Federal Reserve's Survey of Consumer Finances, Federal Reserve Working Papers, and the *Review of Income and Wealth.* See also Wolff 1995.

4. Many readers might want to add "and in the world."

5. Goods and services are sold in even the poorest of communities. Makers of addictive goods such as tobacco and alcohol products, which are especially attractive because they provide temporary relief from physical and psychological pain, know good markets when they see them.

6. For analysis of what happens to the social surplus created by a typical fast-food franchise see Gunn and Gunn 1991, chap. 2.

7. Local business leaders are unlikely to welcome the effect on wages in the local labor market, where they think they should be in charge of such a vital matter.

Chapter 4

1. In Ford's film these changes were nicely captured in the argument offered by the corporate-employed tractor driver for why a distraught, dispossessed farmer should not shoot him as he is about to demolish the farmer's house. The driver makes clear that the changes are a product of greater efficiency through mechanization. If he were shot, he points out, he would quickly be replaced driving the "cat" by another job-hungry former farmer.

2. This is not to argue that all residents of the United States get enough to eat.

3. "Slow food" is a counterattack on fast food and on the culture of which it is a part. The "movement" began in Italy in 1986; its U.S. branch can be reached via www.slowfoodusa.org.

4. This description draws heavily from the Centre for the Study of Co-operatives 2000.

5. An example of a brokerage for these unusual shares can be found at http://www.agcoopstock.com.

6. See, for instance, Curl 1997.

7. The role of foundations in assisting other nonprofits is assessed in chapters 10 and 11. An example of their controversial history and practices is provided by the Weinberg Foundation's activity in Hawaii. See a summary by Lind 2001.

8. One of its valleys is designated the "wettest spot on earth" (Rand McNally 2000, 63). The designation presumably excludes the surrounding Pacific Ocean.

Chapter 5

1. An ongoing problem for owners of the mobile home form of manufactured housing is the tendency of those homes to depreciate in value. Homes built on-site are less likely to depreciate and more likely to appreciate than manufactured homes are.

2. This description of the rise of mobile home cooperative parks in New Hampshire is based heavily on Bradley 2000.

3. The average new, privately owned one-family house in the United States has increased in size from 1,500 square feet in 1970 to 2,225 square feet in 1999 (United States Census Bureau 2000a, tbl. 1197).

4. I am indebted to Liz Walker, director, EcoVillage at Ithaca, New York, for many of the details of this history.

5. A food cooperative started during the 1930s operated until the 1970s. A food buying club begun near the time of its demise has become the successful Greenstar Cooperative Market. Two former school buildings were converted into housing cooperatives, and Longhouse, a housing cooperative begun in 1975, is located close to the EcoVillage site.

6. The 1999 median home value in Tompkins County was $110,698 ("Tompkins by the Numbers" 2000).

Chapter 6

1. The FHA worked on the premise that racial integration threatened a (white) neighborhood's property values. The FHA guidelines for mortgage insurance essentially controlled bank lending, making insured mortgages unavailable in neighborhoods that were racially diversified (Jackson 1987, 205–7). For areas that had been redlined property values were driven down because transferring homes was difficult. The practice opened a market for other, more predatory lenders.

2. In one study the loan default rates for CDCUs were approximately twice as high as those for conventional credit unions (Isbister 1994, 144, tbl. 5.22). Given this the National Credit Union Administration requires CDCUs to carry higher reserves against loan losses than those required for conventional credit unions.

3. Secondary capital investment provides stability in the early years of CDCUs. See Williams 2002.

4. LISC provides funding and technical assistance for development initiatives based in community development corporations (CDCs). It has brought over $3 billion in grants, equity, and loans to development activity since its inception in 1979 (LISC 2002).

5. Reflecting the early status of NCB and its start-up funding from the U.S. Treasury, three of the fifteen NCB board members are appointed by the president.

Chapter 7

1. Blue Cross/Blue Shield organizations were traditionally nonprofit, community-based insurers of an inclusive demographic group in the communities in which they operated. In the 1980s their more exclusionary behavior mimicked for-profit insurers closely enough that the United States Congress eliminated their tax-exempt status, and this accelerated their conversion to for-profit corporations (Salamon 1999, 89–93).

2. In 2000 the United States spent 13 percent of its GDP on health care. By comparison Switzerland and Germany spent between 10 and 11 percent, and Norway and Denmark spent 8 percent of their GDP on health care while providing coverage for much higher percentages of their populations (OECD 2002, tbl. 10).

3. According to the National Cooperative Business Association cooperative HMOs provide health care to nearly 1.4 million families in the United States (National Cooperative Business Association 2003).

Chapter 8

1. Renovation required work on approximately four thousand windows (Trainer 2000, 5), and by the end of phase one of the project forty-eight hundred tons of debris had been hauled from the site (Nicholas Whitman in Trainer 2000, 92).

2. The economic slump of 2000–2001 took a heavy toll on dot.com jobs.

3. Clarification of these missions and other aspects of the history of developments at MASS MoCA were provided by written communication with Joseph Thompson (Thompson 2002). For an overview of the history of MASS MoCA see the film *DownsideUP* (Nancy Kelly, www.downsideupthemovie.org, 2002).

4. In this regard GMDC is a nonprofit example of many of the arguments put forward by Michael Porter (1995, 1997) and his Harvard-based "Initiative for a Competitive Inner City". On the cultural side it also reflects Richard Florida's "creative class" arguments (Florida 2002).

5. The original warehouse district was smaller, ending at Magazine Street. The district has been expanded northwest to Loyola Street to incorporate new museums, several blocks of St. Charles Street, and part of the downtown business district of New Orleans (Blumenthal 2000).

Chapter 9

1. According to the Children's Defense Fund, in 2000, 65 percent of women with children under six and 78 percent of those with children between six and thirteen years old were in the labor force (Children's Defense Fund 2001).

2. Rates were set at the level of federal government long-term borrowing (National Rural Electric Cooperative Association 1990, 26).

3. See Gunn and Gunn 1991, 143–45, for the case of a municipal electric distribution company begun in Massena, New York, in 1981. Public utilities are more numerous than energy cooperatives in the United States, although they tend to serve an even smaller customer base (eighteen hundred) than the co-ops with an average of eleven thousand customers (National Rural Electric Cooperative Association 2002, 3).

4. A more significant criticism of these loans could be directed to the issue of land use. With fewer than 2 percent of the workforce now employed producing food, under what conditions do people want to promote expansion of rural living? A parallel argument could be made about subsidizing highways that lead to suburban sprawl.

5. The Association of America's Public Television Stations (APTS) is a nonprofit membership association.

6. The story of Highlander Research and Education Center is told directly in Glen 1996 and indirectly in Horton et al. 1998.

Chapter 10

1. Lack of sustainability was illustrated by Maine's electric energy generating capacity, almost a third of which in the early 1990s was based on nuclear generation. With the decommissioning of the Maine Yankee nuclear reactor Lincoln County lost 93 percent of its tax base (Dickstein 2001). People paying for electricity from this Yankee reactor were also paying for schools and roads in Lincoln County.

2. This demonstration is the subject of the film *This Is What Democracy Looks Like*, Seattle Independent Media Center, Seattle, September 2000 (www.thisisdemocracy. org).

3. This history is constructed from Rosenthal 1999 and written communication from Clifford Rosenthal to the author, August 2002.

4. Although the *NonProfit Times* top-one-hundred table indicates that income figures are for 2000, the accompanying article states that income and expense data for some organizations are for 1999 (*NonProfit Times* 2002).

5. The Supreme Court ruling of 2002 allows tax dollars to fund school vouchers that can be used for children's education by religious schools. It echoes the Clinton-era Charitable Choice program.

6. See, for instance, the Web site of the Foundation Center (*www.fdcenter.org*), and for a critical evaluation see Dowie 2001.

Chapter 11

1. A 1995 estimate of the impact of a tax credit of two hundred dollars per taxpayer found that it would have cost the federal government 1.5 percent of its revenue if all taxpayers had used the credit in full (Bowles and Gintis 1995).

2. It might be argued, tongue in cheek, that the IRS could use some revenue-enhancing, unrelated business activity to help fund its own operations.

3. For instance, Burton Weisbrod suggests that data from the Form 990-T be aggregated in a way that would preserve the confidentiality of individual filers, and then made available to researchers (Weisbrod 1998, 302).

4. In 1980 there were two states that enabled workers' cooperatives to be variations on the more common agricultural co-op form (Gunn 1984, 70). One of the significant accomplishments of the Industrial Cooperative Association was to assist groups around the country in championing new legislation to make it easier to create this form of enterprise.

5. Some within the credit union movement argue that the benefit of not paying tax on the organizations' earnings is outweighed by the leverage this provides the banking industry in trying to constrain credit unions. Credit union profit margins are kept low because they exist to provide their members the best service at the lowest possible price; hence the tax they would pay would be low as well.

6. Why would contributors to religious organizations put up with providing this subsidy? The likely answer is to enhance growth of the religion.

Chapter 12

1. It could be argued that two international exceptions to this statement are the impact of the Mondragon co-ops on Basque Spain and the use of cooperatives as part of the distinct development strategy of the Kerala region of India.

2. This phrase, sometimes translated as "the sentiment of a heartless world," is a less-well-known part of Karl Marx's description of religion as the "opium of the people." It appears in the 1844 introduction to his *Contribution to the Critique of Hegel's Philosophy of Right* (Marx in Tucker 1978, 54).

3. This omission was partly addressed in *Voice and Equality: Civic Voluntarism in American Politics* (Verba et al. 1995). As its title suggests, emphasis in the book is on traditional nonprofit, civic associations and the political realm, but the authors' use of a class analysis is grounded in the mainstream sociological realm of social stratification.

4. For nonprofits that are heavily dependent on contributions, being able to write a big check can be an important criterion for membership on governing boards.

Works Cited

Abelson, Reed. 2000. "Some Foundations Choose to Curb Donations and Pay More Taxes." *New York Times,* 24 February, 1, 10, Business section.

Agricultural Marketing Service. 2002. "Farmers Market Facts!" http://www. ams.usda.gov/farmersmarkets/facts.htm [28 February 2003].

American Association of Fundraising Counsel. 2002. "Giving USA 2002." http://www.aafrc.org/trust/charts.html [5 June 2003].

Anderson, John E., and Robert W. Wassmer. 2000. *Bidding for Business: The Efficacy of Local Economic Development Incentives in a Metropolitan Area.* Kalamazoo, Mich.: W. E. Upjohn Institute.

Anheier, Helmut K., and Wolfgang Seibel, eds. 1990. *The Third Sector: Comparative Studies of Nonprofit Organizations.* New York: de Gruyter.

Appleby, Terry. 2000. *General Manager's 2000 Annual Report.* Hanover, N.H.: Hanover Consumer Cooperative Society.

——. 2001. "The Business of Cooperation." *Co-op News,* May/June, 1.

Association of Public Television Stations. 2003. "Frequently Asked Questions." http://www.apts.org/html/faq/faq.html [27 February 2003].

Barlow, Maude, and Tony Clarke. 2002. *Blue Gold: The Fight to Stop the Corporate Theft of the World's Water.* New York: New Press.

Barrett, John. 2001. Interview by author with mayor of North Adams, Mass. North Adams, 22 January.

Bellah, Robert N., Richard Madsen, William M. Sullivan, Ann Swidler, and Steven M. Tipton. 1985. *Habits of the Heart: Individualism and Commitment in American Life.* Berkeley: University of California Press.

Ben-Ner, Avner, and Benedetto Gui, eds. 1993. *The Nonprofit Sector in the Mixed Economy.* Ann Arbor: University of Michigan Press.

Ben-Ner, Avner, and Louis Putterman, eds. 1998. *Economics, Values, and Organizations.* New York: Cambridge University Press.

Benner, Jeffrey. 2002. "Getting a Lock on Broadband." http://www.salon.com/tech/feature/broadband/html [7 June 2002].

Berman, Katrina V. 1967. *Worker-Owned Plywood Firms: An Economic Analysis.* Pullman: Washington State University Press.

Berman, Marshall. 1988. *All That Is Solid Melts into Air: The Experience of Modernity.* New York: Penguin Books.

Bibbie, Janie. 2002. Telephone interview by author with human resources director of Kendal. Ithaca, N.Y., 4 December.

Bishop, Lauren. 2001. "EcoVillage Expansion Plans Receive Only One Question." *Ithaca Journal,* 20 June, 1A.

Blumenthal, Ralph. 2000. "A Skid Row Turned SoHo in Downtown New Orleans." *New York Times,* 4 September, 1E, 5E.

Boston Community Capital. 1998. "BCC Annual Report 1997–98." Boston: Boston Community Capital.

———. 1999. "BCC Annual Report 1998–99." http://www.bostoncommunity capital.org/annualreport.pdf [16 May 2000].

———. 2000. "BCC Annual Report 1999–2000." http://www.bostoncommunity capital.org/invest.html [26 July 2002].

———. 2001. "Our Impact." http://www.bostoncommunitycapital.org/impact/ index.html [25 February 2003].

Bowles, Samuel, and Herbert Gintis. 1995. "From the I.R.S. to the P.T.A." *New York Times,* 19 April, 23A.

Bradley, Paul. 2000. "Manufactured Housing Park Cooperatives in New Hampshire." http://www.weown.net/ManufacturedHousinginNH.htm [26 May 2001].

Brigham, Jay L. 1998. *Empowering the West: Electric Politics Before FDR.* Lawrence: University Press of Kansas.

Catholic Charities USA. 2003. "Who We Are." http://www.catholiccharitiesusa. org/who/ [28 February 2003].

Center for Corporate Citizenship. 2002. *A Productive Partnership.* Boston: Boston College.

Center for Digital Democracy. 2002. "Cable TV and the Future of Broadband." http://www.democraticmedia.org/issues/cabletv/ [5 March 2003].

Center on Hunger and Poverty. 2002. "National Facts and Figures on Hunger and Food Insecurity in the U.S." http://www.centeronhunger.org/fsifacts. html [2 March 2003].

Centre for the Study of Co-operatives. 2000. "New Generation Co-operatives." http://coop-studies.usask.ca/NGC/NGC.html, 2 [11 November 2000].

Children's Defense Fund. 2001. "Child Care Basics." http://www.childrens defense.org/cc_facts.htm [5 March 2003].

City of Seattle. 2001. "Duwamish Coalition." http://www.cityofseattle.net/ business/dc/ [28 February 2003].

Cliburn, Jill K. 2000. "The New Co-ops." *Rural Electrification* 59, no. 1 (October). http://www.1strochdalenyc.net/Articles/RuralElectMain.html [26 June 2002].

Coastal Enterprises, Inc. n.d. *An Illustrated Guide to Coastal Enterprises, Inc.* One-page poster. Wiscasset, Maine: Coastal Enterprises.

——. 2000. *Annual Report.* Wiscasset, Maine: Coastal Enterprises.

——. 2003. "Profile." http://www.ceimaine.org/cei/profile.htm [27 February 2003].

Cohousing Network. 2002. "What Is Cohousing?" http://www.cohousing.org [20 November 2002].

Crawford, Stanley. 1988. *Mayordomo: Chronicle of an Acequia in Northern New Mexico.* Albuquerque: University of New Mexico Press.

Credit Where Credit Is Due. 2003. "Financial Literacy Education." http:// www.cwcid.org [5 March 2003].

Curl, John. 1997. "The Rise and Fall of the Berkeley Food Co-op." http:// www.red-coral.net/BerkCoop.html [3 March 2003].

Dakota Growers Pasta Co. 2000. "Going Organic: Dakota Co-op to Produce Pasta," 27 April. http://www.dakotagrowers.com/news/organic.shtml [27 February 2003].

——. 2002. "Dakota Growers Pasta Company Members Approve Corporate Change," 23 May. http://www.dakotagrowers.com/news/index.shtml [27 February 2003].

Dawson, Graham. 2001. "Measuring Welfare: Are People Better Off?" In *Microeconomics: Neoclassical and Institutionalist Perspectives on Economic Behaviour,* edited by Susan Himmelweit, Roberto Simonetti, and Andrew Trigg, chap. 4. London: Thomson Learning.

Dawson, Steven L. 2000. "Home Health Care for the Elderly Is Wasting Away Because of Neglect." *Boston Globe,* 1 January.

——. 2002. Written communication to author, 15 September.

Dawson, Steven L., and Sherman L. Kreiner. 1993. *Cooperative Home Care Associates: History and Lessons.* Bronx, N.Y.: Home Health Care Training Institute, January.

Dawson, Steven L., and Rick Surpin. 2002. Interview by author with president, Paraprofessional Health Institute, and chair, Cooperative Home Care Associates. New York, 9 July.

Dees, J. Gregory. 1998. "The Meaning of Social Entrepreneurship." http://www. gsb.stanford.edu/services/news/DeesSocentrepPaper.html [28 February 2003].

Dickstein, Carla B. 2001. Interview by author with senior program officer of Coastal Enterprises, Inc. Wiscasset, Maine, 8 June.

Direct Care Alliance. 2000. *The Launch of the Direct Care Alliance.* Conference (Washington, D.C., June 14–16) proceedings, appendix. Bronx, N.Y.: Paraprofessional Healthcare Institute.

Dowie, Mark. 2001. *American Foundations: An Investigative History.* Cambridge: MIT Press.

Drucker, Peter F. 1994. "The Age of Social Transformation." *Atlantic,* November, 53–80.

EcoVillage at Ithaca. n.d. "An Experiment in Sustainable Living." http://www.ecovillage.ithaca.ny.us/ [25 February 2003].

——. 2003. "EVI Newsletter, Summer." http://www.ecovillage.ithaca.ny.us/ [5 June 2003].

Etzioni, Amitai. 1994. *The Spirit of Community: The Reinvention of American Society.* New York: Touchstone.

——, ed. 1995. *New Communitarian Thinking: Persons, Virtues, Institutions, and Communities.* Charlottesville: University Press of Virginia.

Federal Reserve Board. 2002. "Community Reinvestment Act." http://www.federalreserve.gov/dcca/cra/ [26 February 2003].

Filkins, Dexter. 2001. "In Some Immigrant Enclaves, Loan Shark Is the Local Bank." *New York Times,* 23 May, 5B.

Florida, Richard. 2002. *The Rise of the Creative Class.* New York: Basic Books.

Foley, Duncan. 1986. *Understanding Capital: Marx's Economic Theory.* Cambridge: Harvard University Press.

Forero, Juan. 2000. "In Harlem, Loans without the Sharks." *New York Times,* 17 July, 3B.

Foundation Center. 2000. *Foundation Growth and Giving Estimates, 1999 Preview,* 4. New York: The Foundation Center.

Freeman, Douglas, Roopchand Ramgolam, and Joshua Wallack. 2000. *Manchester Craftsman's Guild and Bidwell Training Center: Governing Social Entrepreneurship.* Cambridge: Harvard Business School, case MGC005.

Galaskiewitz, J. W., and W. Bielefeld. 2001. *Nonprofit Organizations in an Age of Uncertainty.* New York: Aldine.

Galbraith, John Kenneth. 1958. *The Affluent Society.* New York: Mentor.

Gay, Patricia, and Stephanie Bruno. 2001. Interview by author with executive director, Preservation Resource Center, and director, PRC Operation Comeback. New Orleans, La., 5 January.

Giloth, Robert P., ed. 1998. *Jobs and Economic Development: Strategies and Practice.* Thousand Oaks, Calif.: Sage.

Glen, John M. 1996. *Highlander: No Ordinary School.* Knoxville: University of Tennessee Press.

Glendon, Mary Ann. 1991. *Rights Talk: The Impoverishment of Political Discourse.* New York: Free Press.

Gollhofer, John G. 2000. "Insurance Consolidation Puts Health Care at Risk." *Seattle Post-Intelligencer,* 8 January.

Goodin, Robert E., Bruce Headey, Rudd Muffels, and Henk-Jan Dirven. 1999. *The Real Worlds of Welfare Capitalism.* New York: Cambridge University Press.

Grassroots Economic Organizing. 2001. "Case Studies in Economic Democracy and Cooperative Economics." Case 5: "Childspace Development Training Institute." Issue 47. http://www.geo.coop/article4.htm [5 March 2003].

Greenpoint Manufacturing and Design Center. 2001. "Awards." http://www.gmdconline.com/doc.asp?id=97&pid=199 [27 February 2003].

Greider, William. 2000a. "If Politics Got Real." *Nation,* 7 February, 6.

———. 2000b. "The Last Farm Crisis." *Nation,* 20 November, 14.

Group Health Cooperative. 2003. "Group Health Overview." http://www.ghc.org/about_gh/co-op_overview/index.jhtml [26 February 2003].

GuideStar. 2002. "Kauai Food Bank, Inc." http://www.guidestar.org, plus search using keywords "Kauai Food Bank" [7 June 2002].

———. 2003a. "About GuideStar." http://www.guidestar.org/about/ [28 February 2003].

———. 2003b. "Kauai Food Bank Inc." http://www.guidestar.org, then conduct a search using keywords "Kauai Food Bank" [3 March 2003].

Gunn, Christopher. 1984. *Workers' Self-Management in the United States.* Ithaca, N.Y.: Cornell University Press.

———. 1992. "Plywood Cooperatives in the United States: An Endangered Species?" *Economic and Industrial Democracy* 13, no. 4 (November): 525–34.

———. 1997. "The Nonprofit Organization: Radical Potential?" *Review of Radical Political Economics* 29, no. 3:92–102.

Gunn, Christopher, and Hazel Dayton Gunn. 1991. *Reclaiming Capital: Democratic Initiatives and Community Development.* Ithaca, N.Y.: Cornell University Press.

Hammack, David C. 1998. *Making the Nonprofit Sector in the United States: A Reader.* Bloomington: University of Indiana Press.

Hanover Consumer Cooperative Society. 2000. *Annual Report.* Hanover, N.H.

Harl, Neil E. 2001. "Converging Forces Afflict Farms." *New York Times,* 29 April, 5BU.

Healy, Beth. 2002. "Three Harvard Endowment Managers Reap Over $15 Million Each." http://www.boston.com/dailyglobe2/337/business [3 December 2002].

Henshaw, Nathaniel V., and Mark D. Kaplan. 2001. Interview by author with president and vice president of Coastal Enterprises, Inc. Ventures. Portland, Maine, 5 June.

Herel, Suzanne. 2001. "Food Co-Op Closing after 65 Years." *San Francisco Chronicle,* 28 March, 15A.

Herman, Tom. 1995. "Tax Report." *Wall Street Journal,* 8 February, 1A.

———. 1997. "Tax Report." *Wall Street Journal,* 18 June, 1A.

Higgins, Dan. 2001. "Kendal Fights Tax Bill." *Ithaca Journal,* 29 November, 1A.

Highlander Research and Education Center. 2002. *Annual Report 2001–2002.* New Market, Tenn.

Hochman, Leni. 2001. "Livable Wage Study Updated." *Alternative Currents* (April): 1–2.

Horton, Miles, Judith Kohl, and Herbert R. Kohl. 1998. *The Long Haul: An Autobiography.* New York: Teachers College Press.

Hu, Winnie. 2002. "Farmers in Short Supply at Farmers' Markets." *New York Times,* 20 July, 1A, 4B.

Inserra, Anna, Maureen Conway, and John Rodat. 2002. *Cooperative Home Care Associates: A Case Study of a Sectoral Employment Development Approach.* Washington, D.C.: The Aspen Institute.

International Co-operative Alliance. 2003. "ICA Rules, Section II." http://www.ica.coop/ica/ica/rules/rules1.html [7 May 2003].

Isbister, John. 1994. *Thin Cats: The Community Development Credit Union Movement in the United States.* Davis: University of California Center for Cooperatives.

Ithaca Health Fund. n.d. "Does Health Insurance Cost More than You Can Easily Afford?" Informational flyer. Ithaca, N.Y.

———. 2002. "Balance Sheet." http://www.ithacahealthfund.org/balancesheet.htm [10 December 2002].

———. 2003a. "How It Works." http://www.IthacaHealth.org/howwork.htm [26 February 2003].

———. 2003b. "Introduction." http://www.ithacahealth.org/intro.htm [26 February 2003].

Jackson, Kenneth T. 1987. *Crabgrass Frontier: The Suburbanization of the United States.* New York: Oxford University Press.

James, Estelle. 1998. "Commercialism among Nonprofits: Objectives, Opportunities, and Constraints." In *To Profit or Not To Profit: The Commercial Transformation of the Nonprofit Sector,* edited by Burton Weisbrod. New York: Cambridge University Press.

Johnston, David Cay. 1997. "United Way, Faced with Fewer Donors, Is Giving Away Less." *New York Times,* 9 November, 1, 28.

Kendal. 2000. *Values and Standards.* Kennett Square, Pa.: The Kendal Corporation.

———. 2001. *Annual Report.* Kennett Square, Pa.: The Kendal Corporation.

———. 2002. *Disclosure Statement.* Ithaca, N.Y.: Kendal at Ithaca, November.

———. 2003. *Schedule of Fees for 2003.* Ithaca, N.Y.: Kendal at Ithaca.

King County Labor Council. 2003a. "We're Forwarding the Goals of 'Union Cities.'" http://www.kclc.org/union.htm [28 February 2003].

———. 2003b. "Who We Are." http://www.kclc.org/whoweare.htm [28 February 2003].

Kolko, Gabriel. 1985. *Triumph of Conservatism.* New York: Free Press.

Levine, Mark. 2001. Interview by author with executive director, Credit Where Credit Is Due, Inc. Washington Heights, N.Y., 23 April.

Levin-Waldman, Oren M. 2001. *The Case for the Minimum Wage: Competing Policy Models.* Albany: State University of New York Press.

Lewin, Tamar. 2001a. "Fund for Investors Moves Higher on the Philanthropy List." *New York Times,* 28 October, 20A.

———. 2001b. "In an Uncertain Climate, Philanthropy Is Slowing." *New York Times,* 19 February, 8A.

Lind, Ian. 2001. "Weinberg's Legacy." *Honolulu Weekly.* www.honoluluweekly.com/archives/controversy%/202001/5-22-02%20/Weinberg [8 January 2002].

LISC. 2002. "LISC Facts at a Glance." http://www.liscnet.org/whatwedo/facts/ [26 February 2003].

Lutheran Services in America. 2002. "Windows on the Faith-Based and Community Initiative." http://www.lutheranservices.org/public%20policy%20documents/faith%20based%20windows/lsaandfbciaug01.htm [5 March 2003].

———. 2003. "Who We Are." http://www.lutheranservices.org/whoweare.htm [28 February 2003].

Maker, Steve. 2002. "Report of the Board of Directors." *Co-op News,* April. http://www.coopfoodstore.com/news/Archives/arch_4_02/b_pres_report.html [28 February 2003].

Malveaux, Julianne. 2000. "Fair Pay for Home Health Aides." *Essence* (April): 192.

Massachusetts Division of Employment and Training. 2001. "Employment in North Adams." http://www.detma.org/1mi/local/North_Ad.html [5 May 2003].

Minneapolis Telecommunications Network. 2002. "MTN History." http://www.mtn.org/Video/history.html [6 June 2003].

Mishel, Lawrence, Jared Bernstein, and John Schmitt. 1999. *The State of Working America, 1998–99.* Ithaca, N.Y.: Cornell University Press.

Mishkin, Frederick S., and Stanley G. Eakins. 2000. *Financial Markets and Institutions.* Reading, Mass.: Addison-Wesley.

Moe, Richard, and Carter Wilkie. 1997. *Changing Places: Rebuilding Community in the Age of Sprawl.* New York: Henry Holt.

National Association of Counties. 2001. "Success Stories: 'World Class' Telecommunications System to Spur Economic Development in Berkshire County, MA."http://www.naco.org/programs/comm_dev/rural/story.cfm?success_story_ID=54 [16 January 2001].

National Cooperative Bank. 1999. "1999 Annual Report." http://www.ncb.coop/ [18 October 2000].

———. 2002. "Financial Information." http://www.ncb.coop/ [26 February 2003].

———. 2003. "NCB Co-op 100." http://www.co-op100.coop [3 March 2003].

National Cooperative Business Association. 2003. "Co-op Primer." http://www.ncba.coop/primer.cfm [2 March 2003].

National Credit Union Administration. 2002. "What Is a Credit Union?" http://www.ncua.gov/indexabout.html [28 November 2002].

National Federation of Community Development Credit Unions. 2000. Press release. http://www.natfed.org/i4a/pages/index.cfm?pageid=1 [27 November 2000].

———. 2002. "About Us: The Federation's Membership." http://www.natfed.org/i4a/pages/index.cfm?pageid=256 [5 March 2003].

National Rural Electric Cooperative Association. 1990. *Sourcebook.* Arlington, Va.: NRECA.

———. 2002. "America's Cooperative Electric Utilities: The Nation's Consumer Owned Electric Utility Network." http://www.nreca.org/nreca/coops/elecoop3.html [23 June 2002].

New Hampshire Community Loan Fund. 2001. "An Introductory Guide to Manufactured Housing Park Cooperatives and the Services of the New Hampshire Community Loan Fund." Consumers Union. http://www.consumersunion. org/other/mh/FromTenantToOwner-1.html [25 February 2003].

New York Stock Exchange. 2003. "NYSE Mission Statement." http://www.NYSE.com [2 March 2003].

Nonprofit Pathfinder. 2003. "Governance: Childspace Management Group." http://www.independentsector.org/pathfinder/innovations/govern/chil_man.html [27 February 2003].

Nonprofit Times. 2002. "NPT100." http://www.nptimes.com/Nov02/npt_100 charts02.pdf

North Dakota State Data Center. 2003. "Population Trends in North Dakota by City 1900–2000." http://www.ndsu.nodak.edu/sdc/data/census2000/NEWCities1990_2000 Change.pdf [6 June 2003].

Nyhan, Paul. 2002. "On the Job: Group Health Employees Authorize Union Leaders To Call Strike." *Seattle Post-Intelligencer,* 3 June. http://seattlepi.nwsource.com/business/72983_onthejob03.shtml [26 February 2003].

Odendahl, Teresa, and Michael O'Neill, eds. 1994. *Women and Power in the Nonprofit Sector.* San Francisco: Jossey-Bass.

OECD. 2002. *Health Data 2002.* 4th ed. Organization for Economic Cooperation and Development. http://www.oecd.org/xls/m00031000/m00031380/xls [6 June 2003].

Palmer, Eric. 2002. "Farmland Industries Reports Record Net Loss." *Kansas City Star*, 28 November. http://www.kansascity.com/mld/kansascity/business/4621093.htm [28 February 2003].

Paltrow, Scot J. 1998. "Mutual Insurer Found Way to 'Demutualize' That's Fast and Cheap." *Wall Street Journal*, 1 December, 1A.

Patrie, William. 1998. "Fever Pitch: A First-hand Report from the Man Who Helped Spark Co-op Fever in the Northern Plains." http://www.rurdev.usda.gov/rbs/pub [July 1998].

Pencavel, John. 2001. *Worker Participation: Lessons from the Worker Co-ops of the Pacific Northwest*. New York: Russell Sage Foundation.

Perry, Nick. 2002. "Group Health's Eastside Hospital Might Be for Sale." *Seattle Times*, 11 June. http://archives.seattletimes.nwsource.com/cgi-bin/texis.cgi/web/vortex/display?slug=grouphealth11e&date=20020611&query=Nick&Perry [26 February 2003].

Pollin, Robert. 2002. "What Is a Living Wage: Considerations from Santa Monica, California." *Review of Radical Political Economics* 34, no. 3:267–73.

Pollin, Robert, and Stephanie Luce. 1998. *The Living Wage: Building a Fair Economy*. New York: New Press.

Porter, Michael. 1995. "The Competitive Advantage of the Inner City." *Harvard Business Review* 73 (May–June): 55–71.

———. 1997. "New Strategies for Inner-City Economic Development." *Economic Development Quarterly* 11, no. 1 (February): 11–28.

Preservation Resource Center of New Orleans. 2003. "Twenty-Six Years of Preservation in New Orleans and the Nation." http://www.prcno.org/about prc.html [27 February 2003].

Pristin, Terry. 2002. "Nonprofit Official Indicted in Embezzlement." *New York Times*, 10 February, 36L.

Prud'homme, Alex. 1999. "Off the Urban Rust Heap, a Factory Goes to Work." *New York Times*, 10 January, 1BU, 8BU.

Putnam, Robert. 1995. "Bowling Alone: America's Declining Social Capital." *Journal of Democracy* 6, no. 1:65–78.

Rand McNally. 2000. *Large Scale Road Atlas USA*. Skokie, Ill.: Rand McNally.

Rimer, Sara. 2000. "Home Aides for the Frail Elderly in Short Supply." *New York Times*, 3 January.

Rose-Ackerman, Susan. 1996. "Altruism, Nonprofits, and Economic Theory." *Journal of Economic Literature* 34 (June):701–28.

Rosenthal, Clifford. 1999. "Before the National Federation." *World View NFCDCU* @25, National Federation of Community Development Credit Unions, 4–5.

Salamon, Lester M. 1999. *The Nonprofit Sector: A Primer*. 2d ed. New York: The Foundation Center.

Schor, Juliet B. 1991. *The Overworked American: The Unexpected Decline of Leisure*. New York: Basic Books.

Schor, Juliet B., and Douglas B. Holt, eds. 2000. *The Consumer Society Reader*. New York: New Press.

Seley, John E., and Julian Wolpert. 2002. *New York City's Nonprofit Sector*. Toronto: University of Toronto Press.

Showrank, James. 2001. Interview by author with director of community and governmental relations of Manchester Bidwell Corporation. Pittsburgh, 21 September.

Shuman, Michael H. 2000. *Going Local: Creating Self-Reliant Communities in a Global Age*. New York: Routledge.

Shutkin, William A. 2000. *The Land That Could Be: Environmentalism and Democracy in the Twenty-First Century*. Cambridge: MIT Press.

Spitzer, Ted. 2001a. Interview by author with president of Market Venture, Inc. Portland, Maine, 5 June.

——. 2001b. "Letter from the Director." *Portland Public Market Crier*, no. 6 (winter): 2.

Strom, Stephanie. 2002. "Red Cross Pressured to Open Its Books." *New York Times*, 5 June, 1A, B7.

Swedish Cooperative Centre. 1997. "Message from Swedish Co-operative Centre." http://www.wisc.edu/uwcc/icic/orgs/ica/mem/country/Sweden/Message from-the-Swedish-Cooperative-Cen1.html [6 June 2003].

Sweeny, J. David. 2002. Interview by author with CEO of Greenpoint Manufacturing and Design Center. Brooklyn, N.Y., 9 July.

Thompson, Joseph. 2001. Interview by author with director, Massachusetts Museum of Contemporary Art. North Adams, Mass., 22 January.

——. 2002. Written communication with author, 20 October.

"Tompkins by the Numbers." 2000. *Ithaca Journal*, 18 August, 8E.

Toqueville, Alexis de. 2000. *Democracy in America*. Indianapolis, Ind.: Hackett.

Trainer, Jennifer, ed. 2000. *MASS MoCA: From Mill to Museum*. North Adams, Mass.: MASS MoCA Publications.

Tucker, Robert C., ed. 1978. *The Marx-Engels Reader*. 2d ed. New York: W. W. Norton.

United Jewish Communities. 2002. "About Us." http://www.ujc.org/aboutus_home.html [1 July 2002].

United States Census Bureau. 1998. "Foundations—Number and Finances by Asset Size, 1998." *Statistical Abstract of the United States: 2000*, table 841. http://www.census.gov/prod/www/statistical-abstract-us.html [3 March 2003].

——. 2000a. "Construction and Housing." *Statistical Abstract of the United States: 2000*, section 25. http://www.census.gov/prod/2001pubs/statab/sec25.pdf [25 February 2003].

——. 2000b. "Health and Nutrition." *Statistical Abstract of the United States: 2000*, section 3. http://www.census.gov/prod/2001pubs/statab/sec03.pdf [25 February 2003].

———. 2001a. "American Housing Survey for the United States: 2001." http://www.census.gov/hhes/www/housing/ahs/ahs01/tab1a1.html [29 November 2002].

———. 2001b. "Civilian Consumer Expenditures for Farm Food: 1980–1999." http://www.census.gov/prod/2002/01statab/agricult.pdf, table 815 [6 June 2003].

———. 2001c. "Housing Vacancies and Homeownership Annual Statistics: 2001." http://www.census.gov/hhes/www/housing/hvs/annual01/ann01t15.ht ml [25 July 2002].

———. 2001d. "Labor Union Membership by Sector: 1983 to 2000." http://www.census.gov/prod/2002pubs/01statab/labor.pdf, table 637 [6 June 2003].

United States Department of Agriculture. 2000. "Rural Development, Rural Utilities, Service Electric Program for Rural America." http://www.usda.gov/rus/electric/fs/pa1677.htm [27 February 2003].

United States Department of the Treasury. 2003. "CDFI Fund Overview." http://www.cdfifund.gov/overview/index.asp [28 February 2003].

Vanek, Jaroslav. 1977. The Labor-Managed Economy: Essays. Ithaca, N.Y.: Cornell University Press.

Verba, Sidney, Kay Lehman Schlozman, and Henry E. Brady. 1995. *Voice and Equality: Civic Voluntarism in American Politics.* Cambridge: Harvard University Press.

Walker, Liz. 2000. "The College Connection." *The Village at Ithaca Newsletter* 10, no. 2 (winter): 3.

———. 2001. Interview by author with director of EcoVillage at Ithaca. Ithaca, N.Y., 20 June.

Walljasper, Jay. 1998. "Story Time in Philadelphia." *Nation*, 30 November, 15–20.

Weisbrod, Burton. 1988. *The Nonprofit Economy.* Cambridge: Harvard University Press.

———, ed. 1998. *To Profit or Not To Profit: The Commercial Transformation of the Nonprofit Sector.* New York: Cambridge University Press.

Wheelock, Jane, and Elizabeth Oughton. 2001. "The Household in the Economy." In *Microeconomics: Neoclassical and Institutionalist Perspectives on Economic Behaviour,* edited by Susan Himmelweit, Roberto Simonetti, and Andrew Trigg, chap. 5. London: Thomson Learning.

Williams, Marva. 2002. "How Secondary Capital Investments Help Low-Income Credit Unions Hit Their Stride." http://www.woodstockinst.org/criticalcapital.pdf [26 February 2003].

Wolff, Edward N. 1995. *Top Heavy: The Increasing Inequality of Wealth in America and What Can Be Done about It.* New York: New Press.

World Hunger Year. 1999. "The Harry Chapin Self-Reliance Award Winners for 1999." http://www.worldhungeryear.org/programs/winners.asp?year=1999 [25 February 2003].

Zeuli, Kim, Gary A. Goreham, Robert King, and Evert van der Sluis. 1998. "Dakota Growers Pasta Company and the City of Carrington, North Dakota: A Case Study." Unpublished report prepared for the U.S. Department of Agriculture Fund for Rural America, March, 8.

Zinkin, Justine. 2002. Interview by author with executive director of Credit Where Credit Is Due. Washington Heights, N.Y., 8 July.

Index